ReSearch

ReSearch
A Career Guide for Scientists

Teresa M. Evans
University of Texas Health and Science Center at San Antonio
San Antonio, TX, United States

Natalie Lundsteen
University of Texas Southwestern Medical Center
Dallas, TX, United States

Nathan L. Vanderford
University of Kentucky, Lexington, KY, United States

ACADEMIC PRESS
An imprint of Elsevier

Academic Press is an imprint of Elsevier
125 London Wall, London EC2Y 5AS, United Kingdom
525 B Street, Suite 1800, San Diego, CA 92101-4495, United States
50 Hampshire Street, 5th Floor, Cambridge, MA 02139, United States
The Boulevard, Langford Lane, Kidlington, Oxford OX5 1GB, United Kingdom

Notices
Knowledge and best practice in this field are constantly changing. As new research and
experience broaden our understanding, changes in research methods, professional practices,
or medical treatment may become necessary.

Practitioners and researchers must always rely on their own experience and knowledge in
evaluating and using any information, methods, compounds, or experiments described herein.
In using such information or methods they should be mindful of their own safety and the safety
of others, including parties for whom they have a professional responsibility.

To the fullest extent of the law, neither the Publisher nor the authors, contributors, or editors,
assume any liability for any injury and/or damage to persons or property as a matter of products
liability, negligence or otherwise, or from any use or operation of any methods, products,
instructions, or ideas contained in the material herein.

Library of Congress Cataloging-in-Publication Data
A catalog record for this book is available from the Library of Congress

British Library Cataloguing-in-Publication Data
A catalogue record for this book is available from the British Library

ISBN: 978-0-12-804297-7

For information on all Academic Press publications visit our website at
https://www.elsevier.com/books-and-journals

Working together
to grow libraries in
developing countries

www.elsevier.com • www.bookaid.org

Publisher: Sara Tenney
Acquisitions Editor: Mary Preap
Editorial Project Manager: Mary Preap
Production Project Manager: Chris Wortley
Designer: Alan Studholme

Typeset by TNQ Books and Journals

Contents

About the Authors   xi

Section 1
Introduction

1. Introduction   3

2. Common Career Characters   5
    Teresa M. Evans

Section 2
Understanding the Landscape of Your Challenges and Choices

3. Realities of the Job Market: Charting Your Career Path   11
    Nathan L. Vanderford

    Changes in the Academic Landscape   12
    Know Your Career Options   13
    Narrow Down Your Career Choices   14
    Scientists Working Outside of the Academy   15
    Unexpected Obstacles   16
    Summary   17
    References   18

4. Understanding the Career Game: Figuring Out
    "the Rules" of Career Planning and Getting
    Motivated to Plan for a Successful Career   19
    Teresa M. Evans

    Rule #1: Trainees Do Not Get Hired   20
    Rule #2: Be Visible and Network   20
    Where to Find Opportunities if They Are Not Readily Offered   21
    How to Choose Which Opportunities to Attend
        From Among the Options   21

Rule #3: Just Ask 22
Rule #4: Find at Least One "Career Mentor" 22
Rule #5: Have a Plan to Plan 23
Rule #6: Know Yourself 25
Concluding Remarks 25
Reference 27

Section 3
Taking Care of Yourself

5. Managing Stress and Staying Healthy 31

Lindsay Bira

Graduate Training Is Stressful 32
The Stress Response 33
Chronic Stress 34
Preparing for Stress—Choosing Balance 35
Physical Activity 35
Social Support 36
Communication 38
Cognitive Restructuring 39
Mindfulness Practice 40
Hobbies 41
Trusting in the Process 42
References 43

6. The Importance of Staying Positive in Your Job Search 45

Teresa M. Evans and Natalie Lundsteen

Understand the Challenges 45
Bouncing Back: Practicing Adaptability and Resiliency 46
Cultivating Confidence 48
Always Seeking to Learn: The Growth Mind-Set 50
Learn to Be Optimistic 51
Creating a Career Search Support Network 53
Managing Your Job Search Expectations 54
References 57

7. Fake It Till You Become It: The How-To Guide for Behaving Like a Professional 59

Teresa M. Evans

"Act" Like a Professional, Not a Trainee 60
A Genuine Smile, the Excalibur of True Public Relations Pros! 60
Tit for Tat, There Is Power in Taking Interest and
   Doing Favors for Those in Your Workplace 61
Reciprocity Styles 61

You Are Always Being Watched—Dress Like a Professional!   62
Casual Versus Professional Business Attire   62
Other Tips and Common Mistakes   63
How Do You Dress Professionally on a Budget?   63
Professionals Are on Time   64
The Professional Way to Party   64
Tips for the Professional Woman… and Man   65
So, Here They Are, in No Particular Order   65
References   69

Section 4
Managing Your Career Development

8. Taking a Personal Inventory: Assessing Your Skills,
    Strengths, Interests, and Values   73

    Natalie Lundsteen

    Thinking About Your Skills   74
    Additional Skills and Strengths Assessments   80
    Thinking About Your Interests   81
    Thinking About Your Personal Traits and Qualities   82
    Thinking About Your Values   83
    References   86

9. Overcoming Knowledge and Experience Gaps   87

    Nathan L. Vanderford

    So What Does Practical Experience Really Look Like?   88
    Concrete Ways to Gain Practical Career Experience   89
    How to Expand Your Career-Related Knowledge   93
    How to Sell Your Current Knowledge and Experience   96
    Finding a Balance   97
    References   103

10. Transferable Skills: How to Describe What You
    Really Know   105

    Nathan L. Vanderford

    What Is a Transferable Skill, Anyway?   107
    Skills Employers Really Want   107
    Recognizing Your Transferable Skills   109
    Finding the Hidden Skills in Your Academic Profile   109
    Analyzing Your Work, Sports, and Leadership Profile   110
    Garnering Feedback From Nonacademics   111
    Assessment Instruments   112
    Accomplishment Statements   114
    Look Beyond the Obvious   115
    References   117

11. **The "Me Brand": Tips for Successful Personal Branding**   119

Nathan L. Vanderford

What Is Branding, Anyway?   121
Figuring Out Your Four W's   121
Beginning to Build Your Brand   124
Your Resume   125
Cover Letter   126
Letters of Reference   126
Elevator Speech   127
LinkedIn   128
Facebook   130
Twitter   130
Personal Website   130
Personal Blog   131
Science Blogging   132
Bringing All Aspects of Your Brand Together 133
Wrapping Up Your Branding Efforts   133
References   137

12. **Building Your Professional Network**   139

Natalie Lundsteen

Networking   140
Don't Assume Networking Is Only for Scientists
   Seeking a Career Beyond the Bench   141
Every Minute Spent Building Your Network Is Time
   Well Spent   141
How Do You Network Effectively?   141
Informational Interviewing   144
How Do You Find People for Informational Interviews? 144
Conducting a Successful Informational Interview   145
Above All, Do Not Ask for a Job   146
Maintaining Your Network   147
Building Your Network: Putting It All Together   148
An Unexpected Connection, Thank You Twitter! 148
Reference   153

13. **Create Balance in Your Life and Career**   155

Teresa M. Evans

Knowing Your "End"   156
What's Your One Thing?   157
Get a Dog   158
Learn to Speed Read and Write   160
References   163

14. **The Art of Communication**   165

Teresa M. Evans

Would You Consider Yourself Confident?	166
Are You Thoughtful in Your Communications?	166
Oral Communication	167
Verbal Communication	172
Written Communication	173
Communication Struggles: Overcoming International Barriers	176
Personal Communication Success Story	177
References	178

Section 5
Finding a Job

15. **The Career Search**   181

Teresa M. Evans and Natalie Lundsteen

Things to Consider Before You Begin	183
How to Be What Employers Are Looking for	184
Assessing Your Fit	184
Making a Plan	186
Sample Job Search Plan	187
Step 1 Assess Your Circumstances	187
Step 2 Begin Your Search	187
Step 3 Network	189
Step 4 Submission and Preparation	189
Step 5 Be Realistic	189
Working With Recruiters	190
Wrapping-Up Your Career Search	193
References	194
Further Reading	194

16. **Creating Application Materials, Applying, and Interviewing for Jobs**   195

Natalie Lundsteen and Sharon Kuss

Consider the Importance of Timing in Your Applications	196
Take a Deep Breath Before You Get Started	196
Preparing and Tailoring Application Materials	198
Targeting Materials for Each Job Application	200
Following Application Directions (Dos and Don'ts)	201
Interviews	203
Stages of a Typical Interview Process	204
Types of Interviews	204
Preparing for Interviews	204
How to Answer Interview Questions	205

Structuring Your Interview Answers   206
Interview Practice   207
During the Interview   208
After Your Interview   209
Getting an Offer   210
Considerations for Academic Interviews   211
Postdoc Interviews   211
Faculty Interviews   212
Final Words of Application Wisdom   213
Further Resources for Job Interview and Preparation   214
References   214
Further Reading   214

17.   The International Perspective   233
Natalie Lundsteen

Manage Expectations in Your Job Search   234
Understand Your Visa and Work Options   235
Build Your Transferable Skills   237
Building and Expanding Your Network   238
References   240

Section 6
Quick Tips, Summary and Conclusion

18.   Career Planning Quick Guide   249
Teresa M. Evans and Lily Raines

Quick Guide   250
Step 1: Seek Help   250
Step 2: Assess the Time You Have Available   251
Step 3: Determine Your Short-Term Versus Long-Term Career Goals   251
Step 4: Make a Plan   251
Step 5: Determine Your Current Marketable Skills   252
Step 6: Acquire Additional Marketable Skills Quickly   253
Step 7: Network: Assess Current and Identify Future Allies   253
Step 8: Prepare Your Documents   254
Step 9: Know Where/How to Apply Efficiently   254
Step 10: Stay Positive   254
References   254
Further Reading   254

Index   255

About the Authors

Teresa M. Evans, PhD

Teresa Evans is a graduate of the University of Texas (UT) Health Science Center in San Antonio where she received her PhD in neuroscience in 2014. During her graduate training she built a foundation of career development programming for graduate students and postdoctoral fellows in biomedical science. These efforts grew into the foundational programs of the Office of Career Development that she now directs. As the director of Workforce and Career Development, Teresa provides guidance and consultation through one-on-one meetings that can focus on the discussion of resume and CV preparation, mock interviews, dissertation planning, strategic networking, and skills and values assessments necessary for effectively navigating the graduate education journey. Teresa also facilitates monthly workshops that focus on a variety of topics and hosts regional symposia tailored toward a graduate STEM audience.

As a faculty member in the Department of Pharmacology, Teresa's research interests focus on mental health in graduate students and postdoctoral fellows around the globe. Teresa is an advocate of career development efforts for graduate trainees at the UT System and national society levels where she has presented at multiple conferences such as Experimental Biology, the Association of Plant Biologists, and Sigma Xi.

Teresa is passionate about the communication of science and science outreach at the local and national levels, for which her efforts have received independent funding, have been published, and have resulted in her founding the nonprofit organization San Antonio Science. Through science communication and outreach Teresa hopes to empower trainees to communicate their science, pursue a career that they find fulfilling, and provide the tools trainees need to determine what career path that is.

As a recent graduate and a highly networked STEM professional, Teresa has a breadth and depth of knowledge in careers available to trainees as well as the dynamic biomedical workforce. As a certified career development facilitator, she has specialized training in career guidance practices and is well suited to provide tailored career guidance to STEM professionals. As a scientist, faculty member, and academic administrator, Teresa helps scientists to consider the challenges faced in pursuing a career both inside and outside of academia. Teresa's career has recently expanded to include a role outside of academia. She has recently taken on a role as

Partner at a business accelerator in San Antonio. In this role, Teresa is establishing a novel 15 month business acceleration process for the technology industry, leading operations for the accelerator, and providing one-on-one guidance to portfolio companies. Teresa is a life long learner who is passionate about empowering others to achieve their goals in life, career, and business.

Natalie Lundsteen, PhD

Natalie leads the University of Texas (UT) Southwestern Medical Center's career development program for all PhD and postdoctoral biomedical science researchers, and she is confident that her background as a career advising professional and workplace learning researcher have prepared her for writing this book.

She has spent nearly 20 years working in research universities, including Boston University, Stanford University, the University of Oxford, and MIT. She currently works as the director of Graduate Career Development and is an assistant professor in psychiatry in the Graduate School of Biomedical Sciences at UT Southwestern Medical Center, where she provides career development advising and resources to graduate students, alumni, and postdoctoral researchers.

After many years of university academic advising and career counseling work, Natalie undertook doctoral research at the University of Oxford, which focused on the transition experiences of students moving from academia to workplaces. Her current research examines how doctoral students are trained for careers, and what universities can do to better prepare candidates for professional workplaces. Natalie's broad research interests are in workplace learning—particularly the development of expertise in practices, along with interest in student development theory and student transition experiences. Her research interests in workplace learning and doctoral education developed concurrently with a changing and difficult economic landscape, so she has a deep understanding of the difficulties of the academic job market for doctoral students/researchers.

She is a regular contributor to *Inside Higher Ed*'s Carpe Careers advice for PhD jobseekers and has presented career workshops at annual meetings and conferences for the American Association for the Advancement of Science, the American Society for Cell Biology, and the Society for Developmental Biology, along with being an invited career development speaker to STEM campuses around the world. Having worked with thousands of graduate students and postdocs in a range of international institutions, Natalie is familiar with the pressures faced by science trainees in navigating their career choices and understands the specific challenges of science careers.

Nathan L. Vanderford, PhD, MBA

Nathan earned a PhD in biochemistry in 2008 from the University of Kentucky (UK). Over the last several years, he has primarily focused on an academic-based research administration career path and, in the process, earned an MBA. In his current positions at UK, he is an assistant professor in the Department of Toxicology and Cancer Biology, instructor in the Graduate School, the assistant dean for Academic Development within the College of Medicine, and the assistant director for Research for the Markey Cancer Center (MCC). In these positions, he plays a key role in facilitating research and education initiatives that take place within the MCC and across the College of Medicine. He has scholarly interests in the areas of lung cancer etiology and epidemiology, academic-based research commercialization and in improving the state of graduate education. He is deputy editor for the *Journal of Research Administration* and an associate editor for the journal *Technology Transfer and Entrepreneurship.*

At UK, Nathan provides ad hoc and formal career development mentorship and career counseling to undergraduate and graduate students as well as to postdoctoral fellows. He has also been involved in conducting workshops focused on enhancing PhD trainees' workforce readiness. And, he has developed a course (titled Preparing Future Professionals) at the level of the Graduate School focused on developing trainees' interest in various career paths and enhancing the skills needed for such career paths. Nathan has also published several articles on the topic of improving the education and training of the next generation of STEM professionals with a focus on addressing the current and future state of PhD education and training. These articles have been published with *Science, Nature, Nature Biotechnology, Biochemistry and Molecular Biology Education, F1000Research, Technology Transfer and Entrepreneurship,* and *The Scientist.* He has also been invited to speak on these topics at annual meetings of the American Association of Colleges of Pharmacy and the American Historical Association as well as at numerous academic institutions. Ultimately, through his experiences, Nathan has a unique perspective on providing career guidance to graduate trainees.

Lindsay Bira, PhD

Dr. Bira is assistant professor of psychiatry in the School of Medicine at UT Health Science Center, San Antonio and also runs her own business as a clinical health psychologist, consultant, and speaker. She received her PhD from University of Miami and competed residency at VA Boston Healthcare System as a Harvard Medical School and Boston University School of Medicine fellow. She currently lives in San Antonio, TX, where she focuses on clinical research to reduce combat-related posttraumatic stress disorder and treats a range of issues in private practice.

Sharon Kuss, PhD

Sharon Kuss is both a postdoctoral researcher in virology and a postdoctoral intern in career development at the University of Texas Southwestern Medical Center, where she also completed a PhD in Microbiology.

Lily Raines, PhD

Lily Raines received her PhD in Biochemistry, Cellular, and Molecular Biology from Johns Hopkins School of Medicine. Following her PhD she served as the Global Projects Manager for International Activities for the American Chemical Society where she now manages their Office of Science Outreach. In this position she coordinates the National Chemistry Week, Chemists Celebrate Earth Day, and the Chemistry Festival Programs.

Section 1

Introduction

Chapter 1

Introduction

We, the authors of *ReSearch: A career guide for scientists*, are passionate about ensuring that graduate students and postdoctoral fellows are afforded the opportunity and resources required to pursue the careers of their choice. It is our goal to provide insights that will guide individuals on their career journeys in a way that is clear, concise, and appropriate for science, technology, engineering, and math (STEM) professionals. We are aware that some of our readers may have already gone through one, two, and even three or more career searches to find themselves in the positions that they currently have. Therefore, we have designed this book as a guide for our readers as they research their next career transition.

Throughout the book our readers will find activities to catalyze their career planning, expert insights from STEM professionals in a variety of careers, and key chapter takeaways designed to ensure that *ReSearch* is a valuable resource that our readers return to throughout their careers.

We hope that you enjoy this book as much as we have enjoyed collaborating to create it. Please reach out to us with questions, via social media, and share this book with others. It is our hope, and that of our contributors, that the resources throughout this book will be utilized by graduate students and post-doctoral fellows far and wide.

ReSearch. http://dx.doi.org/10.1016/B978-0-12-804297-7.00001-X

Chapter 2

Common Career Characters

Teresa M. Evans

Chapter Takeaways:

- As a scientist you have been taught the fundamental skills to research and plan for your career path.
- It is possible to overresearch and plan so remember to REFLECT regularly on your career plan.
- **In this chapter, we outline the three most common types of trainee career planners**:
    - *The optimized observer*: This is the trainee who is always observing and exploring options, learning from the experiences along the way, and managing the journey accordingly.
    - *The midway modifier*: These individuals have a clear and thought-out plan for their career from the beginning.
    - *The conclusion changer*: Our final example is the conclusion changer. These ladies and gentlemen experience an unforeseen whammy near the journey's end that causes a need for the plan to be changed.

Just as we know that every fingerprint is unique, it is also true in career planning that every career path is unlike any other. It is important to understand that there is no "one-size-fits-all" protocol for devising a successful career path. There can be many variables that impact a journey just as there are variables that impact our data collection processes within the laboratory. For example, the economic landscape has impacted the way that we view research and funding, industry development, and downturns have shifted the needs of the job market, and, more fundamentally, each of us have personal variables that impact where our career path may lead.

As scientists we are trained to manage entropy and identify variables within the lab. We are here to tell you that these same skills will be fundamental to the very existence of your future career. It is also notable to consider that the process for researching career paths and developing skills and knowledge to build a career can spin out of control. Let's consider a student, *Stan*, who attends every career development workshop offered at his university, conducts countless informational interviews, and is left with nothing but the realization that

ReSearch. http://dx.doi.org/10.1016/B978-0-12-804297-7.00002-1

there is no one prescription for the perfect career path. This feeling can be a lot to handle. Stan, if you are reading this, it is going to be okay. Take a step back from your career research extravaganza! It is time to reflect. We are here to teach you how to not only collect useful career planning information but also teach you how to reflect on what you find and apply it to your choices. We'll unwrap this information in future chapters.

Scientists are unusual adults. Many of us turn out to be career learners in many regards. Many of us also have little experience working in "the real world." And for the sake of this discussion, working at the mall does not count because that is likely not the work experience that will be useful for you to obtain your dream job. While we are trained specialists in our areas of research, it is rare for individuals, in their 20s and 30s to not have had any experience in the professional workplace. Just take one look at your Facebook feed, and if you are like us, it is clear…those friends who left undergrad for an industry position are in a different place than you…just accept it now but know that your time is coming! Unlike those fellow undergrad students on Facebook, your summers have been spent in the lab working under sometimes quite extreme pressure rather than interning and learning about various professions and work cultures as they might have done. This is further complicated by the fact that the outside world also has a very limited understanding about what goes on inside the depths of the laboratories within the Ivory Tower. For these reasons, we will also teach you how to translate and sell your skills to the outside world in a way that is appropriate for any career path you might choose.

Now, let's shift gears a bit. For the purpose of this scenario, imagine that you are embarking on the longest, toughest, and the most challenging journey of your life. Imagine that this journey at times can be quite pleasant and rewarding but at other times can be down right miserable. Oh, and when you reach what you think is the end of the journey and you see the light at the end of the tunnel, you can only enjoy it for a moment before you realize that the light is a freight train screaming toward you faster than you can get out of the way. Would you go on that journey? Well, the truth is that many of you are already on this journey but you might not yet be aware of what is ahead of you. Now, reread the scenario and think about it as if the journey is analogous to your research training and the train represents the next step in your career. This is the true story of the student who does not plan for their career until they see the light at the end of the tunnel. You need to plan for your career long before you see that light so that the train does not slap you in the face.

As scientists and career guidance professionals, we have observed that there are three common types of trainee career planners as outlined below. Read these and consider where you might fit or whom you might know in each of these areas:

The optimized observer: This is the trainee who is always observing and exploring options, learning from the experiences along the way, and managing the journey accordingly. Beware if this is you. Remember Stan? He is an optimized observer as well, but when not controlled, his observing distracts him and makes his career planning hard to focus. If managed properly, this is the ideal way to go about your career journey. Always being aware of your options by attending diverse events and workshops, networking in multiple communities, and reflecting often on what you have learned and by starting early.

The midway modifier: These individuals have a clear and thought-out plan for their career from the beginning. They are focused on their career destination until a mid-journey event (personal or otherwise) causes the need to modify their career plan. These individuals often worry that they are leaving something behind. For example, Sandy is a midway modifier who has decided to leave basic bench science for a teaching job at an undergraduate institution to accommodate her partner's career. This career is notable in its own right, but Sandy worries that this decision will cause her to miss bench research in a large research university and to be viewed by her colleagues unfavorably. It is our goal to help the midway modifiers, like Sandy, be confident in their decisions. We want you to know that it is okay to focus on yourself and your family. You have to come to terms with the fact that it is your life and you only live it once!

The conclusion changer: Our final example is the conclusion changer. These ladies and gentlemen experience an unforeseen whammy near the journey's end that causes a need for the plan to be changed. The one that most often comes to mind is the story of Christine. She realized that continued research training was just not for her as she was writing her dissertation. If this is you, you are late to the planning, of course, and that train is coming really fast but we are here to help you. I would suggest you go straight to Chapter 18 and read our emergency plan.

We share with you these three character types in hope that you can see yourself in one of them and then start to modify your behavior accordingly as you read through the following chapters of this book. We also know that these are not one size fits all descriptions but rather generalizable categories to get you to start thinking about how your actions and the actions of those around you have and will affect your career planning process. As a scientist, you have already chosen to embark on a path that would require you to constantly ask questions and to follow your curiosities. Be assured that career planning is no different. Go forth and follow your curiosities, as we want nothing more than to help you prepare for a future career that will continue to provide you with that excitement for years to come.

Section 2

Understanding the Landscape of Your Challenges and Choices

Chapter 3

Realities of the Job Market: Charting Your Career Path

Nathan L. Vanderford

Chapter Outline

Changes in the Academic
Landscape   12
Know Your Career Options   13
Narrow Down Your Career Choices 14
Scientists Working Outside of the
Academy   15
Unexpected Obstacles   16
Summary   17
References   18
For More Information   18

Chapter Takeaways:

- Be realistic about charting your future career path:
  - Only 14% of life sciences PhDs today hold tenure/tenure-track faculty positions within 6 years of graduating, so it's important that you're willing to change your career plans along with the evolving job market.
- Get familiar with your options now:
  - Only 26% of students are aware of their career options upon beginning a PhD program. Make sure this isn't you—consider career possibilities that extend beyond the walls of academia.
- Think about the kind of work you want to do:
  - It could be applied research, developmental research, management and administration, teaching, or something else. Understanding your own interests is crucial to making a career choice that will hold your interest in the long term.

It's important to be realistic about your career path from the very beginning— don't wait until there's only two months left before graduation! Learn the truth about the current job market and how to plan ahead for a variety of possible careers that take into consideration your personal and research interests.

Trust me, thinking about the job market and your career path is very important! Things have turned out fine for me, but when I was a graduate student I did pretty

ReSearch. http://dx.doi.org/10.1016/B978-0-12-804297-7.00003-3

11

much the exact opposite of the advice I am giving you here. I focused on the here-and-now, which were basically just the day-to-day tasks needed to finish my degree. I didn't put that much thought into the jobs I might want or get in the future. I was really just on autopilot and accepted the fact that I would do a postdoc after my PhD and eventually I would get a "real" job. I certainly was not thinking about how difficult it may be to get a job. As a result, I spent the first couple of years after my PhD backtracking to better prepare myself for the realities of the job market and the career path that I wanted to pursue. So, if you are still a graduate trainee, don't do what I did. Act now and prepare for your career while you are still in training! We're going to give you insight into this throughout this book.

So, I am here to tell you that at some point in your academic studies, you may feel a tremendous pressure to take a certain course, write a specific article, or apply for a particular grant. The justification will be that this is what's required to get on the right track to complete the degree of your choice within a set period of time and "succeed on the job market." At this critical juncture, take a deep breath and consider your options—even those that your advisor may not tell you about.

While considering these options, you may agonize over the seeming rigidity of your future studies, seek advice from trusted mentors, and plan a more reasonable route toward degree completion. But, above all, you'll likely realize that you can no longer put off making a serious, detailed plan for your future until a few months before graduation. While your advisor may ignore the realities of a changing work environment, you cannot afford to ignore them, and the harsh truth is that you may never have the luxury of a tenure-track position.

In this chapter you'll learn that, as you complete your graduate training, you also need to weigh and measure how all of your decisions will fit into your long-term career plan. It will be important to recognize that your options extend beyond the academy, and even outside of the industries that are most often related to your research.

This chapter will outline the landscape of the life sciences job market and help you consider the variety of fields open to you as a scientist and PhD, including many roles not traditionally attached to such backgrounds. The statistics and facts presented here are meant to serve as a motivating factor for you to focus on preparing for your career, so please pay attention to and digest them in relation to your career aspirations.

CHANGES IN THE ACADEMIC LANDSCAPE

The biomedical sciences career landscape has changed dramatically in the last half century, according to Gibbs and Griffin, the authors of "What Do I Want to Be with My PhD?"[1] Referring to their study on this subject, they explain that 40 years ago, the majority of PhD scientists went straight from graduate school to faculty positions. Today, only about 14% of life sciences PhDs obtain tenure or tenure-track positions within 6 years of graduating.

Gibbs and Griffin recommend that from the first year of graduate school, your educational institution, faculty, and mentors should begin making you aware of the wide variety of career paths available. While they should encourage you to be more proactive in charting an early course toward your career destination, you may need to make such efforts on your own to be prepared upon graduation.

The article "The missing piece to changing the university culture"[2] reinforces this picture of a changing job market: "Current PhD training programs are focused primarily on the academic career track despite its disheartening outlook: the number of awarded PhDs is significantly outpacing the available positions." Each year, the authors explain, there are seven times more PhDs awarded in science and engineering than there are newly available faculty positions.

Dr. Isaiah Hankel,[3] founder of Cheeky Scientist (http://cheekyscientist.com/) and author of the book *Black Hole Focus*, clearly remembers the day when he suddenly realized he was not likely to find his place in academic life: "I had no ideas of what I could do outside of the narrow career path that I was on. I was confused and felt like a failure."

However, when he changed his perspective, his life changed. "I decided I needed to start with the end in mind. This meant deciding on an endpoint and then working backwards to get there…Suddenly I felt energized. I also started seeing opportunities to reach my new goals in everything that I did." Hankel says that by mapping out his endpoint, he was able to achieve what he wanted. "But I don't share any of this to impress you," he notes. "I share it to impress upon you that any PhD reading this has the ability to change their life in an instant by mapping out his/her endpoint and working backyards to achieve it."

KNOW YOUR CAREER OPTIONS

If you're like most PhD students, it's unlikely that you're genuinely aware of all the career options that exist for you. In fact, only 26% of postdocs report having knowledge about the career options available to a person with a PhD in their discipline when they began their PhD programs.[4] You, on the other hand, are going to be prepared! Reading this book indicates that you are already ahead of the curve in thinking about and preparing for your career.

In a study by Henry Suermann and Michael Roach[5] published in *PLoS One*, across all study sectors, students in the life sciences and physics sectors most often rated a faculty career with an emphasis on research as extremely attractive (34% and 36% of students, respectively). This interest was followed by a preference for teaching careers and research and development positions in government. In the "other" category of careers, interests stretched broadly, including science communication/writer, science policy, nonuniversity teaching, working for a nonprofit, nongovernmental organization, and consulting.

The researchers also noted that students' interest in faculty careers, though high at the beginning of their graduate programs, waned slightly when they came closer to graduation. One theory that Suermann and Roach offered about this changing level of interest was the possibility that toward the end of a PhD program, students start to shift into other career interests as they become aware of them. Another proposed explanation suggests—more pessimistically—that students realize they have no hope of achieving a faculty position as they progress in their programs and thus start to say that they no longer "want" such unattainable jobs.

Suermann and Roach discovered that what does start looking more attractive as students near the end of their studies are careers in research and development within government facilities. In fact, interest in this career averaged an increase of 10.9% as students neared the end of their programs. The researchers' data showed that students' interests swayed in this direction because of perceived high levels of job security and access to funding offered by such positions. Furthermore, they tended to believe that government labs could provide opportunities to conduct research in a manner that is similar to that in academia.

Gibbs et al. conducted another study[6] that surveyed 1500 US citizens and permanent residents who completed their PhD in the biomedical sciences between 2007 and 2012. They discovered that two-thirds of the respondents worked as postdoctoral scientists (66.8%). Other respondents had found work outside of research, such as science policy, law, science communication, or business (9.2%). Still others worked as research scientists or engineers in industry or government (5.7%), tenure-track professors (4.1%), or in other academic positions (4.1%).

One theme ran through all of these studies: very few life sciences PhDs knew about the wide range of career options they had available to them when they started their programs. Yet in the end, many trainees ended up venturing outside of academia for employment.

If your experience is similar to these students, remember that you're not alone. It's common for PhD students to change their areas of interest as their studies progress. In fact, changing one's career direction is actually a positive step—it's the full acknowledgment that with academic knowledge comes self-knowledge as you get closer and closer to understanding the kind of work that you will find purposeful and sustaining for a lifetime.

You should find comfort in the fact that the unemployment rate for PhDs is only around 2% and PhDs have a median income of around $80,000 in the United States.[7] While only 14% of life sciences PhDs are working in academia in a tenure-track position, over 50% of PhDs are working outside of academia in any number of career fields including those for the business sector (nearly 40% of PhDs) and for the federal and state government (around 10% of PhDs).[8] So, PhDs are being highly successful and happy within the confines of the current realities of the job market. You can and will be too!

NARROW DOWN YOUR CAREER CHOICES

The big question for you now is how do I narrow down my career choices?

There are many ways to plot your career path, but all of them involve these three steps:

1. Determine which kind of work really interests you.
2. Research career options using studies and first-hand examples to gain a deeper understanding of what they entail.

3. Gain experience-based learning in the field that most interests you, if possible.

So, the first thing to ask yourself is what kind of work actually interests me? In their study, Sauermann and Roach identified five distinctive work categories:

1. Work that contributes fundamental insights or theories (aka basic research)
2. Work that creates knowledge to solve practical problems (aka applied research)
3. Work that uses knowledge to develop materials, devices, or software (aka development)
4. Work that is commercialized into products or services (aka commercialization)
5. Work within management, administration, and teaching

The researchers found it noteworthy that many students in the life sciences and chemistry demonstrated a strong interest in work involving finding solutions to concrete problems. Simultaneously, the number of scientists interested in building careers in technology commercialization was significantly smaller; indeed, many respondents actually rated commercialization as uninteresting or even extremely uninteresting. This may not be the case for you, but it's important to know your options as well as the trends among your peers.

Notably, however, these students also reported feeling that they were being encouraged toward academic career paths. Furthermore, they described feeling underinformed about their career options outside of academia. This finding demonstrates why it's essential to start researching career options for yourself as soon as possible.

The key is to spend some time seriously contemplating the kind of work that interests you. Then look at what other scientists have done with their doctorates; you can find a plethora of fascinating real-life stories on scientists' websites.

SCIENTISTS WORKING OUTSIDE OF THE ACADEMY

Let's briefly consider some of the scientists out there who took an alternative career direction upon completing their PhD.

Dr. Mayim Bialik,[9] best known now for her portrayal of Amy Farrah Fowler on *The Big Bang Theory*, played the lead role in *Blossom* prior to getting her doctorate in neuroscience. Ultimately she left the lab and returned to television for practical reasons. "I wanted to be with my children. Also, we [she and her husband] had finished graduate school and needed health insurance… I got pregnant with my second son the week I filed my thesis. Once he was about one year old, I started going to auditions." She landed the role of Amy.

Bialik's character wasn't a scientist in the first season, but when she returned for the second season, cocreator Bill Prady made her a neurobiologist because he thought she could help fix things—the science details—if the show's writers got anything wrong. "We had a physics consultant on staff and our writers are generally very intelligent," she says. She found it rewarding to maintain this connection to science in her renewed acting career.

Dr. Camille Delebecque,[10] founder and president of Synbio Consulting, describes becoming frustrated during his own PhD studies. He began to question how research was being managed and the poor innovation transfer in most places, ultimately making the decision to develop a career outside of academia. On his website, www.camilledelebecque.com, Delebecque identifies his area of expertise as synthetic biology, which he describes as the design and construction of new biological devices and systems for useful purposes. In addition to running his own firm, he now works with the European Commission as an expert in synthetic biology.

After you determine the kind of work that you're most interested in and explore the realm of what other scientists have done as a means of broadening your perspective on career options, it's strongly suggested that you find an opportunity to gain firsthand experiential learning. As I'll discuss in a later chapter, nothing gives you insight into the ins and outs of a career more than being exposed to it through employment (temporary or part time), volunteering, or an internship.

Some students first explore their potential interests as a hobby, which later transforms into a career. For example, when Dr. Kate Baldwin[11] (http://www.k8baldwin.com/) entered graduate school in 2005, scientific diagrams were already one of her interests. Although she enjoyed bench work, especially data interpretation, she found herself eager to compile her data and ideas into simple images. She started helping friends and colleagues in that capacity, as well as teaching communication concepts and graphic software tips.

By July 2013, Baldwin had started a freelance business that she continues to run today. She offers services as a scientific visual communicator, translating the ideas of scientists into visual diagrams that help others to understand complex concepts. The training she received while obtaining her PhD in cellular and molecular biology has given her great insight, allowing her to understand the ideas that she now translates into visuals.

UNEXPECTED OBSTACLES

In a perfect world, your ideal career will have room for you, and you'll have no trouble getting hired. But the actual reality can be harsher: sometimes you may find obstacles in your path. These can include the barrier of discrimination toward women scientists and reluctance in some corporations toward building diverse workplaces.

In Gibbs et al.'s article, the researchers noted that increasing the participation of women and scientists from underrepresented minority (URM) backgrounds in the science professoriate remains "perhaps the least successful of the diversity initiatives."[6] For example, in the biomedical sciences field, "women earn more than half of PhDs but represent only 33% of newly hired tenure-track (TTT) professors. Scientists from URM backgrounds earn 10% of life science doctorates, but represent only 2% of medical school basic science TTT faculty and this number hasn't changed since 1980."

If these studies and stories send one clear message, it is that you need to chart your own career path as early as possible during your studies. This is perhaps even more important if you're a woman or you come from an under-represented minority background. Remember that YOU hold control over your future career, and being aware of the potential obstacles that could stand in the way will allow you to steer yourself in the direction that will be the most promising and fulfilling for you.

This is not to say that your ideas won't change during the time it takes to complete your degree, but by determining the kind of work you want to do and the aspects of a job that interest you most, you will grow closer to securing fulfilling work in your future.

"One significant aspect to our PhD training is that we develop the ability to think analytically, to ask questions, to become independent, and to value undertaking new tasks," writes Dr. Vanessa Hubbard-Lucey.[12] "Fortunately, these are many critical skills that ALL employers seek in their top candidates for countless jobs."

Hubbard-Lucey's one piece of advice to PhD students is to "take responsibility for your career development, whether you are pursuing a career in academia or elsewhere." It's important to monitor your progress along the way, she says, and to consistently develop skills and networks to help you achieve your goals. In the following chapters, we will discuss concrete strategies that will aid you with this process.

SUMMARY

The take home message of this chapter is that *you must* put some thought into the career path you would like to pursue. Maybe you do want to be a tenure-track faculty member and that is OK, but the point here is that you need to understand the statistics behind that job path and you need to understand what you really need to do to be successful obtaining that kind of job. The same goes for any career path you choose. The reality is that very few PhDs are now tenure-track faculty and that is also OK. PhDs are finding very rewarding career paths in all types of areas including being staff and research scientists in academia and industry, consultants, program and project managers, writers, editors, graphic designers, and the list could go on and on. You need to decide what career path you would like to pursue and then start working toward being as prepared as possible to be successful in entering that career path once you've completed your training. We're going to give you steps in this book to follow to do just that!

REFERENCES

1. Gibbs Jr K, Griffin K. What do I want to be with my Ph.D.? The roles of personal values and structural dynamics in shaping the career interests of recent biomedical science Ph.D. graduates. *CBE-Life Sciences Education* 2013;**12**:711–23. http://dx.doi.org/10.1187/cbe.13-02-0021.
2. Schillebeeckx M, Maricque B, Lewis C. The missing piece to changing the university culture. *Nature Biotechnology* 2013;**31**(10):938–41. http://dx.doi.org/10.1038/nbt.2706.
3. Cheeky Scientist. Isaiah Hankel, Ph.D. http://cheekyscientist.com/members/isaiah-hankel-ph-d/.
4. Gibbs Jr K, McGready J, Griffin K. Career development among American biomedical postdocs. *CBE-Life Sciences Education* 2015;**14**(4). http://dx.doi.org/10.1187/cbe.15-03-0075.
5. Sauermann H, Roach M. Science PhD career preferences: levels, changes, and advisory encouragement. *PLoS One* 2012;**7**(5). http://dx.doi.org/10.1371/journal.pone.0036307.
6. Gibbs Jr K, McGready J, Bennett J, Griffin K. Biomedical science PhD career interest patterns by race/ethnicity and gender. *PLoS One* 2014;**9**(12). http://dx.doi.org/10.1371/journal.pone.0114736.
7. United States Department of Labor Bureau of Labor Statistics. http://www.bls.gov/emp/ep_chart_001.htm.
8. National Science Foundation. Science and Engineering Indicators 2014.
9. Bialik M. Biography. http://www.mayimbialik.net/2014/02/06/45/.
10. Delebecque C. About. http://www.camilledelebecque.com/.
11. Baldwin K. Dr. Kate Baldwin: Scientific Visual Communicator for Hire. http://www.k8baldwin.com/.
12. Hubbard-Lucey V. December 2, 2013. Vanessa Hubbard-Lucey, Ph.D. [Web log post]. Retrieved from: http://whatareallthephds.tumblr.com/post/68790452944/vanessa-hubbard-lucey-phd-mba-science-postdoc-industry.

FOR MORE INFORMATION

The Versatile PhD's PhD Career Finder

1. https://versatilephd.com/phd-career-finder/.

This dynamic online tool sponsored by the folks at The Versatile PhD—an excellent resource in itself—lists potential careers for PhDs from any discipline. Aside from providing a basic description of the career or industry, it offers tips on how to get your foot in the door and information on advancement opportunities. It also provides a list of disciplines that are best suited for the career, as well as actual resumes and biographies of PhDs who have established a successful career in the industry. Although you have to join for access to the resumes and biographies, membership is free and offers you access to a whole network of nonacademic PhDs.

What Are All The PhDs

2. http://whatareallthephds.tumblr.com/.

Designed as an informal Tumblr blog documenting the stories of various PhDs and their careers, "What Are All The PhDs?" acts as an archive of potential careers for PhDs from a variety of fields. This blog demonstrates the many career possibilities for someone with a doctorate degree who may be interested in a career outside of the academy.

Chapter 4

Understanding the Career Game: Figuring Out "the Rules" of Career Planning and Getting Motivated to Plan for a Successful Career

Teresa M. Evans

Chapter Outline

Rule #1: Trainees Do Not Get Hired   **20**
Rule #2: Be Visible and Network   **20**
Where to Find Opportunities if They Are Not Readily Offered   21
How to Choose Which Opportunities to Attend From Among the Options   21
Do You Know Anyone Else Who Will Be Attending?   21
How Long Is the Event?   21
Will the Event Be Fun?   21
Will There Be Time at the Event for One-on-One Discussion or Is It a Lecture Format With Little Time for Interaction?   22
What Is the Prestige of the Anticipated Crowd?   22
Rule #3: Just Ask   **22**
Rule #4: Find at Least One "Career Mentor"   **22**
Rule #5: Have a Plan to Plan   **23**
Rule #6: Know Yourself   **25**
Concluding Remarks   **25**
Reference   **27**

Chapter Takeaways:

- Trainees do not get hired, professionals do. Remember to be a professional at all times.
- Be visible and network. Get out of the lab and meet people.
- Just ask. Do not be incapacitated by anxiety. Ask questions! This will help you to build your network.
- Find a career mentor or two. They will guide you toward your goal as they have personal experiences to help you.

ReSearch. http://dx.doi.org/10.1016/B978-0-12-804297-7.00004-5

- Have a plan to plan. You will not reach your goals if you do not think about what you need to do to get there.
- Know yourself. The goal to finding a perfect career is knowing what is perfect for you and your personality. Take time to get to know who you are and what you like and do not like.

As scientists we can often remember the moments in our lives that drew us into our current area of study. Maybe it was a personal experience, or a teacher in grade school, but either way it is these moments that fuel our passion to enter this field. But what happens once we cross over to "the dark side" and are members of the professional scientific career field? Often, the guidance we received to make it into our current roles as scientific professionals is behind us, and we are left with finding our way on our own. We are thrown into the game without ever being told what the rules are. We must navigate our way from higher education and into our careers of choice with not so much as basic guidelines.

But worry no more; there are a few tips that I have learned along my own unique career path that have helped me to minimize the variables and maximize my success in navigating the career game.

RULE #1: TRAINEES DO NOT GET HIRED

The first thing that you need to hear as a graduate trainee is, "trainees do not get hired for jobs." What, you might say, does that mean? What I mean is that as long as you continue to view yourself as a student or trainee and continue to have the habits of such, you will not be viewed well in the hiring community. Whether that is within or outside of the "Ivory Tower." An entrepreneur raised me; my mother owned a restaurant in which I grew up. It is in my DNA to "work a crowd," "communicate well," and "be professional." This is not in everyone's DNA and it is not something that is expected always of a student in the laboratory but it is something expected of a faculty member, industry professional, and leader in the bioscience community. So as you read through this book try to remember the take-away message that the skills outlined here are the skills that get people hired. Your technical skills are very important but you cannot stand alone on the skills you learn in the lab. To rise to the top of the workforce you must master additional professional skills.

RULE #2: BE VISIBLE AND NETWORK

As you progress through your graduate training, remember to be visible and get involved. You will receive emails that talk about great events, such as local symposia and workshops, plan to attend! Your future career aspirations will be much more easily attained if you have a network and the only way to get one is to meet people.

Where to Find Opportunities if They Are Not Readily Offered

More and more graduate universities are increasing the professional and career development programs offered for their trainees. Whether you are in one of these universities where there are ample networking and career development programs, or not, you should be seeking out networking opportunities on your own. Thanks to the Internet and social media there are many ways to find places to meet interesting people and expand your network. I encourage you to check-out Meetups.com and Twitter as a start to finding opportunities in your city. Other opportunities to network include getting involved in: BIO chapters or organizations, Young Professionals Groups, Toastmasters, Bioscience Networking Groups, and local nonprofit events.

How to Choose Which Opportunities to Attend From Among the Options

You do not have to go to every workshop, conference, and event that you find in your inbox or read about online. In fact, you shouldn't. Choosing the events to go to is not a science but there are a few strategic questions you should consider before making the decision to attend.

Do You Know Anyone Else Who Will Be Attending?

Yes. If you answer yes to this question and you are new to networking, then this might be a good event to attend. You will have some people who you already know who can help introduce you to those whom you do not. But be sure to make an effort to meet new people. Don't just stay with those whom you know. No. If no, then this would be a great event to attend. Every person you meet will be a new contact! You will be out of your comfort zone, which is good to experience once in a while.

How Long Is the Event?

The length of the event matters when choosing how to spend your time. Ideally, you want to find events that provide you with the most time to meet new people but with the least time invested. An all day event is not a bad thing as long as you feel it will promote your career. Can you present at a conference to build your CV or resume and justify the 3-day excursion to San Diego, as well as satisfy the goal of meeting new people? For each day of a conference set a target number of new people to meet so that you do not let the time pass without building your network.

Will the Event Be Fun?

Not all networking events are "fun." As you progress through your career you will be asked to go to events that are not fun, but, for example, you might go to an event so that others see that you were there. Also, often at these events are other people whom you need to meet. Just suck it up and go!

Will There Be Time at the Event for One-on-One Discussion or Is It a Lecture Format With Little Time for Interaction?

If the event is solely lecture and little time to meet with people one-on-one I tend to think twice before attending. Especially if the purpose of my attendance is to network—but if I am attending to learn from the speaker, or to meet the speaker, then it is a good event to attend.

What Is the Prestige of the Anticipated Crowd?

If it's a late event and I'm exhausted from a long day at work I will often decide about an event based on who I expect will be in attendance. Try to determine if the event will be filled with high-impact network members. If so, shrug off the sleepiness and go!

For more information about networking see Chapter 12.

RULE #3: JUST ASK

Start asking questions now. If you don't know someone and want to have them in your network, ask for a meeting or a conversation or to make a connection on social media. Just learn to ask and don't be afraid. Fear is often what holds us back in our careers and from pursuing our passions. It is that same fear that can keep us isolated and prevent us from meeting new people. You must MEET A LOT OF HUMANS if you are to convince the world that you are not a student or trainee anymore.

Activity: Schedule an informational interview with someone new. An informational interview is just that, an interview for the purpose of gathering information. If it sounds too daunting to conduct an interview, call it an informational chat (a phrase taken from the UK business world). I encourage you to have a list of questions for the individual you decide to meet with. For example, an informational meeting with a CEO of a local start-up company might include questions like the following:

1. What are some things you might suggest that I do to better prepare myself for the transition from academia to industry?
2. What has surprised you most about your current position?
3. Do you know anyone else that I should meet in this area? (THIS ONE IS KEY, always end with the invitation for the person to provide you with another contact.)

RULE #4: FIND AT LEAST ONE "CAREER MENTOR"

As graduate trainees we spend much of our time thinking about, complaining about, and wondering about the feelings of our laboratory mentor. Also, I commonly hear from trainees, "my mentor will get me a job." Well, the reality is our laboratory mentor is not the end all be all. They are not responsible for finding you a job or for leading your career in any way. These individuals can often serve as a guide in preparing for career transitions but they are not there to hand anything to their mentees. Someday, when you become a mentor, you will expect your mentee to take these matters into their own hands, have some eagerness, and be the driver of their career destiny.

This being said, we all need more than one mentor to assure our success. Not all laboratory mentors will be career mentors or life mentors, and we often need multiple mentors. These mentors will shift and change their focuses and purposes throughout your life (see Chapter 12, for more on how to build a personal board of directors). But as this book is focused on making career decisions, I will focus this discussion on what it takes to be a good career mentor. If I were to write a personal ad for a career mentor it would read as follows:

> *Seeking a career mentor. Someone who is a good listener and willing to meet regularly. A person who has experience with the career area that I am interested in but also willing to help me debate other options as I progress through my career. Someone who can ask good questions to help me to work through complex career planning steps. Overall, I am seeking a mentor who will promote and support me as I transition from trainee into a professional.*

In looking for your career mentors I encourage you to keep this passage in mind and know that you will need to build a mentoring team to meet all of your needs. Your mentors will develop along with the relationships you build, and the impact of your different mentors will "ebb and flow" over time, according to where you are in your career journey. Keep in mind you cannot force mentor or sponsor relationships. Rapport will develop only when you get to know people—so if you aren't making connections, you can't begin building mentor–mentee pairings. Mentorship (either being mentored or becoming a mentor yourself) is a lifelong activity.

RULE #5: HAVE A PLAN TO PLAN

We are acutely aware that not everyone is the same type of career planner. Let's think back to Stan, Sandy, and Christine from Chapter 2.

Stan, the optimized observer, is always planning and observing his options along the way. Stan would most likely create a plan like the one pictured below, (Adapted from the 5-year plan, found in *The Professor Is In*[1]), which includes not only deadlines for his entire graduate career but also for planning his future career path. This is key. Although as an optimized observer, Stan can become too focused on planning and might get lost in the process of making plans rather than taking action, setting aside this time should help him to avoid this issue (Fig. 4.1).

Sandy, the midway modifier, has a similar plan, but due to her never-changing focus on her long-term career goal she has neglected to plan any time to think about her career. For this reason, when she makes it to year 3 of her PhD program and decides she wants to change her mind, she will have to meet more frequently with a career mentor to discuss her career plan and put her networking into overdrive. This is not uncommon—but can be avoided if you make taking time to reflect on your career and build a solid plan B a priority from the beginning. Even if you don't think you will need it.

5-YEAR PLAN

	January	February	March	April	May	June	July	August	September	October	November	December
'15								Orientation and Grad School Starts Start: CV, 5-year plan IDP LinkedIn	18-19 Career Symposia / Waitlist for Better Parking	Lab Rotations →	Career Update	
'16	Laboratory Chosen; Career Planning Meeting	Career Update; Discuss Dissertation Topic			Career Update	Finalize Dissertation Topic	Career Planning Meeting	Career Update			Career Update	Start Writing Qual Exam
'17	Career Planning Meeting	Career Update		Complete Candidacy Qual Exam	FTROOP; Career Update	Form Dissertation Committee FTROOP	Career Planning Meeting FTROOP	B-F Grant Submission; Career Update			Diss. Committee Meeting; Career Update	
'18	Career Planning Meeting	Career Update			Diss. Committee Meeting; Career Update		Career Planning Meeting	Dissertation proposal; Career Update	Attended Dissertation Boot Camp START WRITING		Career Update	
'19	Career Planning Meeting	Diss. Committee Meeting; Career Update			Begin the application process; Career Update		Career Planning Meeting	Diss. Committee Meeting; Discuss Date and Draft; Career Update		Career Planning Meeting	Career Update	
'20	Diss. Committee Meeting; Career Planning Meeting; Career Update		Defense	Career Update; Job OFFER?	Graduation	NEW JOB!						

Application and Interview Preparation

FIGURE 4.1 Stan's plan: This is an example of a 5-year plan adapted from *The Professor Is In.*[1] You will see that the months are across the top and five years are listed down the table. In this way you set deadlines and goals for yourself across a 5-year timeline and can visualize them all on ONE PAGE. Remember, you need to begin planning for a career change at least 1 year in advance. You will see that Stan did that with the *blue arrows* (dark gray in print versions) labeled, Application and Interview Preparation.

Now, Christine had a plan and followed it to a "T," but…in year 5 of her graduate program she has realized that she no longer wants to stay at the lab bench. What does she do? How could she have better prepared? Well, everyone's plan should include a plan B, as we already stated. You need to be sure that, no matter how determined you are, you have a back-up plan at all times. Life is unpredictable just as science is unpredictable. So in this case, Christine has worked to diversify her CV by including teaching courses at a local undergraduate institution and is now looking for positions with a focus on teaching.

This is just one example of how to prepare a career plan. Many people use simple lists or event plans in a larger scale with blank monthly calendars. I encourage you to find what works for you and stick with it! No matter the method you choose to plan your career make sure to include time to plan and time for fun! Also, be sure to share your plan with someone else to keep you accountable, possibly one of your career mentors.

RULE #6: KNOW YOURSELF

In the career-planning game, this is often overlooked because people say "of course I know myself." But most scientists have never turned analysis and investigation on their own preferences and aspirations. There are many tools available to help you to better know yourself: to determine your likes, values, and personality type (see Chapter 8). As you work through these tools, remember this is an evolving journey. As your life changes, so will your priorities. Also, know your limits and don't hesitate to reach out for help if you need it (see Chapter 5 for tips on personal well-being and how to achieve it). If you are a planner, dedicate even a small amount of time to focus on yourself and what makes you "you." I encourage you to find time to sit and reflect. Simply think about what you like and do not like.

Activity: Use the checklist in Fig. 4.2 as you plan your own career. Be sure to revisit the checklist often as this is not a one and done approach to career planning.

CONCLUDING REMARKS

Taking on career planning is like having a second job. It takes time, it takes effort, and it's ongoing. Even once you land a fantastic job, wherever that may be, you will still be thinking about how to thrive in that new position. You will need to navigate a new work environment and learn to interact with a set of colleagues and managers. You also will want to set and reach professional goals, continue building your network, and perhaps even be looking toward a promotion. This is why business self-improvement books are a multimillion dollar industry! So once you take on the job of career planning, recognize that you will have that job, to some extent, for the rest of your professional life.

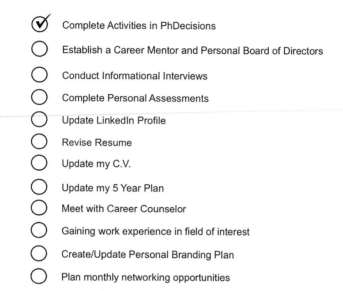

FIGURE 4.2 This is an example of a checklist of basic career-planning steps. Use this as a starting point as you begin your career planning journey.

Right now, the job of career planning is going to be more difficult and take more time, because you are a novice. However, in a few years, you will be grateful to have the foundation of self-knowledge and career tools (resumes and cover letters, for example) and over time each move along your career trajectory becomes easier.

For current students and postdocs, it may be simplest to undertake your career-planning "job" in a set period of time each day or week, for example, setting aside just 5 or 10 min a day is a great way to start and avoid the possibility of feeling overwhelmed. It is okay to break down the career planning process because you simply can't give it large amounts of dedicated time. If you work at a laboratory bench and are surrounded by colleagues or in view of a boss whom you are not comfortable sharing that you are investigating your next steps, you'll have to find time to do things, such as update your LinkedIn profile on your lunch break. Also, many institutions now have staff and/or faculty in place who are trained to help with career planning, and it is your job to seek out these individuals to ask for help. They will not come knocking on your door! If you are working in a lab you may not have time or flexibility in your work setting to do Internet searches, fill out career assessment instruments, or have informational chats without raising eyebrows. All of the career-planning advice and activities in this book can be done in small segments of time and during your personal time—it's up to you to create the time and space for career planning to achieve your unique work–life balance.

Now that you have a few quick rules to get you started, it is important to remember that your career is a journey. You will definitely not have all the answers overnight or even after completing all the activities in this book. As you continue down your path you will find rules of your own and techniques that work for you, in fact, we encourage you to look for them. In conclusion, be mindful along the way that you are surrounded by people who are supportive of you and are there to help if you ask. Do not go on this journey without knowing that there are people rooting for you to succeed.

REFERENCE

1. Kelsky K. *The professor is in: the essential guide to turning your PhD into a job.* Three Rivers Press; August, 2015.

Case Study

Dr. Nicole C. Woitowich holds a PhD in Biochemistry and Molecular Biology. She is currently the director of Science Outreach and Education for the Women's Health Research Institute at Northwestern University.

You Must Prepare for Your Professional Career in Graduate School

I was lucky enough to find my dream job straight out of graduate school. But in all honesty, it wasn't luck. It was incredible timing and the fact that I had relentlessly prepared myself to be the best possible candidate for the job I wanted. Hopefully by sharing my path, you might gain some insight on how to get started on yours.

Early in my graduate training, I realized that I did not want to continue my career at the benchtop. I had found a passion for science outreach and education that trumped my love for X-ray crystallography. I quickly realized that I needed to develop additional skill sets, beyond pipetting and western blot analysis, that would make me an attractive candidate for these types of positions in academia, government, nonprofit, or private industry. This meant participating in extracurricular activities outside of the laboratory.

I must admit, I didn't think of it as "skill building" at first. Instead, I just wanted to explore what other options were available for scientists, beyond the bench. I noticed that my professional society was hosting a Capitol Hill Day where graduate student and postdoctoral members could travel to Washington, DC, to speak with their elected officials about the importance of biomedical research. I thought this would be a great way to learn more about science communication and science policy—and it was! But it was also so much more! I finally realized why science communication is so incredibly important on multiple levels, and that all scientists should be engaged members of the scientific community. I also realized that this is what I might be good at!

I took the excitement and energy of my experience on Capitol Hill back to my home institution, eager to get involved with more science outreach activities. As a graduate student on a medical school campus, I found that the majority of outreach programs had a health-care focus. In fact, I could not find a single science

Continued

Case Study—cont'd

outreach program which was active in my local area. The next step just seemed so logical to me—why not start my own? At the time, I did not think of it as something to add to my CV. Instead, I saw a need for this type of programming in my community and decided to fill that role. I ended up developing a science outreach organization which promoted the advancement of women in science and medicine through mentorship. It was originally going to be a small partnership with a local undergraduate institution, but soon expanded to include middle-school and high school programming once other graduate students became interested in participating. I soon learned how to manage volunteers, develop marketing, and attract stakeholders (all things that definitely weren't covered in my graduate-level molecular biology courses).

Throughout this time, I remained engaged with my scientific society. I noticed that they had an entire session dedicated to science outreach at their national meeting. I applied to present my outreach work, and unbeknownst to me, that this would be one of those "life-changing" moments in my career. I was like a kid in a candy shop at that poster session, I could barely contain my excitement and energy. There I learned three important lessons: (1) There are actually scientists who get paid to do science outreach (I had thought this was some sort of mystical career option like dragon-training or underwater basket weaving). (2) There is a dedicated community of scientists who actively support and encourage science outreach. (3) *This is what I want to do with the rest of my life.*

I networked with as many people as I could at that meeting. I found out that my scientific society had a Public Outreach Committee and before you know it, I was their newest member. Armed with a new found confidence and clarity, I began conducting informational interviews with people in positions I aspired to hold. Did I know them personally? Not at all. But I found that most people are more than willing to talk about their career to anyone who is interested. I began applying to jobs early—almost 8 months prior to my scheduled defense date. I did not want to miss any opportunity that may come across. The next thing you know; I am applying for a position which sounds like it was created just for me. Like a substrate bound to the active site of an enzyme, it was a perfect fit.

I can guarantee you that I would not have gotten my dream job had I remained in the laboratory waiting for things to happen. I went outside of my comfort zone, on more than one occasion, to create opportunities for myself. The best piece of advice I can give to you is the following: **You are your own best advocate**. No one is going to pluck you out of your laboratory and into some fantastic role in the government, industry, or academia, no matter what the field. But there are numerous people who are willing to support and mentor you along the way, as long as you show the initiative.

Section 3

Taking Care of Yourself

Chapter 5

Managing Stress and Staying Healthy

Lindsay Bira
University of Texas Health San Antonio, San Antonio, TX, United States

Chapter Outline

Graduate Training Is Stressful	**32**	Communication	38
The Stress Response	**33**	Cognitive Restructuring	39
Chronic Stress	**34**	Mindfulness Practice	40
Preparing for Stress—Choosing		Hobbies	41
Balance	**35**	**Trusting in the Process**	**42**
Physical Activity	35	**References**	**43**
Social Support	36		

Chapter Takeaways:

- Understanding what stress is and how it affects the body is crucial to managing stress more effectively.
- Prestress conditioning describes how you can prepare yourself to be more resilient in the face of stress.
- Get tips for keeping healthy activities in your schedule, such as exercise and hobbies.
- Utilizing social support is a skill. Understand when to reach out, to whom, and under what circumstances.
- Learn techniques for effective communication that will help get your needs met. Also learn how to work with your thoughts when things aren't going as planned.
- Life brings many changes and unexpected hurdles. Trusting in the process is half the battle!

As a clinical health psychologist, a large part of what I am interested in is how stress affects the mind and body. Physiological and emotional issues can result from a range of stressful circumstances, from a punishing career to a severe trauma. I work with people in therapy to help them better manage these issues and

ReSearch. http://dx.doi.org/10.1016/B978-0-12-804297-7.00005-7

I'm passionate about sharing tools and techniques broadly *before* chronic stress results in health issues. Looking back on my own graduate training, I realize that being unaware of simple ways to manage my stress led to some emotional and physical difficulties. On top of the already-stressful circumstances related to graduate training, I would also get sick, or become irritable, which only added fuel to the fire. When a mentor or professor discussed the importance of "self-care" and "balance" when I was in the midst of my studies, I heard unrealistic ideas from someone who was already out of the process. I tried to focus on managing school, relationships, and life responsibilities in the best way I could at the time, but that meant they all suffered to some extent because I didn't know how to manage them well.

Now, I am out of the process and speaking to you about the same things that made me roll my eyes, but I understand what would have helped me relate to and absorb this topic and I want to share that with you. This is more than just advice. Stress management tools are based on solid research and the techniques are effective if presented properly and utilized well.

There are simple and helpful ways to form new habits, if you are willing to put in the work now for benefit later (and let's be honest, that's your mind-set if you've taken on any kind of higher education!). Graduate training is a long path with a giant reward at the end, and that reward will be even more enjoyable if you take care of yourself along the way. This chapter will focus on the stress related to graduate training, but keep in mind that the information you'll find here can be applied to any phase of life.

GRADUATE TRAINING IS STRESSFUL

To start, it's important to understand what stress is and how it affects us. Stress happens when the demand of a situation exceeds our current resources and/or abilities, which leads to feeling out of control.[1] Clearly, graduate training is often synonymous with stress. This has positive aspects (we grow the most when we're stretched the thinnest) and negative ones (obviously). Although the graduate path is structured to provide access to resources and build abilities, there is a learning curve and most tasks are meant to challenge you…deeply. Even life after your training will bring curveballs of many kinds that will throw you off track. Stress is inevitable.

The issue to consider here is not how to avoid stressful situations. That would be impossible: we cannot avoid an exam, a difficult advisor, the beloved dissertation, or catastrophes that may pull us away from our work. Instead, it is important to focus on how to limit the negative effects that those situations can have. If we step back and take an objective look, we see that we do have some control over certain aspects of a stressor, and particularly, over our behaviors and habits. It's important to identify and work on those areas to set the stage for resilience early in your training so that you can be the best, healthiest version of yourself, no matter what comes your way.

The specific strategies I discuss here will keep you moving on a steady path if you make them a part of what you do throughout the next few years. But why is this so important? What will stress actually do to you if left unchecked?

THE STRESS RESPONSE

To fully understand the power of stress, it is necessary to understand a little bit about the biology behind acute and chronic stress. Our biological response to stress is very tied into mental and emotional processes, so it's referred to as the "psychobiology" of stress.

Let's consider the sympathetic nervous system's response to something stressful (also called the "fight-flight-or-freeze"[2] response):

You are camping. You decide to explore a trail that weaves into the woods and suddenly...there's a bear in your path. What happens in your body? What would you feel? We react quickly for survival in response to such an acute stressor. The brain immediately gears up and the sympathetic nervous system implements a fight/flight/freeze response, depending on the factors of the situation. Does it make the most sense to fight the bear, run away, or play dead? The body springs into action. Blood quickly gets pulled from inner organs and shunted to large muscle groups. Heart rate and respiration increases. Digestion stops because the immediate threat of death supersedes metabolizing breakfast. Glucose is pulled out of storage and flushed into the bloodstream for quick energy for the brain and muscles. The immune system shuts down because there's no need to fight off pathogens to avoid a cold tomorrow if you have to fight off a bear right now. Senses become heightened, pupils dilate, and time seems to slow. Within the brain, our frontal lobes (responsible for drawn-out decision-making and filtering emotions and behavior) go offline and our amygdala, which controls the fear response, is more active. We react with speed for survival.

The nervous system has evolved this stress response to fight off threats to our well-being and it's extremely effective in keeping us alive. As soon as the threat is gone, these responses subside almost as quickly as they began—the system calms and the body returns to normal.

However, there is a problem with this system when we consider the complexity of our daily lives today. We don't have the life-threatening attacks that our ancestors once did in the wild and they didn't have the multifaceted stressors that we do now. Regardless, the nervous system views stress as a threat. Many of our most significant stressors today include deadlines, daily hassles, difficulties in relationships, and unexpected events that derail us. These happen on a daily basis: we're stuck in traffic, we have a paper due, and/or we have a fight with our partner. Because we lead such complex social, personal, and professional lives, the brain often simplifies these events and activates the fight-or-flight response. Thus, the nervous system may be continuously activated on a low level, chronically. It doesn't get a healthy chance to slow down because daily stress is rarely gone, and we don't tend to notice the stress response as much because chronic stress becomes the norm.

CHRONIC STRESS

The same chemicals that help us stay alive in the face of an acute stressor can harm the body if activated chronically. Work stress and daily hassles of life activate chronic stress. Over time, the body becomes worn down and mental as well as physical health can be affected.[3] Stress makes existing problems worse[4] and can even lead to disease, either through changes in the body or through unhealthy coping behaviors. Acute stress has been linked to sudden heart attacks and chronic stress is related to coronary artery disease[5]...and we know heart disease is the leading cause of death in the United States. It's safe to say that due to our complex lives, we've all suffered from chronic stress at some point or another, and the graduate training path can lead to negative chronic stress outcomes if individual stressors are not managed properly. See the list below for symptoms of chronic stress and make a note about which ones you've experienced:

- Anxiety
- Depression
- Difficulty concentrating
- Feeling keyed up or on edge
- Irritability and anger
- Upset stomach
- Change in appetite
- Difficulty falling asleep or waking up when you don't want to
- Headaches
- Muscle pain
- Weak immune system

When we experience uncomfortable symptoms, we try to cope with them. If the right tools aren't in place, we might engage in unhealthy coping behaviors, such as overeating, smoking, abusing substances, and isolating, all of which reinforce problematic mood symptoms and lead to further complications over time. In fact, problematic behaviors (e.g., alcohol consumption, smoking, obesity, and sedentary lifestyle) are risk factors for the three leading causes of death in the United States (i.e., heart disease, cancer, lower respiratory disease[6]).

We are all at risk for chronic stress issues, especially when we have a heavy workload. Knowing this can help us look at what we can do to combat it, which is of high importance in graduate training and other times of our life when responsibilities may become difficult to manage. Think about the many assignments and hoops you will be expected to jump through in the next few years. How are you going to take care of yourself and train your nervous system so that you can stay balanced and healthy as you move through them?

PREPARING FOR STRESS—CHOOSING BALANCE

We cannot control a hurricane that is coming but we do have control over preparing for it so that it affects us less. When we get the weather forecast, we can buy food and water supplies, board up windows, and bring important things inside. Even better, we could prepare these things in the off-season and make sure the house is inspected and sturdy, so that we are more efficiently protected when the time comes.

The same idea of preparation relates to the storms of graduate training and the human body under stress. Preparing for extreme conditions before they even start is something I call "prestress conditioning." We condition our hair, our leather shoes, and even our grass to withstand future harsh conditions, so why is it so easy to forget about conditioning our mind and body? Well, it's an abstract concept, the reward isn't immediately seen and we get busy with other obligations. One of the first areas of importance to fall off the radar when we are busy is self-care, and sometimes it's not given attention even when we aren't busy. Unfortunately, we may begin to pay attention to it when suffering has already begun. Along with exercising the body, we need to exercise the mind and form positive habits to build the muscle of a healthy lifestyle. It's important to do this before stress happens to maximize rebound and resilience when it does.

You should always practice prestress conditioning, and this is even more important to do if you know a storm is coming (i.e., the stages of graduate training). There are several areas to consider and specific ways to begin to make small adjustments for long-term gain are elaborated on in the sections ahead:

1. Physical activity
2. Social support
3. Communication
4. Cognitive restructuring
5. Mindfulness practice
6. Hobbies

Physical Activity

Whether we exercise or not, we know that physical activity is good for our bodies. Exercise drastically reduces the risk for many diseases[7] and has a positive impact on mental health.[8] The World Health Organization recommends that adults get 150 min of moderate intensity exercise plus muscle exercise each week.[9] People who meet this standard have lower rates of death, heart disease, lower blood pressure, stroke, diabetes, cancer, and depression.

Today, many companies recognize the health benefits of exercise and offer on-site facilities or gym memberships to their employees to encourage physical activity. Insurance companies offer wellness programs and incentives to employees because they know that active employees are healthy employees who utilize less insurance resources. Your training or employment site may or may not have these perks. Even if there is a gym you can use, fitting in exercise is going to be entirely up to you.

How can you incorporate exercise into your busy schedule? Here are some ideas:

- Walk between buildings and avoid taking the bus.
- Park further out in the parking lot.
- Instead of coffee, do a few rotations of push-ups/squats in the morning and throughout the day when you feel tired.
- Transform your desk to a stand-up desk, using books and other objects, so you sit less and stand more.
- Go on a walk after lunch.
- Combine a meeting with a colleague with exercise.
- Utilize your campus recreation center.

Social Support

Having supportive network is a crucial factor for doing well during and after a stressor. It's not just about having someone to talk to; it requires good social skills and a thoughtful strategy for selecting *who* can meet your different needs at a given time. Developing a strong social support network on several levels (e.g., friends, family, professors, professionals) and knowing who can help with what is key to riding the waves of life. To understand this, let us take a look at the different types of social support:

- **Emotional**—Emotional support is emotional intimacy and openness. This is shown as empathy, love, concern, trust, affection, encouragement, and caring. *Someone is a good emotional supporter if you feel understood and loved after sharing how you feel about something with them.*
- **Tangible**—Tangible support is an act of service or concrete assistance being provided to you. This is shown as financial assistance, help with daily activities (e.g., doing chores, delivering food, providing a ride), or the provision of some other good material. *Someone is a good tangible supporter if they run an errand for you, cook you food, or give you a massage.*
- **Informational**—Informational support is the act of providing information needed to complete a task or make an informed decision. This is shown as advice, suggestions, professional opinions, research, or guidance. *Someone is a good informational supporter if they provide helpful information that would be hard to get on your own.*
- **Companion**—Companion support is time spent with someone that leads to positive feelings of belongingness. This sounds like emotional support but is different in that it is simply a companion with whom to enjoy an activity; it doesn't have to be deeper than that. *Someone is a good companion supporter if they're fun to be around and available when you want to do something.*

When we are unaware of these different types of support, it's easy to make the mistake of trying to get all types from one person or expecting a certain type from someone who may not be good at providing it. If you've ever tried to get support and felt worse afterward, you may have been seeking the wrong kind of support from the wrong person. Failing to understand what we need and who can best provide it set the stage for conflict and more stress.

If you take a look at the people in your life, you can identify who is good at providing which type of support and who generally fails at it. Have you ever known someone who is always there if you need a ride but is pretty bad at keeping a secret? Maybe another person who is great at giving you good information to help you make a decision but makes you feel worse about things if you open up emotionally? You might have one person in your life you reach out to immediately for most things, and can't understand why you sometimes feel worse after talking to them. By forgetting to assess your primary needs and differentiate your supporters, you're only setting them up for failure and piling more stress on yourself.

You can probably think of a few people who fit nicely with each type of support. The person who always makes you feel good about yourself or is always willing to listen would be a good emotional supporter. Someone who is always available to go for a walk or do another activity that clears your head would be an example of a companion supporter. It's also good to have someone in mind to lean on in a time of need (e.g., your car breaks down) so that you can meet your tangible support needs. Similarly, that person who always seems to know helpful information about a topic or gives good advice on where to turn to get a better understanding is a good informational supporter. Before a stressful situation arises, ask yourself what type of support would be most helpful and which person could best provide that type of support. You protect relationships and get things done this way. Keep this mental list handy.

Another source of social support of particular importance at all stages of your career is your professional network. Undoubtedly, something will go wrong at some point in your training. The best thing you can do for yourself is find an advocate early on and nurture the relationship. You will hopefully have your research advisor in your corner but it's also helpful to build a relationship with another professor as well. How do you do this? Spend what little time you have sitting in their office hours with questions and pursuing their interests. Be thoughtful: remember their birthday or boss' day and think to bring them back something small from your vacation. Making small efforts to show that you care about your studies and about what professors are offering can be instrumental in gaining their faith in you as a student and their extra support when you need it.

In graduate training in particular, we often have the idea that it is important to excel in all areas (e.g., research, coursework, clinical work). However, I would argue that there is also a lot of value in doing very well in *some* areas and good enough in others, while you develop and maintain great relationships. If someone enjoys working with you and thinks you bring something special to the table, that can be more powerful than excelling at a subject with weak personal relationships. I realized this the first time I taught a college course. I am much more likely to write a strong letter of recommendation for a C student who asks questions in class and comes to my office hours than an A+ student who seems disengaged and uninterested in the process. It's simple: I understand and know the C student better. They have made the effort to engage on a personal level and have shown me what they are passionate about as well as what they struggle with. Thus, I am more inclined to support them in a time of need. Make good impressions with advisors and faculty. When people like you, they want you to do well, and when you have that support, you can keep stress levels from jumping too high too quickly. To read more about developing your professional network, see Chapter 12.

Communication

Consistently working on our communication skills is something everyone should do throughout life. At work and at home, we are a part of complex interpersonal relationships that provide daily challenges. We have to effectively navigate difficult situations with the people around us and the better we understand how to balance their needs and ours, the more we will succeed in getting both met. If we do that, we have less relationship breakdown, more productivity, and overall less stress.

This warrants a discussion about assertive communication. *Assertive* communication is achieved when you maintain control over your emotions, are aware of your needs as well as the other person's, and communicate effectively to get both sets of needs met. This may sound straightforward, but it's a hard balance to strike, especially in a difficult situation. It's extremely easy to swing to the *passive* side (i.e., considering only other's needs and disregarding your own) or the *aggressive* side (i.e., considering only your needs). Assertiveness is a skill that is especially hard to implement in difficult situations. There will be times during your training and career where someone disregards your needs and you may be the only person who can stick up for yourself. When you are trying to address an interpersonal problem, ask yourself: "Am I being passive, aggressive or assertive?"

A simple approach that works well when you need to identify and address a problem is the "I notice; I worry; I wonder" sentence structure. It goes as follows:

I notice there's a problem with the spreadsheet and it shows you were the last one entering data; I worry that data points are getting lost because things aren't closed down properly; I wonder how we can work together to fix this/make sure it doesn't happen again.

or

I notice I am consistently doing poorly on these quizzes; I worry that this means I'm not understanding the material/may not do well in the class; I wonder what else I can do to make sure I understand and raise my score.

or

I notice we've been distant since our argument; I worry that my apology wasn't enough; I wonder what I can do to make things right again.

Take a second to think about the top two problems in your life right now and see if you can plug them into the "I notice; I worry; I wonder" sentence format. The more you practice this, the easier it will be to access in the face of an unexpected problem to elicit collaboration from another person; the better you are able to communicate in those moments, the better the outcome will be. You will be able to read more about communication in Chapter 14.

Cognitive Restructuring

Cognitive restructuring[10] is a technique that psychologists use to help people gain control over their thoughts, thereby reducing the intensity of unhelpful emotions. Thoughts are largely automatic and they change the way that we view the world, which affects how we feel and how we behave. We all get stuck in certain thought patterns that become habit and paint our reality. This can especially be present during the stress of graduate training and other times of life that bring increased stress levels. Although these thoughts usually run underneath our awareness, we do have some choice about how we view something. To exercise this choice, it is important to develop insight into how your thoughts are skewed and why they may be damaging. This list of common thinking traps is a good starting point for developing greater awareness:

Unhelpful Thinking Styles:

1. **All-or-nothing**—Thinking in black-or-white terms and forgetting the gray area. For example, "If I'm not the best then I have failed."
2. **Overgeneralizing**—Using one event to draw conclusions about future events. For example, "I received poor feedback so I'm not good at this and probably will do poorly in the future."
3. **Mental filter**—Only noticing certain types of evidence that supports a thought. For example, "I'm a failure because look at all the times I've done poorly."
4. **Disqualifying the positive**—Ignoring positive things and discounting good things you've done. For example, "Yes, I did well on this test but that doesn't count."
5. **Mind reading/fortune telling**—Jumping to conclusions about what others are thinking or what is going to happen. For example, "he thinks I suck; I'm going to fail."
6. **Catastrophizing/minimizing**—Blowing something out of proportion or shrinking its significance. For example, "if I fail this, I will fail grad school; she said I did great but she was just being nice."
7. **Emotional reasoning**—Using your emotions as proof that something must be true. For example, "I feel like a failure so therefore I must be; I feel guilty so I must have done something wrong."
8. **Shoulds and musts**—These words hold us to an unrealistic standard and lead to feelings of guilt and shame. If we use them when thinking about others, we'll get angry that others aren't matching up. For example, "I should be among the best in the class; she should appreciate what I'm doing."

9. **Labeling**—Using labels to describe yourself or others. For example, "I'm an idiot; He is a bad person."
10. **Personalization**—Blaming yourself or others inaccurately or taking things too personally. For example, "I am to blame for my mom's sickness; He is to blame for my unhappiness; She was talking about me when she made that comment."

What thinking patterns do you fall into most often? If you're human and alive, you will probably be able to relate to all of them. It's important to begin taking a look at your thoughts and compare them to each category. Copy this page to refer to it easily. As you examine what your mind gives you, you may begin to notice a pattern. Becoming familiar with your weak spots to understand why some thoughts aren't realistic helps you practice keeping them in check. This is the key to developing better resilience and improving your ability to think critically during times of stress.

This can be effective if done on your own, but sometimes it is a difficult process. When we're used to thinking a certain way, it seems like fact. This can drive symptoms of depression and anxiety as well as maintain chronic stress. If it's difficult to get a handle on your thoughts, look into what kind of mental health services your program offers. It is likely that there is a counseling center you can visit, free of charge. You can work with someone to identify sneaky patterns, adjust your thinking, and remove the fire behind difficult emotions. To find a community therapist in your zip code, visit the Psychology Today Therapist Finder[11] tool online.

Mindfulness Practice

When you are stressed, your body is on edge, your mood is off, and your thoughts are maintaining it all. Thus, teaching the body how to relax and teaching the brain how to better control thoughts are very effective when done together. Above, I discussed how to identify and readjust unbalanced thoughts into thoughts that are more realistic and helpful. The other side of that is learning how to clear the mind and relax the body, which is where mindfulness comes into play.

Mindfulness is about training the brain to stay in the present moment, on purpose, without judgment. Another aspect of mindfulness is paying close attention to sensations in the body and noticing the difference between feeling tense and feeling relaxed. There are many exercises you can do that will help you strengthen these skills. Meditation and diaphragmatic breathing, both under the umbrella of mindfulness, are a couple of them.

When practiced consistently, mindfulness has been shown to have many benefits. It can reduce stress, boost working memory, improve attention, improve control over emotions, increase flexible thinking, and increase feelings of contentment.[12] Training your brain to stay in the moment and being aware of your body's reactions keeps baseline stress low and allows your body learn to relax more quickly. Try the following breathing script to practice mindfulness and physiological relaxation:

Diaphragmatic breathing script:

Begin by settling in where you are, allowing your body to sink into that space. Bring your awareness to your breath, noticing how you breathe naturally, without trying to change it or wishing it was different. Notice how that natural breath feels as it enters your body and leaves again. Now, with the intention of making a healthy shift, adjust your breath. Take a long, deep, slow inhale, allowing your lungs to fill completely, deeply. Pretend there's a balloon in your belly that inflates as you inhale. Use your diaphragm to pull the air in, allowing your stomach to expand. Now, simply allow your breath to flow out…gently, slowly…letting the balloon deflate and drawing your belly button to your spine. Notice how it feels to use your belly to breathe, like a baby or a puppy does before stress shifts the breath. As you breathe in again, pay particular attention to how the air feels as it enters your body…feel the coolness around your nose, moving down your throat. Notice what your lungs and chest feel like as you allow them to fill as much as they can. And take a second to pause in the space between the breaths…the space before the in-breath turns into the out-breath…and notice that stillness, quietness…and then allow your breath to flow out. Repeat this several times, allowing the breath to become slower and deeper, allowing the body to become quieter and more relaxed.

Do you feel more relaxed? If the answer is no, it's usually because it's a new exercise. We aren't used to breathing in healthy ways or paying close attention to our body, so it can feel odd when we do. Physiologically, a deep breath stimulates nerves that tell the brain that everything is ok and tell the muscles to relax. Just like learning an instrument, using the breath to clear the mind and promote relaxation takes practice. For more guided mindfulness audios, see www.DrLindsayBira.com/mindfulness and find more resources at www.mindful.org.

Hobbies

Activities we are passionate about fall to the side quickly when our schedules get busy. What hobbies have you given up over the years? Arts, sports, volunteering, or nature? Maybe you are still involved in an activity you love but don't see it fitting in as you work to meet the demands of graduate training. Unfortunately for our hobbies, there is no limit to the work that can be done in graduate training and beyond. The pressure to write/publish/collect more data is constantly nagging, and there will always be someone who is pumping out more work than you. By knowing that the workload at any stage of your career can easily become all-consuming, you can decide right now to plug balance into your schedule; thinking about an activity you are passionate about and committing to it is a good place to start.

Often, when we engage in something we are passionate about, we enter a state called "flow."[13] Flow, in contrast to stress, is when the demands of an activity are just slightly above our resources but still within what we are capable of, so that we are challenged and stimulated in a positive way. The brain releases reward chemicals, so the task feels good and increases our motivation to attend to it. Our ability to focus increases, and we may even forget about time or have the sense that time passes quickly. Sometimes we even forget to eat because we are consumed by the activity. Many musicians, artists, dancers, coders, and sports players experience this state when involved in their work because it's based on passion.

If you go through a period where all work-related tasks seem punishing (we've all been there), at least you have something separate to look forward to and feel good about when you have a scheduled hobby. This relates to how we derive self-value from the structure of our lives. If you can't meet your dissertation deadlines, you just can't do well in statistics, and you're struggling financially, can you still be good at the harmonica? Yes you can. If that's all you have for a period of time, then you're doing ok. Plus, if you feel good about your musical gains, you may feel more motivated to sit down and do other, less-enjoyable work. Even though time management is an ongoing struggle, we tend to do better at difficult, time-consuming tasks if we schedule in activities that we really enjoy; it makes us feel good about ourselves and provides motivation that will spill over into the other areas.

Need to find a new hobby or meet other people who are doing what you're interested in? Check out www.meetup.com to see what's going on in your zip code. From scuba diving to book clubs and jam bands, people are meeting up for free and doing what they love while making new friends.

TRUSTING IN THE PROCESS

How we prepare for, interpret, and react to stress can drastically change the way stress affects us. Create insight into your own patterns, practice these techniques before the hurricane hits, and continue to carve a path to resources that can be used in a time of need. Trust that if you do good things for your mental and physical health, you will get good things in return.

It's also important to remember that you were accepted into your current position for a reason and the process is *meant* to be challenging. Dealing with rejection is simply a part of it for everyone. You will write grants that will not be accepted. You will submit papers that will get turned down with harsh reviews. Toward the end of your studies, you will be applying to jobs and other positions, and may not get them. Use the skills I discussed when these events happen. In particular, utilize the cognitive restructuring techniques and maintain awareness about when you are allowing thinking errors to skew your thoughts, drive negative emotion, and cloud your judgment. Catastrophizing after rejection is a common one: it may seem like something is the end of the world, or at least, a detriment to your training or career. Just remember thousands of people have struggled in the same ways and have still completed the process successfully. You will get through it, too, and can focus on your health in the process.

REFERENCES

1. http://www.stress.org/what-is-stress/.
2. Jansen ASP, Nguyen XV, Karpitskiy V, Mettenleiter TC, Loewy AD. Central command neurons of the sympathetic nervous system: basis of the fight-or-flight response. *Science* October 27, 1995;**270**:644–6.
3. Baum A, Polsusnzy D. Health psychology: mapping biobehavioral contributions to health and illness. *Annual Review of Psychology* 1999;**50**:137–63.
4. Kiecolt-Glaser J, Glaser R. Stress-induced immune dysfunction: implications for health. *Natural Reviews. Immunology* 2005;**5**(3):243–51.
5. http://www.stress.org/stress-and-heart-disease/.
6. http://www.cdc.gov/nchs/fastats/leading-causes-of-death.htm.
7. http://www.heart.org/HEARTORG/GettingHealthy/PhysicalActivity/FitnessBasics/American-Heart-Association-Recommendations-for-Physical-Activity-in-Adults_UCM_307976_Article. jsp#.Vosph8CAOko.
8. http://www.apa.org/monitor/2011/12/exercise.aspx.
9. http://www.who.int/dietphysicalactivity/factsheet_adults/en/.
10. https://www.mindtools.com/pages/article/newTCS_81.htm.
11. https://therapists.psychologytoday.com/rms/?utm_source=PT_Psych_Today&utm_medium-=House_Link&utm_campaign=PT_TopNavF_Therapist.
12. http://www.apa.org/monitor/2012/07-08/ce-corner.aspx.
13. https://www.psychologytoday.com/blog/the-playing-field/201402/flow-states-and-creativity.

Chapter 6

The Importance of Staying Positive in Your Job Search

Teresa M. Evans, Natalie Lundsteen

Chapter Outline

Understand the Challenges	45	Creating a Career Search Support	
Bouncing Back: Practicing		Network	53
Adaptability and Resiliency	46	Managing Your Job Search	
Cultivating Confidence	48	Expectations	54
Always Seeking to Learn:		References	57
The Growth Mind-Set	50	Resources	58
Learn to Be Optimistic	51		

Chapter Takeaways:

- Job searches have many ups and downs but you can manage them.
- Learning to adapt and be resilient will help you stay healthy and optimistic.
- Positive self-talk can help overcome imposter fears.
- Maintaining a growth mind-set in a job search helps improve your talents through learning and skill development.
- Creating a career support network during a job search makes the whole process less stressful.

UNDERSTAND THE CHALLENGES

Your career search is a huge, multifaceted project. As a researcher you understand the pressures of managing a large research project with a lot of data points to collect and variables to account for. Well, a job search is no different. This is a big undertaking, a huge life transition, and just like completing a thesis or dissertation, a job search comes with lots of pressure. In addition to the regular pressures of conducting science (experiments, writing, funding), the need to conduct a thorough job search simply adds to these already real pressures. This is in part because for many scientists a job search is a "double unknown." It is unknown what paths and options there are, and it is unknown how long it's all going to take (or even if it is going to end positively!).

ReSearch. http://dx.doi.org/10.1016/B978-0-12-804297-7.00006-9

We know firsthand the difficulties of navigating the job search process, having done it ourselves, as well as having advised hundreds of scientists and researchers on their job searches and career development paths. We have also seen mental health harmed by too much pessimism and anxiety, as well as the damage to a professional image and future professional prospects when the pressure of a job search results in the portrayal of a constantly negative impression. But we are not saying you can't be confused and challenged in your job search—it's a natural and necessary part of the process. What we hope to offer in this chapter is some advice on how to be self-aware, to be mindful of your mental state, and to work toward managing your job search pressures.

Your career search will probably be tough and may have a few setbacks or challenges, but there is no failure in figuring out what career path you want to take. It's a process less like the serious pursuit of a Nobel Prize, and more like doing childhood mazes where the crayon or pencil hits the solid line—just back out and try another path. There is no single best way to pursue career exploration or to undertake a job search. Every person is different, with different interests, skills, values, and career desires. There are many tried and true actions you can take (like networking and informational interviewing) that will ease your travel to the right career path, but the pace of the journey will vary depending on the individual. And, as in any kind of journey, there will be detours, missed turns, and setbacks. Try and adapt a "road trip mentality" of enjoying the journey.

BOUNCING BACK: PRACTICING ADAPTABILITY AND RESILIENCY

The best way to combat negativity and work toward positivity is to think about the concept of resilience. To build mental strength, you can think of resiliency as a mind-set, a way of responding to life's challenges, setbacks, or even failure. It is the process of adapting to a challenge instead of letting it defeat you, as well as recovering quickly when setbacks occur. To become resilient is to gain knowledge and develop attitudes and skills to overcome life's challenges. Also, resiliency has been shown to protect from depression or anxiety.[1]

Often we feel like science is built on invisible failures. Our ideas don't pan out and our experiments don't work, and while we do see success in science, through the funding and publication celebrated all around us, there's often a lot going on we **don't** hear about. When looking at an iceberg, there is a lot under the surface of the sea, and similarly, there can be a lot of invisible struggle underneath the surface of success in science. This can help us to remember that although on the surface things might seem easy, nice, organized, and successful, under the surface there has been an uphill battle of failed experiments, rejected manuscripts, and unscored grants. Those who succeed (in science and in life) are those who do not give up, and it's a rare success that comes easily.

Activity: Think about a time when you had to face a tough challenge, but eventually succeeded. How did you handle the event? How did you overcome the obstacle?

As lifetime students and learners, we can imagine that we stepped on a train that first day of elementary school and have been riding that train on a straight track of academic learning and research ever since. Maybe we have stopped at a few stations along the way, but we find ourselves getting back on the train and advancing to the next stage in our educational career one mile of track at a time. Well, once your education is over you must step out of the train and onto a winding path. This path is not one that goes in a straight line but one that can have twists, turns, and setbacks. Applying for jobs is one of these times in life where we might experience setbacks and most definitely will experience transitions. It may take time to find the right path. Then, once you find the path, it may take more time to find the position that is the best fit for you. As a part of this process, we need to be mindful of the setbacks that occur for all of us. For example, there are going to be amazing jobs you are very excited about that you won't even get an interview for. You may go for an interview and do well—but not get the position. You may not do well interviewing the first few times at all. You may hear of others finding career success, getting multiple offers, maybe even a signing bonus.

This is when you need to be adaptable. Learn to "roll with the punches" and realize that setbacks, as well as successes, will occur in times of transition, and transition is rarely smooth. Adaptability is defined as the ability of an entity to alter itself or its responses to the changed circumstances or environment. Being adaptable means that you have the ability to learn from your own experiences. Furthermore, the goal is not just to learn but to improve as a result.

Another way to recover quickly from job search difficulties is to build your resiliency. Resiliency is not something that everyone is born with, but rather a skill that can be learned and cultivated. It does not stem from boundless optimism, but rather comes from understanding reality and possibility. Rising above the suffering in the moment to have an eye on the bigger picture marks out a resilient person from one who gets knocked down and cannot recover. You can cultivate your resilience by understanding that circumstances can change and that you have some control over situations—at least in going forward.

When setbacks occur, as they inevitably will in a job search, it helps to have a strong sense of yourself and what is important. Resilient people make the most of what they have wherever they are, and focus on the future. Understand your values, your goals, and your purpose. Know that the job search setback is just temporary and new opportunities will certainly arise. Don't see yourself as a victim and allow yourself to sink into despair. When things don't turn out as you planned, it's certainly okay to be disappointed, even to wallow in a bad mood for a short time. You don't always have to "turn that frown upside down," so to speak, but resilient people limit the time they allow themselves to feel sadness and self-pity. Practicing resilience means learning and growing from setbacks, even if it takes you a while at first to get into the groove of putting disappointments into perspective. There will always be elements of a job search completely out of your control, but what you do have control of are your own reactions to adversity.

Remember, stress from one thing in your life affects everything else in your life. You can't put your best self forward in your career search if you are over-whelmed or unable to manage. Dr. John Medina, author of *Brain Rules: 12 Principles for Surviving and Thriving at Work, Home, and School*, reminds us that we only have one brain and if it's stressed out with your career search that will affect work, family, and everything else.[2] Tips in Chapter 5 on staying healthy and taking care of yourself will definitely come in handy when job search stress starts creeping in.

CULTIVATING CONFIDENCE

When we see great achievements in science, they are usually attributed to both expertise and hard work. But confidence also plays a part in reaching goals—whether at the bench or beyond.

You have probably heard reference to "imposter syndrome," but we prefer the gentler term "imposter fears." Imposter fears, which can manifest in high-achieving individuals as low self-confidence, or a feeling that you don't belong in whatever environment in which you are studying or working, seem to bubble up to the surface during a job search, particularly for scientists who are moving away from the bench and the academic environment where they have been for many years. These imposter fears can be very severe and result in decreased confidence, missed opportunities, lack of interest in taking part in things, isolation, and self-sabotage. For example, you might know of someone who chooses to not take part in career or leadership activities even though you know they would benefit. (This might be you, or it might be someone you know!) When asked why they do not participate, these individuals will say something like, "Because I don't feel I'm good enough," "I have nothing to offer," or "nobody cares about my ideas." We might remember those students who had a fear of speaking up or sharing ideas in class—whether because of shyness or lack of confidence. We might also know colleagues who, when told they have a strength or are given a compliment, disagree or cannot simply smile and accept the compliment.

Imposter fears can absolutely manifest within the career search process—individuals might find themselves not applying for positions for which they would be a great fit, or not being able to articulate ideas and demonstrate confidence in interviews. We see this often with the scientists who we guide through this process. When asked to list their transferable skills, using a card sort task, the scientists we work with often won't admit to having a skill unless they feel they are the world's expert in that area. After further discussion, it is clear that often this feeling of needing to be the expert to claim you have a skill stems from the academic research culture of trainees comparing themselves to their mentors or leaders in the field in which they study. This is not how the career field looks at applicants. They will not compare you to the world's experts and you should not either.

Even if you don't have imposter fears (or if you do, but have managed to contain them!), many of us engage in negative self-talk. This is the way you might speak to yourself and can be conscious or unconscious. Your inner voices can be destructive or nurturing, but during times of stress (like a job search), the negative voices somehow seem the loudest. Come to terms with your inner voices! Everyone has them—even the most successful people have internal critics.

Negative self-talk can sound something like, "I will never get out of this postdoc because I must not be good enough" or "I am never asked to present at meetings because people do not like me or my work." The first step in combating negative self-talk is to teach yourself to recognize these types of thoughts; the second (more difficult) step is to put these thoughts out of your mind. As we have mentioned in other places throughout this book, you are in control of your own mental state and you can choose to put these things out of your mind if you work to train yourself to do so. In addition to simply removing the thoughts, you can convert them into positive self-talk. Think rather, "How can I improve my application package to increase my odds of transitioning out of my postdoc?" or "Who should I contact for guidance in my career search to gain feedback and improve?". However, you can edit out or mute the voices that stop you from moving forward and consciously create gentle, calm, and accepting inner voices to compete with the strident negative ones. Athletes have long known the power of positive self-talk and its effects on the parasympathetic nervous system—think of the phrases Olympians mutter to themselves before medal-winning performances: "I've got this" and "I'm going to do my best." Athletes also spend time in self-visualization, imagining themselves first at the finish line or at peak performance, which is another method for optimizing your outlook—try picturing yourself confidently answering questions at an interview. Improving how you speak to yourself and focusing on successes will yield great benefits not just in your attitude toward the job search, but in your overall mind-set.

These phrases from the wellness website MindBodyGreen (www.mindbodygreen.com) are helpful for times when you need some positive self-talk and an accepting inner voice[3]:

- I am capable.
- I know who I am and I am enough.
- I choose to be present in all that I do.
- I choose to think thoughts that serve me well.
- I choose to reach for a better feeling.
- I share my happiness with those around me.
- My body is my vehicle in life; I choose to fill it with goodness.
- I feel energetic and alive.
- My life is unfolding beautifully.
- I am confident.
- I always observe before reacting.

- I know with time and effort I can achieve.
- I love challenges and what I learn from overcoming them.
- Each step is taking me to where I want to be.

In addition to changing the tone of your inner voices, find outer voices to provide support, such as friends, mentors, or authors. Some supportive online author voices we recommend to create positivity: Brene Brown's *Gifts of Imperfection*,[4] Susan Cain's *Quiet* and the Quiet Revolution website,[5] Martha Beck's *Find Your Own North Star*,[6] and Amy Cuddy's TED talks on power poses and confidence.[7]

Activity: Write about a time you felt powerful (reached a goal, finishing a marathon, getting a PhD, submitting a manuscript, seeing experimental results). Think about the who/what/where/why of that experience.

ALWAYS SEEKING TO LEARN: THE GROWTH MIND-SET

Undertaking a job search is a new experience for many scientists, who may have moved seamlessly from undergraduate to PhD research, through to a post-doctoral fellowship, without having to make too many choices about the path ahead, and might not even had to interview. The novelty of the job search experience is a challenge in itself, but on top of that are the challenges of mastering aspects of job search activities such as finding and completing self-assessments, exploring career paths, and setting up (and going to) informational interviews. Once you get through those activities, you can look forward to preparing for job interviews, dealing with rejections or lack of response from applications, and then, eventually—undertaking job offer negotiations. It's a steep learning curve! Even people who have undertaken a few job searches cannot be completely confident because every career transition situation is different. Job searching is never the same twice. One way to cope with the learning curve overload is to adopt a way of thinking known as the "growth mind-set."

A growth mind-set is simply the belief that you can work hard and learn from just about any situation. Dr. Carol Dweck, Professor of Psychology at Stanford University has spent much of her career studying and writing about the growth mind-set.[8] Her work shows that individuals who believe their talents can be developed through hard work and feedback from others tend to be higher achievers when compared to those with a "fixed mind-set" (believing talents are unchanging and can't be changed or developed). Dweck has found that those with a growth mind-set worry less about "looking smart" and focus more on learning. A growth mind-set doesn't just mean being open-minded or flexible, it means setting goals, having a commitment to reach those goals, and working toward them through obtaining knowledge as well as working hard.

So, as you work toward your career goals, aim for a growth mind-set and cultivate within yourself the idea that while some of the tasks, activities, and challenges of a job search are new to you, you won't be a novice forever. Identify times when you are not the expert and can benefit from the advice of others. There are endless resources to help you understand and overcome career search challenges, from the advice in this book (and others), to online tools such as blogs and website, to the advice of mentors, advisors, and friends. Understanding that you can expand your talents through continued learning in the job search will then help you to soar throughout your career as a lifetime learner.

Activities to build a growth mind-set in the career search (these are just a few ideas):

- Get involved in teamwork activities outside of the lab, such as an intramural sport or a club or society.
- Build transferable skills (like communication) through participation in activities both inside and outside of science.
- Read blogs and articles on preparing for an interview.
- Gain feedback by participating in a mock interview.
- Share your resume and CV with colleagues and ask for revisions.
- Attend career development talks or workshops.
- Meet regularly with a career mentor or career counselor to ensure you are staying on track.

LEARN TO BE OPTIMISTIC

You might be familiar with the concept of "learned helplessness," a condition in which you feel a sense of powerlessness, arising from trauma or persistent failure. In "Learned Optimism," Dr. Martin Seligman discusses the idea that, even amid setbacks or trauma, we can also learn to be happy and optimistic.[9] Just as at the core of pessimism is the feeling of helplessness that nothing we can do will make a difference, at the core of optimism is the feeling that we are in control of many things around us and that we can choose to be optimistic and happy. If we look at these choices as habits that we must ingrain in ourselves and our psyches, then we can find that pessimists have habits of thinking which include blaming themselves for bad events, believing that bad events will last a long time, and that bad consequences will undermine all that we do. On the other hand, optimists believe that circumstances, simple bad luck, or even other individuals are responsible for bad events, that the defeat experienced is temporary, and that the effects of negative events are limited to this specific area of their lives rather than generalized to their whole life.

Applying these ways of thinking to a PhD job search, a pessimist assumes that not getting an interview for a coveted job means he or she will never get an interview anywhere, ever, much less an offer, which means they will never get a job, and by the way, the rest of life is going to be terrible now too. An optimist puts job search setbacks into perspective by recognizing the reality: competition for PhD jobs is fierce, and there can be many factors at play in an application—including the possibility of an internal candidate, someone with direct experience in the role, or some other reason for the job rejection that has nothing to do with the qualifications or suitability of this candidate. Optimists are disappointed, but can move on from that disappointment to a new possibility.

These ways of thinking can be reinforced by certain types of environments and situations. Pessimistic learned helplessness seems to be common among postdocs, who have spent a considerable number of years working for scientific goals under the supervision of a single individual. If that mentor–mentee relationship is not positive and the trainee feels he or she is not growing, the trainee can feel trapped and hopeless. It surprises us as career advisors how many scientists don't recognize the many available career paths and opportunities, and instead choose to focus on unchangeable static situations.

That mind-set can be changed through retraining our minds and relearning the way we process how we look at events beyond our control. The process of looking for a job or exploring career opportunities can offer motivation rather than demotivation. It's all in how you view it. The challenges won't change, but your viewpoint can. Frame your job search as the opportunity to move beyond a negative situation, and don't put a lot of weight or pressure on yourself or your actions. Take small steps such as attending a career panel or talk, or going for a one-on-one meeting with a career advisor. Find opportunities for successes in low-stress situations before attempting those activities in more high-stress activities, such as practicing an informational interview with someone in an adjacent lab, rather than reaching out to a stranger for the first one.

Even if you see your career search full of unknowns, by channeling your inner optimist you might see that the career search process provides multiple possibilities (instead of unknowns), and can be an avenue to something different and hopefully better.

Activity: Ask a friend or colleague to share five positive words that describe you. Keep those words somewhere you can see them—such as posted on your computer monitor or the dashboard of your car.

In addition to taking incremental steps to increase your motivation and outlook, we cannot stress enough the importance of celebrating the big and little wins in your career and life. Celebrate all of your career search successes. Did you make a key LinkedIn connection? Great! Sent a networking email? Great! Got invited to an interview? Great! Think of small rewards to grant yourself for each career success you achieve. For example, if you reach a goal of sending three networking emails, reward yourself with time reading a book or watching a favorite show.

We have so many advisees who come into our offices defeated because they have had three interviews and didn't get the job—our first thought is always "Wow, you got THREE interviews! That's fantastic!" The job market for PhDs is competitive, no matter the industry, with literally hundreds of applicants for jobs, thus making selection for interview a great success. But this is not our trainees' first thought—they only see the negative. Don't let this be you. Remember to see the positive, or if you can't quite see the positive, put things into context. And if you can't see the context, make a point of talking to someone (like a career advisor or friend) who can put things into perspective.

Activity: For one week, keep a daily log of five positive things that have happened to you. At the end of the week, review what you have written and think about ways that you can celebrate more of the positive things in your career in life.

CREATING A CAREER SEARCH SUPPORT NETWORK

If possible, don't go through the job search alone. Finding camaraderie is a great way to break through some of the negative mental aspects of a job search. You are probably not the only person in your lab, department, or institution going through a job search. Identifying even just one person to talk to or share resources with will make you feel less alone and may keep you going through difficult times. It also can be surprisingly motivating to offer help to others.

Graduate career advisors are a logical first step in finding others who are job searching. They can connect you to other scientists individually, or suggest targeted career and professional organizations and groups in your institution or community. Most graduate schools have career-focused groups for students and postdocs, and if not, why not consider starting one? Attending career or social events in your graduate school puts you right in the middle of crowds of people with similar interests. You may even find that you have some advice or information to share!

Beyond your academic institution, meetup groups can be found around the world in local communities, where people with shared interests arrange to gather. Meetup's website (www.meetup.com) has a Business & Career category to find groups of people interested in science, job searching, or networking.

Other resources for finding career support:

- Women (and men) can find a local Lean In circle (or use the resources online at www.leanin.org) for improving leadership and communication skills and building confidence.[10]
- VersatilePhD meetup groups occur in nearly every major city, check VersatilePhD's website (www.versatilephd.com) for information. You may find virtual job search support in the "Forums" section of VersatilePhD.[11]
- The Cheeky Scientist (www.cheekyscientist.com) is an online PhD career resource and association (joining fee required) which takes a no-nonsense and practical approach to the challenges many scientists face when moving from academia to industry. Many of the articles on the site focus on the emotional aspects of science career transition.[12]

Another job search support option is to find a job search "buddy," someone who is also going through the career search process, with whom you can give and receive feedback on materials, share networks, and attend events with. Dr. Tom Magaldi, administrator for career and professional services at Memorial Sloan Kettering, suggests up-front conversations with a potential PhD job search partner, laying down ground rules about your career goals and expectations of working together (in case you and your buddy are in competition for the same jobs).[13] He recommends connecting with a job search buddy who has similar professional interests, but perhaps not someone targeting exactly the same jobs. That way, you can share resources and networks, but not be in direct competition. Discuss what you each hope to get out of working together, set regular meetings, and be prepared for the inevitable—one of you will get a job first! If it's you, be supportive and generous to your buddy. If it's your buddy, be happy for him or her, and put your efforts immediately to finding another job search partner or other methods of support.

MANAGING YOUR JOB SEARCH EXPECTATIONS

Sometimes the challenges of a job search come from impractical expectations: Your first batch of applications probably will not lead to a job offer. Not everyone on LinkedIn is waiting to talk to you. Sometimes jobs are posted only to satisfy a legal requirement before an internal candidate is hired. Sometimes jobs are left posted even after they have been filled for months. Once you have been in the job search for a short time, you will probably adjust some of your expectations as you learn more about the reality of how your target industry operates, and you are able to observe the "landscape" of the careers you are pursuing, as well as when you get to know more by informational interviewing. Related to this, try and recognize when you might have too narrow or perhaps an unrealistic focus on one particular career path, which can lead to disappointment. Broaden your search and options. Don't give up on what you really want, but allow yourself to see multiple solutions and opportunities.

An example of this is the number of PhDs targeting jobs with global strategic consulting firms, positions that are massively competitive. If you step back and consider what is it about those consulting jobs that appeals to scientists, there may be scope for including other types of similar jobs, or jobs that include some of the appealing aspects of the strategic consulting work, but are in a different setting. Consulting jobs appeal to scientists for many reasons: the responsibility, the problem-solving challenges, the strategic focus, the ability to work on teams with really smart people, the constantly changing projects, and even the financial rewards. But consulting is not the only occupation that offers those aspects. If you can identify the characteristics of certain jobs or work environments that appeal to you (see Chapter 8 on self-assessment), you can expand your search to include related industries or occupations. So, while consulting is a "dream job" for many PhDs, there are many similar jobs in business intelligence, operations, or business development across many different types of employers. This same comparison works in nearly every industry or occupation.

In closing, challenges and setbacks in your career search are inevitable, but letting those challenges overcome you is not! Stay healthy and strong by identifying imposter fears and negative responses, and stopping them before they take over your mind-set.

Practice positive self-talk, accept praise, and celebrate successes. Look for opportunities to learn at all times during your job search, and adopt a growth mind-set that you can continue even after you have started your new job role. Surround yourself with people who support you and work to minimize time with those who undermine or are negative (this includes both your PI and peers!). With these tips we hope that your search is one that can be successful and empowering.

Case Study
_____

Advice on Imposter Syndrome and Self-Doubt

By Joseph Trombello, PhD

Joe is a Licensed Psychologist and Assistant Professor of Psychiatry at the University of Texas Southwestern Medical Center, as well as an Adjunct Clinical Assistant Professor at Southern Methodist University. His PhD is in Clinical Psychology from UCLA.

The imposter syndrome and self-doubt within graduate school (and beyond!) are true phenomena. I know this because I was once a graduate student who dealt with these issues, and also because, through years working in University Student Counseling Centers and other therapy settings as a psychologist, I have direct experience listening to and helping individuals with these concerns.

Graduate students are, by definition, high achievers. Admission rates to many programs, including the one I am most familiar with—clinical psychology—are incredibly low. Graduate school selection is typically made on a combination of GPA/GRE scores and research match with a potential mentor. Graduate students therefore enter their programs already being not only very smart but also very hardworking, often at or near the top of their university cohort members. In under-graduate studies, you may have been a big fish in a small pond, but now in graduate school, you are with many other big fishes in a much bigger pond. So, it's very normal to wonder how you get into your program, to think that everyone around you is "smarter" and "better" than you, and to doubt yourself and your abilities.

My first piece of advice: If you start to doubt yourself or fall into the "imposter syndrome" way of thinking, relax. You are not alone in this. Talk to other friends and classmates about what you are thinking and feeling and what you are going through. It is likely that others are in a similar position as you, and you may be pleasantly surprised and relieved to learn this.

Second, continue to do the things that help you take care of yourself. Nurture your passion and interests both in and inside of graduate school. Travel, work out, do yoga, breathe deeply, take a relaxing bubble bath, spend time with friends and family, whatever you need to decompress after a difficult work day. Behaviorally, staying active is one of the best strategies to avoid rumination, or thinking deeply and critically about yourself and your flaws and mistakes.

If you notice yourself falling into negative ways of thinking, consider some evidence to the contrary. You might try writing down one or two things you are

Continued

Case Study—cont'd

---

grateful for each day, or one or two things you think you've done well. Through these small exercises, you will begin to gather some evidence that you are worthwhile rather than worthless. You might also try an exercise called thought stopping, which is just what it sounds like: When you notice yourself thinking too negatively, tell yourself simply to "stop it," or imagine a stop sign, etc. Interrupting these negative thinking cycles, and replacing them with something else (another way to think positively about yourself, an activity you enjoy) is an excellent strategy to move on from negative thinking patterns.

Finally, you are not alone on campus. Reach out to the University Counseling Center (or whatever the institution is called on your campus) for additional help and support. Many offer specific therapy groups aimed at graduate students that deal extensively with similar worries. Other typical services include individual therapy, medication consultation and management, and brief psychoeducational workshops. Please reach out if you are struggling in graduate school.

Case Study

Managing and overcoming stress, imposter syndrome, and depression
By Lily Raines

Lily Raines is currently a Global Projects Manager at the American Chemical Society in the Office of International Activities in Washington, DC. She has a PhD in Biochemistry, Cellular, and Molecular Biology from the Johns Hopkins University School of Medicine. She started at the ACS immediately after completing her PhD.

As already discussed in this chapter, graduate school is very difficult. For me, it was definitely the most challenging task I have undertaken to date. My challenges did not lie solely in the sheer volume of material one must master to become a proficient scientist, nor in learning the way that scientists think. In fact, I found this very rewarding. What I found most challenging was staying positive during my PhD in spite of years of "failure."

As a scientist, I love data. I feel more comfortable making any claim, including claims about my own worth, if there is objective evidence to support them. I felt confident in my intelligence and my abilities after I was accepted into graduate school. I felt more confident after I passed my qualifying exams in my second year, and after I won a predoctoral fellowship from the NIH in my third year. However, after that I went for years without what I would consider an experimental success.

While initially I knew to expect this, as my main project was a high-risk endeavor to crystallize a unique fusion protein relevant to breast cancer, I did not expect how hard it would be for me. Particularly once my "safe" backup project did not work. Neither did my second "safety" project, nor my third, nor my fourth. I began to question if the one thing common throughout these projects—me—was why I continued to face experimental failure after failure.

I had previously been able to ward off feelings of inadequacy and imposter syndrome by falling back on my old friend—data. I could look at my resume and see

Case Study—cont'd

recent successes. But as I continued to struggle in lab it became harder and harder to keep my positive attributes in mind, and easier and easier to write those off as lucky breaks. I wrote off the skills I still had evidence for as the "easy" skills—writing, presenting, and explaining my work to the public. If I were an acceptable scientist, why couldn't I accomplish anything in lab?

My negative feelings continued to worsen. My advisor is always supportive and I have funding, so why can't I make this work? How could I ever graduate if I cannot finish a first-author paper? If I quit, won't I be enforcing stereotypes that women are not tough enough for STEM careers? Is it my duty to continue? If I continue this way, will I be miserable my whole life? How did I become so worthless? How could I go on like this?

This was a very dark time for me. I later discovered that I have what qualifies as a family history of depression, and it is unsurprising that I began to show "depressive tendencies." I cannot emphasize enough how valuable therapy is and how much less I would have suffered had I gone to seek the counseling services at my graduate institution sooner.

Remember: hard work and discipline are necessary but not sufficient for success in science. If you are struggling in any arena—be it your experiments or your health—use all the resources available to you.

REFERENCES

1. Mayo Clinic Staff. Build skills to endure hardship. 2016. http://www.mayoclinic.org/tests-procedures/resilience-training/in-depth/resilience/art-20046311.
2. Medina J. *Brain rules: 12 principles for surviving and thriving at work, home, and school.* Pear Press; 2008.
3. Anderson B. 14 Mantras to help you build positive self-talk. 2014. http://www.mindbodygreen.com/0-12637/14-mantras-to-help-you-build-positive-self-talk.html.
4. Brown B. *The gifts of imperfection: let go of who you think you're supposed to be and embrace who you are.* 2010.
5. Cain S. *Quiet: the power of introverts in a world that can't stop talking.* 2012.
6. Beck M. *Finding your own north star: claiming the life you were meant to live.* 2002.
7. Cuddy A. TedTalks: your body language shapes who you are. http://www.ted.com/talks/amy_cuddy_your_body_language_shapes_who_you_are.
8. Dweck C. *Mindset: the new psychology of success.* Ballantine Books; 2007.
9. Seligman M. *Learned optimism: how to change your mind and your life.* Vintage; 2006.
10. LeanIn. www.leanin.org.
11. Versatile PhD. Website: www.versatilephd.com.
12. The Cheeky Scientist. Online resource for PhDs transitioning to industry. www.cheekyscientist.com.
13. Magaldi T. The job search buddy system. *Inside HigherEd* 2016. https://www.insidehighered.com/advice/2016/05/16/advantages-working-buddy-job-search-essay.

RESOURCES

Authentic Happiness: website for positive psychology resources. https://www.authentichappiness.sas.upenn.edu.

Clance P, Imes S. The imposter phenomenon in high achieving women: dynamics and therapeutic intervention. *Psychotherapy: Theory, Research & Practice* 1978;**15**(3):241–7. http://dx.doi.org/10.1037/h0086006.

Covey S. *The 7 habits of highly effective people.* Free Press; 2004.

Magaldi T. Don't be a professional downer. *Inside HigherEd* 2016. https://www.insidehighered.com/advice/2016/02/08/strategies-combat-pessimism-essay.

Quiet Revolution. Website: www.quietrev.com.

The Thesis Whisperer, online blog supporting PhD level research and thesis-writing, 'dedicated to helping researchers everywhere'. www.thesiswhisperer.com.

Young V. *The secret thoughts of successful women: why capable people suffer from the impostor syndrome and how to thrive in spite of it.* 2011.

Chapter 7

Fake It Till You Become It: The How-To Guide for Behaving Like a Professional

Teresa M. Evans

Chapter Outline

"Act" Like a Professional, Not a Trainee **60**

A Genuine Smile, the Excalibur of True Public Relations Pros! **60**

Tit for Tat, There Is Power in Taking Interest and Doing Favors for Those in Your Workplace **61**

    Reciprocity Styles **61**

You Are Always Being Watched— Dress Like a Professional! **62**

    Casual Versus Professional Business Attire **62**

    Other Tips and Common Mistakes **63**

    How Do You Dress Professionally on a Budget? **63**

Professionals Are on Time **64**

The Professional Way to Party **64**

Tips for the Professional Woman… and Man **65**

    So, Here They Are, in No Particular Order **65**

References **69**

Chapter Takeaways:

- Professionals get hired—NOT graduate students and postdoctoral fellows.
- In your career you must establish that you are a genuine colleague who follows through and cares about the needs of others.
- Do not forget the art of tit for tat. This is something that is mastered by business professionals but rarely taught.
- You can meet your future employer anywhere, so always look like a professional.
- Punctuality is key. Plan to be on time or early to any engagement. You must make this a habit.
- There is a professional way to party. Every business engagement requires your professional behavior. Be mindful of this even when others are not!
- Do not be afraid to be a strong business professional irrespective of your gender.

ReSearch. http://dx.doi.org/10.1016/B978-0-12-804297-7.00007-0

This chapter will discuss professional behavior, how to develop and maintain that behavior, and the importance of **not** modeling the "bad" behavior that is often "trained into" scientists. I have never seen a graduate student or postdoctoral fellow get hired into any position. I have only seen professionals get hired. When you are applying for a position you must leave behind the "trainee" version of yourself and embrace nothing more than pristine professionalism. The sooner you do this the better! You might not feel like the professional you are at first. If this is the case, act like the professional you wish to become and before you know it you will be that professional. Go forth and "fake it until you become it!"

"ACT" LIKE A PROFESSIONAL, NOT A TRAINEE

At the time of writing this chapter, the United States was at the start of a presidential race. One might think that there is no one more professional than the president of the United States and that the candidates to fill this position would be professional. Well, I caution the readers to be aware that the title does not always equal the expectation of professionalism. The image of a professional is not the same everywhere you look, as you can tell from presidential candidate to candidate. But there are fundamental behaviors that are expected around the world in all professional settings. There are standards of conduct in any setting and in any profession. These standards often align with qualities that are valued and appreciated and are opposite of qualities that are frowned upon. I am sure we can list the positive and negative qualities of presidential candidates, right? It is clear that those candidates who ignore the norms, and act as if they are unaware of the expectations of behavior, are not viewed as positively and just might not be successful in their career field. If you are not aware of the professional customs of your industry, occupation, or profession you will never truly succeed.

As the daughter of a lifetime restaurateur, my mother instilled in me the importance of strong public relations, communication skills, and professional behavior. Furthermore, growing up within a restaurant allowed me to hone my skills in entrepreneurship and professionalism. As I began my journey into the field of science, I quickly realized the value of what my mother and the restaurant business had taught me. There is no replacement for one's experiences in life but I gain great pleasure in sharing my knowledge with those who did not grow up in the environment that I did. Therefore, I wish to share with you a few tips to help you transition now from trainee to professional in the eyes of those around you.

A GENUINE SMILE, THE EXCALIBUR OF TRUE PUBLIC RELATIONS PROS!

Notice I did not just say a smile but rather a *GENUINE* smile. This is not something that comes naturally to everyone, as I believe it does for some. But it can be practiced and honed.

To truly make connections in the business community (throughout this chapter the term business is used to refer to all work environments) and to be viewed as a professional that many want to collaborate with, you must be genuine. How do you define genuine? Webster defines genuine as "sincerely and honestly felt or experienced" but my definition is a bit different. To be a genuine business professional is to be accountable and to be truly concerned for the needs of others. You must follow through on what you promise in a timely manner and also take a real interest in the needs of those around you. Now there is a trick to this step as well. A trick I learned not from within the walls of the restaurant, but from some of my favorite lawyer-filled television shows. No favor comes without a cost.

TIT FOR TAT, THERE IS POWER IN TAKING INTEREST AND DOING FAVORS FOR THOSE IN YOUR WORKPLACE

This point can be surprising for some, as it has to do with doing favors for others with the expectation of something in return as this is not always the expectation. Is doing something with the expectation of something in return not genuine, you might ask? Well, in fact, it is the common practice of many, and as long as you follow through as you said you would, you are being nothing more than a strong colleague. It is good to do things to show that you understand and care about the needs of your colleagues. However, also pay careful thought and consideration as to how this behavior might benefit you in return. The industry and business communities do this very well. Many individuals in the workplace will know the value of a favor and will cash them in whenever they get a chance. If you are someone who does not already think this way, I encourage you to help out others but to occasionally remember that they too can help you in return. Furthermore, if you ask someone to help you, do not be surprised when they come back, maybe weeks or months later, and request help in return. This type of tit for tat behavior will build your accountability with your colleagues that we have already defined as very important.

Adam Grant, in his book *Give and Take,* states that you can summarize the complexity of people into three categories or motives. He calls these reciprocity styles and we list them for you below.

Reciprocity Styles

1. Takers: people who try to get as much from others without giving back, hog credit, step on someone on the way to the top
2. Givers: enjoy helping others, not volunteers, but do a lot of knowledge sharing and make great mentors and connectors
3. Matchers: tit for tat, give an even balance

With these in mind think about the tit for tat scenario and try to determine which one of the styles that most often fits you, your colleagues at work, and family at home, for example.

So, which style is best? Who makes it to the top of the corporate food chain? Well, Adam has answered this for us as well. First, his research and that of others he sights indicate that "takers are good fakers," especially when dealing with superiors. Their peers and subordinates can see through this however. Furthermore, takers use "I" and "me" more than "us" and "we." So the question is that which style sinks to the bottom. An interesting study of medical students found that those with the worst grades in first year were those who most often helped others. Furthermore, studies of sales people and engineers found that the lowest productivity was among those who helped others. So, across these three groups the same result was found, the group that was consistently worse off were the givers.

Does this mean that being a giver automatically puts you at the bottom? If so, who's at the top? Don't you fret, givers are also the more common style to be found at the top. The takers and matchers are consistently more likely to be in the middle. Back to the medical students, it is clear that medical professionals get better reviews and give better care over time if they are givers. To learn more about questions like, "What do successful givers do?," "How to givers build networks?," "Can you turn a taker into a giver?," and "What happens to givers at the bottom?" read Adam Grant's book or watch his presentation on Google.[1,2]

YOU ARE ALWAYS BEING WATCHED—DRESS LIKE A PROFESSIONAL!

I am always prepared to run into my future employer or connection anywhere that I go. My family knows that I would not ever consider going out into public in any fashion not prepared to share my business card and to be proud of the way that I look. This does not mean I wear a suit everywhere I go…it simply means that I am presentable and confident in the way that I am dressed. If you do not feel like this is something that you are sure about, a good place to start to learn the basics is with Sylvie di Giusto's book, *The Image of Leadership: How leaders package themselves to stand out for the right reasons.*[3]

Here is a simple formula to get you started: Lab=jeans/nice shirt; Presentation=business attire.

Casual Versus Professional Business Attire

It is also important to know the difference between business professional and business casual. You should at all times be dressed no less than business casual when at work. I would like to suggest that this be the case even when you are in the lab. You must make a lifestyle change in the way you dress and to do so you should consider dressing your best at all times. Here is a table to help you better distinguish the different categories of professional dress:

	Women		Men	
Type	Casual	Business	Casual	Business
Coat	Jacket/Cardigan	Suit jacket or business dress	Jacket or vest	Suit or sports coat
Shirt	Colored/pattern	Solid is best	Colored or polo shirt	Colored shirt only
Color/Pattern	More colors/ patterns	Black, white, grey, brown, blue	Patterns and colors okay	Black, white, grey, brown, blue only
Pants	Khaki, trousers, fingertip length skirt	Suit pants/slacks, skirts/dresses must extend to the knee	Khaki pants or trousers	Suit pants or trousers
Shoes	Flats or heels	Low-heels or flats acceptable	Dress shoes/loafers	Dress shoes

It is fairly easy to observe the type and style of dress once you are in a workplace, and adapt your own clothing to fit in. (This is another aspect of the helpfulness of informational interviews or workplace visits—a chance to see professionals in their "natural habitat.") You can also attend industry or trade association meetings and pay attention not just to what's being discussed but also to the level of formality/informality in what attendees are wearing. And finally, Pinterest has some great visual examples of professional dress at all ends of the spectrum from casual to formal and even some examples of what **not** to wear.

Other Tips and Common Mistakes

- If the dress code is not clear, always aim to dress in business professional style. Better to overdress than underdress.
- A suit is a good option in most situations (men—do not forget your tie).
- Get rid of the wrinkles. A suit with wrinkles speaks volumes about a person's inattention to detail.
- Women, keep your accessories simple and modest.
- Do not wear too much cologne or perfume.

How Do You Dress Professionally on a Budget?

1. Find your style—you can do this by checking out the Internet, Pinterest, magazines and finding the clothes you are drawn to. Those in the professional dress sections, of course.
2. Clean-Up—you must make room in your closet for the new items. Often you can clean out the old and gain funds for the new by working with a consignment shop.

3. Come up with a shopping plan—stick to the classics and items that can be mixed and matched. It is possible to build a professional wardrobe on a similar budget to that of a nonprofessional wardrobe. Make a list of the must have items to get you started and plan to add one item to your wardrobe each month after you get the essentials. It will not take you long to have enough items to get you by. Also, don't forget to tell the family to buy your professional dress items for birthdays and holidays rather than the new jeans they usually buy. We also would like to encourage you to research free personal shopping services or stylists, which are often offered in large department stores—for both men and women. Also, for men, private clothing companies such as J. Hilburn offer personal consultation.

4. Shop off season—any professional shopper (or mom) can tell you that the best deals are found out of season. Buy your fall/winter clothes in the spring and your spring/summer clothes in the fall. Also, do not miss an opportunity to visit your nearest outlet mall.

PROFESSIONALS ARE ON TIME

Plan to be at an event or meeting 15 min early, no matter with whom the meeting is. This allows for some room for error, so that you will not be late. Being late is the fastest way to ruin your impression with someone and to be viewed NOT AS A PROFESSIONAL. Just don't do it! There is no excuse! You can arrive early, stake out the location, and then wait in your car until the appropriate time to announce yourself.

THE PROFESSIONAL WAY TO PARTY

There have been several instances where I have seen this cardinal rule broken, not only by trainees but by academic professionals. This has often occurred at professional conferences, white tablecloth dinners, and cocktail hours. What do all of these events have in common you might wonder? Well, it is pretty easy to see…ALCOHOL. It is important to note that I feel a strong need to mention this topic, as I have seen the most unprofessional behavior occur under the influence of this powerful compound. There is a right way to partake in a beverage and still maintain your professionalism. The rule should be no more than TWO drinks per event. You will see others around you having more, I am sure, but you must be prepared at any time to meet your future employer, right? If so, you must, in professional company, maintain your professionalism at all costs. Do not do as others around you are doing, but do as you know is best for you and your career.

So how do you make those two drinks last for the entirety of your 4-h presidential gala? Drink water in between and remember to sip, not gulp. Also, the more you network and talk with others, the less you will find yourself drinking the beverage you so professionally carry around with you.

TIPS FOR THE PROFESSIONAL WOMAN...AND MAN

As a woman working her way up the academic ladder, be it in a nonconventional way, I could not pass up this opportunity to share some of the hurdles I have encountered, tips I have used, and mistakes I have made or seen made along the way. Women in academia, or in any professional setting for that matter, face unique challenges but these are not exclusively female in nature SO MEN READ ON. I know that the below tips are just as valuable to men as women but will describe them only from my point of view as a female in the workplace. It goes without saying that, thanks to the strong women who came before us, the next generation of women professionals will face lesser hurdles although they still exist.

So, Here They Are, in No Particular Order

1. Be assertive! This does not make you bossy.
   Sheryl Sandberg, author of the New York Times best-selling book *Lean In*,[4] has stated "I want every little girl who's told she's bossy, to be told instead she has leadership skills." This statement stems from the business world in which an assertive female is often seen as bossy, but an assertive male is referred to as a strong leader. Remember when you leave the lab or graduate training and embark on your career that you, by nature of your educational background, are a trained leader. Be assertive—and if done with grace you will be viewed by your colleagues as a leader.
2. Do not perpetuate the stereotype that the women who came before you fought to extinguish.
   This means dress modestly and professionally, as outlined above. Be mindful at all times that you are held to a very high standard and that you must represent the "women leaders" of your generation in all that you do. This goes for both inside and outside of the office. You will not believe the number of unprofessional interactions I see on social media. Be professional in all facets of your life, you will be better for it![5]
3. Respect other women in the workplace and learn to communicate with each other.
   There will be that colleague that you constantly struggle to get along with. A true business woman will go above and beyond to overcome these challenges and support other woman leaders around them, irrespective of their attitude. Be the example and treat everyone with respect especially other woman professionals. Also, leave jealousy at the door. There is no room for jealousy in a professional environment.
4. Learn to communicate and interact with senior men.
   In this section, I am using the term senior to not reflect the age of a person but rather their position in the hierarchy of the business environment. I have been very lucky to have both senior male and female advocates but have also interacted with some males who are not clearly a sponsor or advocate for me. If you come into contact with one of these not so supportive men,

I encourage you to maintain your course, stay professional, and speak up. You deserve a seat at the table just as they do and you will just have to work a bit harder to convince them, with the reality that you might never do so. If you should find yourself in a situation that veers toward the unprofessional, seek advice from mentors and superiors. Stay strong and focus on the relationships that empower you.[6]

5. You can integrate your family and work.

I must say thank you to all of those wonderful women who have shown me that you can accomplish all that you wish to accomplish! If you do not have a female role model in your life, who has successfully integrated both her family and her career, I encourage you to get out into the world and find one. They are not so hard to find, but when you do find them, listen to their wisdom. I was very lucky to be raised by a woman who had a drive and passion in her career and family life. I watched her and naively thought that she was balancing it all, although what I later realized was that it was not a balancing act but rather an act of integration. I choose this word carefully because the real trick I have found is to allow that which is important to you, i.e., your family, to be included in your daily efforts in the same way that your work tasks are. For example, I include all of my family events on my work calendar. I do not segregate one event as more important than another. Also, for the men who are reading this, it takes a village to raise a family, and by that I encourage you to support one another in your relationships, whether you are a man or a woman—we are all in this as a team. Watching my mother run a business and my father support her in this effort has been a true gift, as I too work very hard to support my spouse as he does. So rather than saying "I can do it" say "we can do it" whenever you get a chance. In those few weak moments when I start to doubt that I can make it all happen, I turn to my family, friends, and mentors to remind me that, in the words of my late grandfather, "this too shall pass!" So ladies and men, go for it all and know you got this and your support system has your back!

6. Know your identity (identities).

When asked to list our roles or identities in life we often will list more than one. For example, I would list wife, daughter, friend, mentor, and scientist. Having multiple roles has been shown to be an advantage as we can gain more social support, career networking, etc. But, alternatively, issues can arise when we are not able to negotiate the combination of identities. Having multiple identities can result in identity interference, which occurs when the pressures of one identity interferes with the performance of another identity.[7,8] An example of identity interference would be a female engineering student who feels she has to suppress her female identity in engineering courses to fit in with her male counterparts. This student has gender scientist identity interference as she feels she should not express both identities at the same time. Another key is to understand your own identity centrality. This is the importance or psychological attachment that one places on their identities. It is clear that identity centrality has an impact on how we understand the relationship between negative events (e.g., racial discrimination, identity-related stress) and well-being. Dr. Isis Settles, University of Michigan, has examined the interrelations among identity interference, the centrality of identities, psychological well-being, and performance of women in science and found that women scientists who experience interference between their woman and scientist identities report lower science performance and lower psychological well-being.[8] Furthermore, studies have found that interference between work and family roles are associated with negative outcomes, including lower work satisfaction.[9] So how do you combat interference?

Activity: Take a moment to draw representative circles of your identities, overlapping them in the amounts that you view your own identity overlapping. Below you will see two examples, one of centrality and one of interference. The goal is to strive toward a mentality where we identify as one individual with multiple roles (centrality) rather than putting on a new hat for each role (interference).

Identity Centrality:

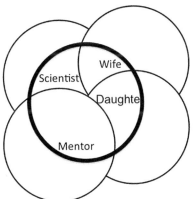

Identity Interference:

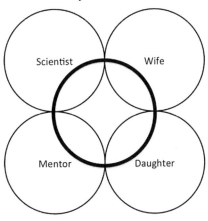

7. Age barriers exist.

So we have discussed the challenges of being a female in the workforce but I want to bring up another unique challenge that I have faced as a young PhD graduate in a nontraditional trajectory. This is one of age. Not being too old...but rather being too young. Yes, you read that right, you can be too young. If you have a baby face you know what I am talking about. You are sitting at the grown-up table (or committee conference table) and it is clear that you don't belong there. In this case, the above tips apply. You must work very hard to show those around you that you belong there. Whatever you do, do not fall into the routine of acting as if those around you are on a different level than you. I struggle with letting my respectfulness, ("Hello Dr. Smith"), serve as a constant reminder that I was once Dr. Smith, I mean Mike's, student. A situation such as one where you are asked to do things like, take the minutes, order the lunch, not be the lead on a project that was your idea, can also feel as if you are being put into a subservient role. This is okay at times but not as a routine. Think to yourself, did you offer to do this task? Is it a part of your job duties? All of these questions can help you to determine if these tasks are tasks that you should be more aware of and work toward changing. Remember, you are an equal now and you need to be respectful and a peer at the same time.

8. Splash size matters!

When you are beginning a new position you should be looking for the big wins. These will set the tone for you and you need one that is strong and assertive but not one that ruffles the feathers of those around you. Find your niche and excel at it. If you are joining a new consulting firm, seek out that big client and do your best work. But don't step on someone's toes by taking a client they had brought to the company. This was once described to me in terms of a high dive. The best high divers know how to enter the pool with a very small splash. This is what you want to be. But you can imagine what it would be like to jump off of the high dive for the first time and the large splash that would follow. Many people will enter into a new work environment this way...this can be fatal. Be thoughtful about your actions and minimize your splash. Take time to observe the work environment that you are in and determine the standards of practice. The definition of a successful professional in each environment can be different but the sooner you figure it out the sooner you can work toward that goal. Take the time to evaluate your workplace will help you to build stronger and lasting relationships in the workplace.

9. Be proud.

In all that you do, be proud of your accomplishments. Celebrate every win. You have come a long way and you are worthy!

REFERENCES

1. Give and Take by Adam Grant.
2. Give and Take YouTube https://www.youtube.com/watch?v=1baNQmnRCVw.
3. de Giusto S. *The Image of leadership: how leaders package themselves to stand out for the right reasons*. Executive Image Consulting; June 20, 2014.
4. Lean In by Sheryl Sandberg.
5. http://www.cnbc.com/2015/06/08/avoid-these-career-killing-social-media-mistakes.html.
6. https://www.insidehighered.com/advice/2015/11/02/how-avoid-awkward-and-unpleasant-networking-situations-essay.
7. Van Sell M, Brief AP, Schuler RS. Role conflict and role ambiguity: integration of the literature and directions for future research. *Human Relations* 1981;**34**:43–71.
8. Settles IH. When multiple identities interfere: the role of identity centrality. *Personality and Social Psychology Bulletin* 2004;**30**:487–500.
9. Thomas LT, Ganster DC. Impact of family-supportive work variables on work-family conflict and strain: a control perspective. *Journal of Applied Psychology* 1995;**80**(1):6–15.

Section 4

Managing Your Career Development

Chapter 8

Taking a Personal Inventory: Assessing Your Skills, Strengths, Interests, and Values

Natalie Lundsteen

Chapter Outline

Thinking About Your Skills	74	Thinking About Your Values	83
Additional Skills and Strengths		References	86
Assessments	80	Resources	86
Thinking About Your Interests	81		
Thinking About Your Personal			
Traits and Qualities	82		

Chapter Takeaways:

- A realistic assessment of your personal interests, strengths, skills, and development areas allows you to determine your best career fit.
- You can develop skills to become more marketable for jobs of interest.
- Being able to articulate your strengths and what you have to offer makes both choosing a career path and the application and interview process much easier.

When thinking about career choices, many graduate students and postdocs immediately want to know "what jobs can I get?" That's a great question, and there are scores of resources to help you learn about potential career paths for scientists, but the short answer is that there are hundreds, maybe thousands of jobs that you can get with a science PhD. A better question to ask is "what jobs are the best fit for what I am good at and what I like to do?" Determining what you enjoy doing and what is important to you in your work is part of the process of self-assessment, which is fundamental to career development (and finding a great job).

The true first step in career exploration is not finding out everything possible about your career options, and it's certainly not launching out hundreds of resumes and cover letters to random employers. Instead, it is most important to take some time to understand *yourself*. Once you evaluate and understand your

ReSearch. http://dx.doi.org/10.1016/B978-0-12-804297-7.00008-2

skills and strengths, and throw in some thinking about your values (personal and work), you are better equipped to determine which of the science career paths will be the best fit for you and where you will find success. If you're a good fit for a job, it is much more likely that you will get an interview, do well in the interview, and land a great job.

You may have heard about Richard Bolles' book *What Color is Your Parachute?*,[1] a career-counseling classic. The idea of the parachute, by the way, comes from the idea of "bailing out" of one career and landing in another. *What Color is Your Parachute?* has been around for over 40 years, but remains one of the world's bestselling books, because it offers a unique way to job search. Through the book's many self-reflection exercises, it guides job seekers beyond the tasks of simply creating resumes and applying for jobs, instead asking them to think about these things: "What do you most love to do, described in terms of the basic transferable skills you most love to use? And to do your most effective work, where would you most love to use those skills, geographically, and with what knowledge, for what purpose, with what target audiences, in what kind of an organization?"

These are questions every scientist should also be asking when embarking on a career transition. This chapter will help you "figure out the color of your parachute," because it includes self-assessment exercises to help you get started thinking about what you love to do and where you might be happiest working. Credit must be given here to the various university career centers where I have worked: Stanford University, Oxford University, and the Massachusetts Institute of Technology, because the activities and exercises I am including in this chapter are an amalgam of self-assessment activities and exercises used in my career-counseling work at these universities. I am grateful to my career-counseling colleagues (and to Richard Bolles!) for creating these ways of thinking about career choices that have been helpful to so many students, postdocs, and alumni. For scientists, identifying personal values, skills, and strengths requires introspection. This can be a new or uncomfortable experience for many scientists. But keep in mind that the benefits of self-awareness will better help you in your career search, and these self-assessment techniques are tried and true.

THINKING ABOUT YOUR SKILLS

Let's start with skills. You have plenty of them! Every day you use skills, ranging from broad communication skills to detailed bench technique skills. Some skills are required for the work you do now, but you don't have to keep using those skills in the future. You can choose what skills you want to use in a career. This idea of choice and "free will" often comes as a surprise to scientists who have been on a research trajectory for many years. You can also do some skill development to make yourself more appealing and marketable for certain jobs. So consider this: you may have great skill at the bench, but you don't necessarily have to select a career that focuses on bench skills. If you have good writing skills, you might consider a career path that includes writing—but you don't have to. If you don't love a skill, you don't necessarily have to use it every day. Your mission is to find a career that focuses on whatever skills **you** choose to use.

Your skills can be classified into three main categories:

- transferable/functional skills
- knowledge-based skills
- personal traits/attitudes

Your transferable/functional skills focus on your work with people, data and information, or objects. As my coauthor Nathan describes these skills in Chapter 10, these are the skills that you'll transfer from your academic world, your volunteer world, your leisure world, and your work world to whatever career path you target. You can further break down your transferable and functional skills by reviewing your natural talents as well as your intellectual, creative, leadership, and problem-solving abilities. You probably have thousands of skills, but beginning to identify which skills might be useful or relevant in your career is best done by making a list of all your current activities, including paid work and hobbies or free time. The worksheet below focuses on your functional skills and gives you the opportunity to identify the skills you have and think about how and where you might have used them.

Functional Skills, part 1:

Underline all the skills you have. Don't think too long about the level of skill, just decide whether or not you have the skill. Next, circle the top 10 from your underlined skills by identifying the skills you would enjoy using most. After completing this section, proceed to part 2.

Communication
Exchange, convey, and express knowledge and ideas.
write
edit summarize
verbal communication listen
facilitate discussion consult
teach train sell
promote
use languages interview
ask questions
make presentations negotiate
think on one's feet conversational ability entertain, perform host
deal with public public speaking teamwork

Information Management *Arrange and retrieve data, knowledge, and ideas.*
math skills
organize information manage information keep records
attend to details logical ability develop systems categorize summarize streamline systems
monitor

Organization Management *Direct and guide a group in completing tasks and attaining goals.*
solve problems
time management make decisions lead
meet deadlines supervise motivate
recruit
resolve conflicts mediate
initiate projects organize coordinate handle logistics
put theory into practice delegate
give directions assume responsibility determine policy interpret policy
apply policy set priorities strategize

Design & Planning
Imagine the future and develop a process for creating it.
    anticipate problems
    plan conceptualize design
    display layout/format design programs
    anticipate consequences brainstorm new ideas think visually
    improvise compose adapt
    create images

Research & Investigation
Search for specific knowledge.
    analyze ideas analyze data research investigate
    read for information interview for information gather data
    evaluate
    critical thinking synthesize information observe
    outline
    formulate hypotheses develop theory calculate/compare

Human Service
Attend to physical, mental or social needs of people.

Functional Skills, part 2:

Write about 10 of your skills on the lines below, and come up with an example of how you have used this skill. This could be in the lab, in work or volunteer experience, a role in a team or an organization, or any other activity.

Your Top 10 Preferred Functional Skills

Example of how you have used this skill

Credit for the development of these skills exercise is gratefully given to Stanford University BEAM/ Massachusetts Institute of Technology GECD.

Knowledge-based skills are those acquired from experience, and will vary among individuals, depending on the subject matter you are focused on. These kinds of skills may include the amount of education you have (such as a PhD) and additional training and work situations. Knowledge-based skills may include physical or technical skills like making things or "having good hands" as a scientist, along with dealing with equipment, computer skills, communication skills, or managerial ability plus many more. There is slight overlap with your transferable/functional skills, but bench skills are probably the best way to think about knowledge-based skills: they are most relevant to bench work and don't really transfer to other tasks or situations. Your knowledge-based skills will most likely be shown on your resume or CV when describing your research.

Assessing your skills can lead to understanding your strengths, which are inherent individual qualities. Strengths might also be skills, but they are skills at which you are REALLY good. Maybe you've developed them over time, or maybe you are just naturally good at something. Has anyone ever told you that you are a great listener? Or do you have a knack for immediately sizing up people or quickly seeing the big picture of a situation? Are you great with finding patterns and analyzing data? Those are strengths. Finding a career in which you can use your strengths means you will probably enjoy going to work almost every day. Being aware of your strengths can be an incredible boost when you are job searching. You can talk about strengths in an interview, but it's also just nice to be reminded that there are some things at which you naturally excel.

Knowing what skills and strengths are common for science PhDs can be useful in your job search. Dr. Peter Fiske, author of *Put Your Science to Work*,[2] asked scientists at various stages of their careers the following question: "Of the many skills people develop in grad school, which are the most valuable in the outside world?" The answers are as follows:

- Ability to work productively with difficult people
- Ability to work in a high-stress environment
- Persistence
- Circumventing the rules
- Ability and courage to start something even if you don't know how yet.

Fiske also surveyed employers who hire PhDs, to ask where they found skill deficits among the PhDs they hired. The answers are as follows:

- Communication skills
- Teaching and mentoring
- Appreciation for applied problems, particularly in an industrial setting
- Teamwork (especially in multidisciplinary settings)

Improving the skills that many PhDs lack can put you ahead of the competition for jobs. You may also want to consider highlighting your skills on your LinkedIn profile, including those skills in descriptions of activities and experiences. One final skills exercise is this lab evaluation worksheet, developed by a PI to assess lab team competencies, which may help you identify some of your science skills.

Evaluation form for laboratory personnel

Name: _____

Date: _____

Use a 1 to 10 ranking (1 = poor performance and 10=great/no room for improvement).

Your performance:

_____Dependability (predictable working schedule, etc.)
_____Number of sick/personal/vacation days is appropriate
_____Number of hours worked per week is appropriate
_____Self-motivation/drive
_____Good use of time
_____Completes tasks in a reasonable time frame
_____Progress on projects/experiments
_____Ability to multi-task
_____Accuracy/attention to detail
_____Plans ahead
_____Independence
_____Ability to work in a team
_____Organizational skills
_____Record keeping/notebook/plasmid bank, etc.
_____Writing skills
_____Participates in lab meeting (ask questions, make suggestions, etc.)
_____Oral presentation skills (lab meeting, WIPS, etc.)
_____Understand techniques
_____Understand concepts
_____Data interpretation skills
_____Willingness to admit mistakes
_____Ask necessary questions
_____Makes PIs job easier (organized for meetings, drafts are complete/on-time, etc)
_____Shares data with PI, Keeps PI up-to-date on experiments/progress
_____Consideration for others in lab
_____Willingness to help other lab members (training, etc.)
_____Good lab citizen (make solutions, ordering, maintenance, proactive, etc.)
_____Level of "trainability" (takes advice, learns from mistakes, etc.)
_____Overall attitude

For Staff:

_____Ordering efficiency
_____Receiving efficiency
_____Animal colony maintenance
_____Flexibility (with changing projects, tasks, etc.)
_____Supply maintenance (tips, tubes, swipes, nitrogen tank, etc.)
_____Lab maintenance (equipment, inspections, etc.)

For Graduate Students:

_____Progress in courses

_____Participation in seminars and journal clubs (ask questions, etc.)

_____Extent of "driving own project"

_____Independently coming up with new ideas/projects/approaches

_____Extent of reading the literature relevant to your project

_____Progress toward papers

_____Progress toward degree

_____Performance at conferences (presentation skills, networking, collecting new ideas)

_____Progress toward next step (identification of postdoc advisor, interviews, etc.)

_____Thesis writing progress

For Postdocs:

_____Participation in seminars (ask questions, etc.)

_____Progress toward obtaining funding (writing fellowships, etc.)

_____Grant-writing skills

_____Progress toward papers

_____Extent of "driving own project"

_____Extent of reading the literature relevant to your project

_____Independently coming up with new ideas/projects/approaches

_____Performance at conferences (presentation skills, networking, collecting new ideas)

_____Progress toward next step (what type of job? Rationale of choices, etc.)

_____Preparation for next step (ready to lead own group, etc?)

PI performance:

_____Accessibility of PI/Ability to communicate with PI as needed

_____Questions answered completely and quickly by PI

_____Interactions with PI satisfactory

_____Experiments/Projects well explained conceptually by the PI

_____PI expectations for day/week reasonable (Do you need help? Less to do? More to do?)

_____Lab Equipment/Supplies suitable and sufficient (I have what I need for my experiments)

_____Safeguards for your health and safety adequate

_____PI ensures a good lab environment/Interactions with other lab members satisfactory

_____PI shows interest in your project, helps you move things forward as needed, etc.

_____My project and job expectations are well suited to my abilities and interests

_____Our lab is well connected to other labs/PIs (PI promotes interactions)

Elaborate on any point covered above:

Are there things about your job, the lab, or interactions that you would like to see change?

Chapter 10 of this book contains a number of activities related to your transferable skills and delves deeper into why understanding your transferable skills makes you more marketable as a job candidate.

Overall, when considering career paths, don't discount the importance of knowing your skills and strengths. There are many jobs out there, but if you want to find a **career**, and be truly happy in the work you do, use your skills and strengths to find career paths and opportunities that are the best match.

ADDITIONAL SKILLS AND STRENGTHS ASSESSMENTS

The following tools may be useful or helpful if you would like to delve deeper into determining your skills and strengths. Some have a cost, so check with any university you are affiliated with to see if you can access the tools free of cost or for a reduced rate.

- **myIDP**: This is an online assessment tool for creating an individual development plan (IDP). This tool was developed by scientists for graduate students and postdocs and takes into account your skills, interests, and values to help you determine an appropriate science career path. The myIDP tool assists you in setting goals and identifying possible career paths. Many universities offer myIDP workshops and resources (including recorded sessions accessible to alumni or those no longer on campus). These can help scientists learn about myIDP and get the most out of using it. You will find myIDP online at http://myidp.sciencecareers.org.
- **Gallup StrengthsFinder**: The StrengthsFinder is the most extensive strengths evaluation tool available, with a comprehensive guide that outlines your talents and strengths and how they influence the way you live life, including how you work. Cost for StrengthsFinder is $15 for learning top five talents and how to maximize them. You can take this assessment online via the Gallup website (www.gallupstrengthscenter.com) or buy the book, which includes a code to take the assessment online.
- **Myers–Briggs-Type Indicator (MBTI)**: The MBTI is an assessment of personality preferences, resulting in classification as one of 16 different types, which assists in understanding how you see, interpret, and act in the world. Several free online versions of MBTI are available. However, these are "knock offs" of the authentic MBTI assessment, which are administered and interpreted by a certified individual. We recommend taking the official MBTI whenever possible. University career centers often provide access to the MBTI for students and alumni for free or at a discount and are the best place to start looking for someone MBTI-certified to administer and discuss the MBTI with you. You might also look to counseling centers or local colleges and continuing educations programs. Many churches, temples, or other religious organizations also use the MBTI instrument. If you **must** use a free version of the MBTI, this is the most reputable version I have

found: https://www.16personalities.com/free-personality-test (but remember the certified MBTI is still the one you should strive to take!) Chapter 10 of this book also contains some description of the MBTI and how it can be helpful in identifying transferable skills.

- **SkillScan**: Many career centers offer skills-based workshops or opportunities for individual skills assessment exercises, including use of a transferable skills card sort activity called SkillScan that helps you identify and map your skills. Alternatively, the SkillScan website (www.skillscan.com) offers individuals an online version of the card sort activity called Career Driver. For individuals to self-assess basic skills and obtain a report, the cost is $15.

THINKING ABOUT YOUR INTERESTS

The activities you most enjoy doing (i.e., your personal interests) can give clues to help clarify possible career directions. Sometimes your interests will intersect with your career path, but it is also likely that many of your interests may remain separate from your work. Still, if you love the outdoors, you could look for work that will allow you to live near nature or provides enough income to allow you to take great camping vacations. If nothing else, thinking about your interests is a great exercise that few people take the time to do. Use the following questions as a jumping-off point for conversations with people you trust or simply as topics to ponder on your own.

Questions to consider in determining your interests include the following areas:

Your general interests:

- What do you most like to do when you have free time?
- What subjects do you most enjoy discussing with your friends?

The things you like learning about:

- In your formal education, what subject areas have always been your favorites?
- Do you have any subject interests outside of formal educational training?
- What issues in the world intrigue you?
- If you could teach courses on any subject, what would you teach, and to whom?

Career areas you have considered:

- When you were young, what did you think you would be when you grew up?
- What careers have you considered throughout your lifetime, and what continues to interest you?
- If you could run a "parallel life" to the one you live now, what would it look like?
- If you could switch jobs with someone else in the world, who would you choose, and why?

Your motivations:

- What accomplishments are you most proud of? Why?
- What goals and dreams do you have? Are they both long term and short term?
- What would you do if you knew there were no risk, no negative outcome, and no chance of failure?

THINKING ABOUT YOUR PERSONAL TRAITS AND QUALITIES

Along with the activities and topics that interest you most, a consideration of your personal traits and qualities can help shape your thinking about the kinds of people you want to work with and how you are perceived. This also affects your preferences for a work environment.

After working through these activities on personal traits and qualities, and the kind of work environment you prefer, ask for feedback from people who know you well to see if they agree with your assessments!

Personal Traits and Qualities

Circle the traits and qualities that fit you, then choose five, and give examples of times or situations where you developed or experienced those qualities.

Attitude
positive
action- oriented
straightforward
open- minded
realistic
objective
caring
imaginative
other _____

Personal Style
assertive
motivated
energetic
independent
responsible
persevering
flexible
calm
other_____

Interpersonal Style
humorous
tactful
adventurous
enthusiastic
cooperative
competitive
other _____

Work Habits
efficient
dependable
resourceful
detail- oriented
takes initiative
decisive
risk- taker
other _____

Trait	Example
1. _____	_____ _____
2. _____	_____ _____
3. _____	_____ _____
4. _____	_____ _____
5. _____	_____ _____

Preferred Work Style

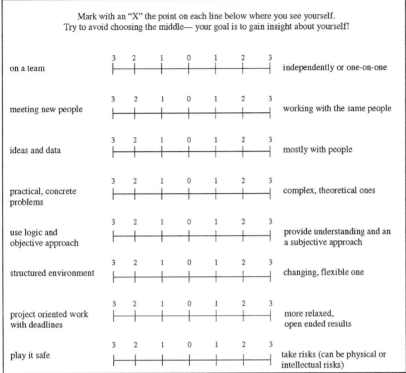

Mark with an "X" the point on each line below where you see yourself.
Try to avoid choosing the middle— your goal is to gain insight about yourself!

on a team	3 2 1 0 1 2 3	independently or one-on-one
meeting new people	3 2 1 0 1 2 3	working with the same people
ideas and data	3 2 1 0 1 2 3	mostly with people
practical, concrete problems	3 2 1 0 1 2 3	complex, theoretical ones
use logic and objective approach	3 2 1 0 1 2 3	provide understanding and an a subjective approach
structured environment	3 2 1 0 1 2 3	changing, flexible one
project oriented work with deadlines	3 2 1 0 1 2 3	more relaxed, open ended results
play it safe	3 2 1 0 1 2 3	take risks (can be physical or intellectual risks)

Credit for the development of these exercises is gratefully given to Stanford University BEAM/ Massachusetts Institute of Technology GECD.

Understanding your work style and work environment preferences will help you in making decisions about various job opportunities. When considering a job role, ask yourself how many and which of your preferences will be met, and when you are able to visit a workplace, compare what you experience with your ideal workplace environment. These exercises also can help when you are undertaking informational interviews!

THINKING ABOUT YOUR VALUES

Values are your personal beliefs and priorities and can be seen as "guiding principles" that serve as an internal compass for your life decisions. Understanding your values allows you to make meaning of your career choices and decisions. If you know what truly motivates you, you will pursue career paths and job roles that align more fully with who you are. When you are starting out in your career, you may prioritize income or location over other values, but if your workplace values do not align with your personal values, you will eventually feel tension and will probably not be very happy in your work.

Work Values, part 1:
- Underline all the values that you possess, or that you imagine will be the most important in your worklife for the next few years.
- Then narrow down the list and circle the top ten values that are absolutely essential to express or satisfy in your work.
- Prioritize those top ten and define them on the next page.

Work Content	Work Setting	Work Relationships	Intrinsic Values
challenging	flexibility	teamwork	integrity status
leading	deadline pressure	trust	prestige
competence	surroundings	cultural identity	achievement
mastery	time freedom	caring	respect
risk	security	competition	responsibility
leading edge	high earnings	cooperation	power
detail-oriented	action-oriented	diversity	influence
social activism	structure relaxed	collaboration	appreciation
learning	pace casual	humor	helping
excellence focus	quiet	harmony	belonging
creativity	organized	autonomy	community
variety	excitement	recognition	equality
growth	pressure	support	independence
knowledge	predictability	open	contributing
control	location	communication	service
adventure	public contact	people contact	authenticity
helping	comfortable	independence fun	commitment
initiating	income		balance honesty
			having an impact
			fairness
any other values:			

Work Values, part 2:

Your Top 10 Values	How I define this work value

Work Values, part 2: — cont'd

Credit for these values exercise is gratefully given to Stanford University BEAM/Massachusetts Institute of Technology GECD.

Here are some further questions to help you start thinking about your values, which you can consider on your own, in conversation with a friend, or with a career counselor:

- What gives your life meaning?
- What does "success" mean to you?
- What are some of your proudest professional accomplishments?
- How do you want to be remembered?

However, even after thinking about values questions, you may not be able to truly discern your core values on your own or may need to delve deeper. Dr. Laura Schram, Director of Professional and Academic Development at the University of Michigan Rackham Graduate School, has conducted training for graduate students on discerning values.[3] She suggests undertaking an exercise asking and answering questions such as the ones above with a colleague or partner, so that one person can answer while the other takes notes, identifies patterns or themes, and then provides feedback.[3] This method of generative interviewing is a powerful, reflective exercise for identifying personal values.

In addition to the career center, your university or research institute may also offer self-assessment resources through the human resources office, usually within an office focused on training and development.

Considering all these things about yourself is a process that will take some time and effort, but none of it should be that difficult. Think of it as organizing your ideas and knowledge or as a personal lab notebook. Taking the time to think about what you value, what you are interested in, and what you are good at doing will allow you to determine the best kinds of job roles and environments, which will make the application process so much easier. You will find this self-knowledge helpful for both informational and regular interviewing, and you can continue to adjust your reflections over the course of your career.

REFERENCES

1. Bolles R. *What color is your parachute?*. 2015.
2. Fiske P. *Put your science to work: the take charge career guide for scientists*. 2001.
3. Schram L. How to identify your core values in your career exploration process. *Inside Higher Ed* August 22, 2016. https://www.insidehighered.com/advice/2016/08/22/how-identify-your-core-values-your-career-exploration-process-essay.

RESOURCES

1. MyIDP. www.myIDP.com.
2. SkillScan. www.skillscan.com.
3. StrengthsFinder. www.strengthsfinder.com.

Chapter 9

Overcoming Knowledge and Experience Gaps

Nathan L. Vanderford

Chapter Outline

So What Does Practical Experience
Really Look Like?   88
Concrete Ways to Gain Practical
Career Experience   89
How to Expand Your
Career-Related Knowledge   93

How to Sell Your Current
Knowledge and Experience   96
Finding a Balance   97
References   103
To learn more...   103

Chapter Takeaways:

- You can gain valuable career-related experience in many ways, including internships, volunteering, short-term employment, or fellowships.
- Filling in knowledge gaps doesn't require formal education—seek out informal avenues such as auditing undergraduate courses, adult education classes, or online training.
- Learning the language of your chosen career is key to selling your academic knowledge and experience in the private sector.
- Be realistic about what opportunities are right for you and know when to say no—you are your biggest advocate in the career preparation process.

Position yourself right for the job market by following this chapter's advice to overcome knowledge and experience gaps in your chosen career!

We know all too well how consuming life in academia can be—we've been there. Aside from having little to no personal or family time, most PhD students and postdocs can barely fathom fitting in other activities on top of their academic work and other obligations. That's why many individuals miss out on gaining professional experience (hereafter referred to as work experience) that is applicable to their future career goals outside of higher education. Even if it is for your own good, it can be hard to find the time or energy to make your career goals a priority when you're stuck in the persistent quicksand of lab work, research, and writing (just to name a few).

ReSearch. http://dx.doi.org/10.1016/B978-0-12-804297-7.00009-4

But you have an advanced degree (or you will soon), you say—doesn't that count for something? When it comes to careers in the private sector, the answer is *yes and no*. Yes, a master's degree or PhD will look good, but in most cases it's simply not enough. Matt Hackett, manager of the Digital & Marketing Recruitment Team at Orchard, has noted that private sector recruiters are less impressed by a degree and now place more importance on experience.[1] There are even some who say that hiring professionals stray away from individuals with PhDs with the thought that they are overeducated or overqualified. But, again, it's all about how you prepare and package your experience and training that will convince a hiring official that you are the right person for a particular job.

In the end, a higher degree might get you a slight bump up in salary over applicants with a lesser degree, but there's no guarantee that it will get you in the door of your ideal employer. The bottom line is this: *work experience is invaluable to be competitive on the job market.*

So does that mean that you're doomed before you've even begun? Not at all! While it may seem initially challenging, gaining applicable experience while completing your master's degree, PhD, or postdoctoral fellowship isn't impossible. Others have done it, and so can you!

There are many different strategies to enhance and supplement your professional knowledge and experience beyond your specific academic program to avoid being at a disadvantage once you're ready to launch your job search. The key is to keep your career goals in mind throughout your graduate training and make them a priority even as you're working on your degree.

In this chapter, I'll walk you through some concrete ways to get more practical experience and knowledge in your chosen career, whether it's in science administration, science policy, or another area entirely. Even if you didn't start right at the beginning of your academic career, there are many opportunities available to help you prepare yourself strategically *before* you enter the job market.

SO WHAT DOES PRACTICAL EXPERIENCE REALLY LOOK LIKE?

You've heard people throw around the words *work experience* and *practical experience*, but what do they really mean? Let's put it this way: when hiring managers at your dream organization start reviewing their applicant pool, there are several types of experience that will stick out to them. While straightforward *paid* work experience is the preferred type of job preparation for most hiring managers, other types of hands-on experience can easily stand in for it.

Think of internships or volunteer opportunities related to your career of interest. Other options include temporary or short-term work or participation in a career-related fellowship or mentorship program. These are all great options for busy scholars like you who have limited free time to commit to nonacademic pursuits.

Let's get one thing straight right off the bat: there is NO reason to feel guilty about pursuing extracurricular opportunities during your academic career, regardless of the stage that you're at. While some graduate programs, supervisors, or principal investigators may discourage outside obligations, in the end it's YOUR career—not theirs—that will be affected by the decisions you make today. Yes, it's important to exercise caution not to violate any formal policies regarding outside employment during your tenure (if your university has such stipulations). But that's where opportunities such as internships and volunteering come in—they're great alternatives to get around such policies and still gain the needed practical experience.

And YES, it's possible to balance your academic responsibilities with outside obligations. Many others before you have mastered this feat, and you can too—it just takes being economic with your time and being honest with yourself and others about your limits. I'll talk more about how to maintain balance in your life later on. First, let's take a look at your different options.

CONCRETE WAYS TO GAIN PRACTICAL CAREER EXPERIENCE

There are many strategies to gain the knowledge and experience needed to be successful within a particular career path. Below I offer several example strategies that are not meant to be all inclusive, but rather are meant to plant ideas for you to consider in relation for going out and executing ways to fill in potential knowledge and experience gaps. Keep in mind that opportunities may present themselves in all types of industries from academic, government, for-profit industry, or nonprofit organizations. And, you must be prepared to be proactive in finding these opportunities and/or in creating your own opportunities around these strategies if you find no other formal programs. You can often create your own opportunity through your academic institution or through your personal connections/network. Also, keep in mind that you don't have to commit an extreme amount of time through these activities to gain the specific knowledge and experience you are looking for. Oftentimes, just 10 hours or so a week for several months can be enough experience to achieve your goals.

Internships: While most people associate internships primarily with high schoolers or undergraduate students, a growing number of internships have emerged that are designed specifically for graduate students or postdocs to help them gain practical experience *beyond* the realm of the university. Most of these internships are paid, offering at least a set stipend, if not hourly pay, for your work as an intern. While unpaid internships still exist, there are strict legal stipulations regarding hiring unpaid interns, so do your homework and make sure the internship will truly benefit—and not exploit—you. Many paid internship programs are offered by private corporations, while others are sponsored by nonprofit and governmental organizations. For example, the National Cancer Institute (NCI) offers several different internship and fellowship programs,[2] including the Health Communications Internship Program.[3] These paid internships are excellent training opportunities. Other organizations offering internships include several nonprofit science organizations, including the Genetics

Society of America. Microsoft and GE Global Research are among the multinational corporations that offer internships for PhDs. Do you already have a dream employer in mind for your future career? Check out their website to see if they offer any type of internship opportunities. If they don't, don't let that stop you from contacting them to see if an opportunity can be created. Or, find a similar employer and apply to their established internship program or contact the company and work with them to create your own experience.

The key to internships is to strategically schedule them around your other academic obligations. Many of these programs may require you to take time off during the summer to dedicate yourself solely to the internship. Or, since some may last longer (6 months–1 year), they may be a better option to pursue after completing your degree. Be sure to read the fine print carefully to see the kind of commitment that each internship requires. And, as with any of these strategies, make sure to check the rules and regulations that may apply to you via your academic program or, if you are an international trainee, your visa requirements.

Volunteering: This is an excellent opportunity to gain experience in a manner that allows you more control over your schedule and time commitment. Since you are essentially donating your time, you can determine how and when a volunteer position will best fit with your current obligations. This allows you more flexibility while still providing you with excellent practical experience in your chosen career. Being proactive about creating spaces for you to gain career-related experience is key during this formative time in your academic career.

The other great thing about volunteering is that it is something that you can offer to just about any organization, brand, or entity even if they don't have an established volunteer program. If you're interested in volunteering with a small life sciences startup or a local environmental magazine, it's more than likely that they would welcome an extra set of hands. Some example volunteer possibilities include:

- *For those interested in science writing*: Becoming a contributor to a relevant science periodical or institution-sponsored publication. Many magazines and journals—both online and print—offer opportunities for unpaid contributors as a way for amateur writers to start building a name for themselves. You might also consider approaching your university's school newspaper and proposing adding a science column to it (if they don't already have one) that you will oversee.
- *For those interested in community outreach/education*: Volunteering for a local youth enrichment/extracurricular program in the sciences. Many of these smaller programs have limited funding and always appreciate volunteers. You can also volunteer with a nonprofit organization aimed at STEM literacy or health education. Examples of this include the Susan G. Komen organization and the American Heart Association as well as many others.

- *For those interested in business or science administration*: Volunteering with or becoming a member of a professional association related to your career of choice or seek out a willing department in your institution that could use some help. Even if you're doing mostly administrative tasks in your role as a volunteer, you'll get a chance to attend events and network with individuals in the field. Plus, you'll learn how organizations are run from the inside—perfect hands-on experience! Women might consider approaching their local Association for Women in Science (AWIS) chapter to see about opportunities. Other options include local or regional biomedical or biotech associations.

Temporary/Short-term Work: A great way to fit in practical experience in the middle of your academic career is to find temporary or short-term work that is brief enough to allow you to work around your other obligations. In today's evolving work climate, temporary or short-term assignments are becoming more and more common. They work especially well for organizations seeking to complete temporary contracts or projects who need to hire outside consultants or freelancers to meet the demands of the job. Many international, governmental, and nonprofit organizations offer short-term opportunities that are ideal for scientists with technical expertise in a specific area. Some examples of employers who offer temporary work include:

- *The International Council for Science (ICSU)*: An international organization dedicated to integrating science into the development of international policy, they often have short-term positions for scientists that offer training in international policy development. Opportunities are available worldwide, many of which require travel outside the United States.
- *BALSA Group*: A unique technology transfer and entrepreneurship consulting group based in St. Louis, Missouri, BALSA links, for example, local companies with graduate students and postdocs for short-term consulting projects. Projects are research based and generally last 6–7 weeks. They are designed to offer training in the business of science (from management consulting to research and development to sales and marketing) to help PhDs and postdocs develop transferable skills for work in the private sector. Seek out similar groups in your geographic area.
- *RAND Corporation*: A global policy think tank, RAND often has temporary opportunities available for researchers and scientists in a wide range of fields in different locations across the United States. Scientists perform research and analysis to advise policymakers on specific topics.

Many other organizations—both local and international—offer temporary employment opportunities, but they are often underpublicized. If you have an organization or corporation in mind that you'd like to work for, don't be afraid to reach out and express your interest in consulting or contract positions. Mustafa El Tayeb, director of the science analysis and policies division of UNESCO, encourages such initiative: "We want to have our databases updated with interested people."[4]

Believe it or not, as a graduate student or postdoc, you are well positioned for temporary consulting or freelance work. The fact that you're looking for *supplementary* work and that you already have another established source of income and professional responsibilities will likely appeal to a company since you won't be asking for more than they can offer. Of course, this is dependent on *how* you present yourself—make sure to make your goals and interest in the position clear in your application (i.e., you're seeking opportunities to contribute to the success of organizations in the field while gaining practical experience in the industry). Always stress the fact that, if hired, this position will be your first priority despite your other obligations and that you have sufficient time to dedicate to the job.

Fellowship Programs: Fellowships are another excellent way to get practical experience. These programs are usually more structured and might require a bigger time commitment than a temporary consulting job or volunteer position. However, formal fellowship programs are also a perfect launching pad for your career. They are an excellent option if you're nearing the end of a degree program or postdoc, as they could help you transition into your career of choice. Some established fellowship programs include:

- *American Association for the Advancement of Science's (AAAS) Mass Media Science & Engineering Fellows Program*: A paid 10-week summer program that places science and engineering graduate and postgraduate students at media organizations across the nation. Fellows work in a variety of roles as writers, editors, reporters, researchers, and production assistants and learn how to communicate technical scientific concepts to the public. An excellent opportunity if you're interested in a career in science writing.
- *Insight Data Science Fellows Program*: An intensive postdoctoral training fellowship lasting 7 weeks, it is designed to teach scientists industry-specific skills for a career in data science. Fellows train in areas such as Silicon Valley, Seattle, or New York City under top industry data scientists in a project-based environment. The program is structured to launch your career into data science, and interviews with top firms in the industry are built into the program. Previous fellows have included biologists, neuroscientists, geneticists, and biophysicists, among others. This can be a promising career opportunity if you excel in quantitative data analysis.
- *American Society for Biochemistry and Molecular Biology's (ASBMB) Science Policy Fellowship Program*: A longer program lasting between 12 and 18 months, it offers PhDs the opportunity to work in the public affairs office at ASBMB headquarters in Washington, DC. Fellows are involved in a wide range of activities related to science policy and governmental relations. A competitive fellowship offering a generous stipend and healthcare benefits, it is limited to one fellow per year. This can be worth pursuing if you're interested in either science policy or science communications.

- *AAAS Science and Technology Policy Fellowship Program*: This highly sought after policy program offers a 1–2 year experience in which individuals have the opportunity to participate in the federal policy making process at the intersection of science and policy. Similar to the ASBMB fellowship program, a generous stipend and benefits package is included, and a professional development program is built into the fellowship. This program can open the door to a variety of career opportunities!

Many large governmental organizations offer some type of fellowship or mentorship program for graduate students or new professionals, so do your research to see what's out there in your chosen field. Since many of these opportunities have a very specific niche, your chances of getting accepted are often higher than you might think!

HOW TO EXPAND YOUR CAREER-RELATED KNOWLEDGE

Gaining practical work experience is all well and good, but there are often concrete skills and knowledge associated with given careers that are important to learn *before* heading out into the work world.

So how does one go about accumulating that invaluable knowledge?

The good news is that there are many ways for you to gain more knowledge related to your chosen career while continuing to uphold your academic obligations. As with gaining work experience, expanding your career-related knowledge base will require being creative with your time and being realistic about the commitments that you make.

While you might initially anticipate needing formal education specifically related to your dream career, that is often not the case. To be a science writer, you don't necessarily need a degree in journalism. Neither do you need an MBA to go into science administration or business, although you can always go back to school later to obtain another degree if it will provide additional value to your career. Here are some of our examples:

Natalie: I am an example of someone who works in an environment very different from my research background. I advise and teach biomedical scientists, but my PhD is in social science. So I bring transferable skills from the social sciences and I can contextualize those skills into a science environment, without actually being a scientist. I've been able to develop an "interactional expertise" that allows me to operate in the world of science. In other words, I have an understanding of how scientists are trained and what their skills, strengths, and career paths might be.

Nathan: When I began a career in academic administration, I had no formal business background. The key value I brought to the table was key business-related transferable skills I picked up in the laboratory (for example, skills such as project management, leadership, communication, analytic and critical thinking, etc.). I was highly valued early on for the ability to speak the language of scientists in a way that allowed me to translate "science speak" to other administrators. I did eventually go back to school to earn an MBA as a way to fill in other business-related knowledge and experience gaps and not only did my MBA experience serve that purpose, but it also made me more competitive for other job opportunities. So, I am an example of how you can transition into a career field and then assess whether there would be an advantage to pursue more formal education that would benefit you now and in the future.

As a trained scientist, what is key for you to understand is that you already possess much of the skills and knowledge needed for a variety of careers. As a first step, it's important to identify your *transferable skills*—that is your current knowledge and skills that can be transferred or applied to a career outside of higher education. I'll talk more about transferable skills in Chapter 10.

After you identify your transferable skills, it becomes a matter of *filling in the gaps*—are there specific areas where you still need to gain additional expertise? Obtaining such knowledge can be done through more informal and shorter-term educational avenues, many of which are specifically aimed at professional development. Let's take a look at some possibilities:

- *Relevant courses at your institution*: Consider enrolling in or auditing classes that are directly related to the career you're pursuing. This is a relatively easy option because it keeps you within your comfort zone. Plus, costs will be minimal if you're already enrolled. If you're a postdoc or you'd like to observe the class more informally, you can always approach the instructor, explain your interest, and ask to audit the class. Make sure to target classes that will fill in specific gaps in your knowledge. If you're interested in science writing but you lack training in journalism, take a class in news writing. If you're interested in a career in technology or administration, enroll in a business course. Be honest with yourself about what your weak areas are, and look for classes that will help strengthen them.
- *Adult education*: Most counties and/or cities have government-sponsored adult education (also known as continuing education) programs that provide more practical, job-oriented classes. Many of these are free to the public and offer training in specific skills such as web programming, graphic design, accounting, business writing, and more. There might even be certificate programs for certain job skills. Check out their offerings and see if any of them apply to your career of choice. Besides being free or relatively inexpensive, another advantage is that adult education classes are often offered at night or on the weekends to accommodate people's work schedules.
- *Massive Open Online Course (MOOC) platforms*: MOOCs can offer a very valuable way to gain exposure, training, and development in a variety of areas that could be important to master your chosen career path. For example, if you want to pursue a career in administration, you could take business courses

through an MOOC platform to build your business knowledge base. Once you have a career path in mind, search the various MOOC platforms (Coursera, edX, Lynda.com, etc.) to find courses that are applicable to knowledge and skills you will need for a particular job within that career path.

- *Workshops or online trainings*: Many larger organizations and professional associations offer workshops and trainings on topics and skills related to their industry. These include local workshops that you can attend in person and online trainings that you can access through the organization's website. While in-person workshops or seminars might be more difficult to attend depending on location and timing, they are also often recorded and uploaded to the organization's website after the event, so you might still be able to gain access that way. Some selected resources include:
  - The Association of Health Care Journalists offers periodic webcasts and online trainings for aspiring journalists covering a broad range of topics, from how to report on hospitals in your neighborhood to how to pitch a story to a top publication. Also check out the World Federation of Science Journalists' free online course in science journalism.
  - The Union of Concerned Scientists' Science Network offers a workshop series involving communication and advocacy trainings for scientists related to science policy. While some workshops are held in person, their on-demand workshops are available online and cover issues such as communicating with policy makers and talking to the media about science.
  - The National Institutes of Health's (NIH) Office of Intramural Training and Education (OITE) offers a variety of career development resources, including workshops on communication, grant writing, and information and tips on job searches and applications. Although the OITE gears its services for NIH trainees, it invites other trainees to participate in events in person for individuals located near their headquarters and the office provides many workshops and tutorials online via their website.

Professional organizations in practically every field offer similar resources, so take the time to do your homework and make the most of free trainings and workshops. If you do make it to an in-person workshop or event, it's an excellent opportunity not only to expand your knowledge but also to *network*—try to connect with as many professionals in the field as possible. Who knows, you just might meet someone influential who can help open the door to the career of your dreams!

More and more institutions are now offering formal certificate or degree programs in some of the most popular science careers such as science journalism and science policy. However, these may not be for you—you already have (or will soon have) at least one graduate degree under your belt. That could be more than enough! Plus, the last thing you need is to get yourself into more debt before you even hit the job market. Focus instead on resources and opportunities that offer you more than they ask for in return.

HOW TO SELL YOUR CURRENT KNOWLEDGE AND EXPERIENCE

All of the ideas I've outlined for gaining career-related knowledge and experience are great, but you may or may not be able to pursue many of them while in academia. My mantra is *be realistic*. It's better to have one solid internship and have audited a couple courses related to your chosen career than to burn yourself out trying to do too much at once. And while it's fine to pursue these opportunities simultaneous to your research or degree commitments, you still need to stay on top of those as well.

So, regardless how much or how little career-related knowledge and experience you've been able to accumulate over the course of your time as a scholar–researcher, there are always ways to sell the knowledge and experience that you do have. Although hiring managers may prefer paid work experience, you CAN make yourself more marketable even if your work experience or knowledge in your career of choice is lacking.

But where do you start?

For many of us, traditional job application documents such as the resume immediately come to mind. While crafting an effective cover letter and a stellar resume—which we'll cover in the upcoming chapters—is important, you need to accomplish something else first.

Learn the language of your chosen career

Every career, from science communication to international policy to data science, has its own vocabulary. Knowing how to apply that vocabulary is the equivalent to paying the toll to gain access to the toll road—it doesn't guarantee that you'll get to your destination, but it sets you on the right path. Especially if your experience isn't traditional, it's important to develop the vocabulary necessary to explain it in a way that recruiters will understand.

Think about your scientific specialty: whether it's cell biology, biochemistry, or pathology, each area has its own language that you had to learn to be accepted by your colleagues. The same goes for careers outside of the university. Danielle J. Deveau, Managing Director at Pop Culture Lab (a research firm), warns: "you cannot simply list intellectual accomplishments and knowledge sets and expect the individual reviewing your resume to equate these abstract skills with the more applied work that they often require."[5] The key is translating those skills into a language they understand. More information about how to craft resumes, cover letters, and job applications will be covered in Chapter 16.

So, how do you learn the language specific to your chosen career? Do your research! One great way to learn how professionals in the industry speak is to *talk* to them. If you've already established contacts in the field, set up an informal meeting over coffee to pick their brain about the keywords that hiring managers will respond to. If you don't have any contacts yet, take advantage of your university's alumni network to get in touch with someone in the industry. They'll likely be happy to share their insight to help an aspiring professional in their field.

Another strategy is to look at job postings in the industry and identify key terms used in them, suggests Deveau. Then read up on what these terms mean within the context of that industry. The key is to connect the dots between industry keywords and your own experience. For instance, a science administration position might emphasize "project management skills," which in the academic sphere translates into the ability to manage a research project or lab—something that you may very well have experience with. You can also look through LinkedIn profiles and other online platforms to find examples of how other people in similar positions have branded themselves, and see the words and phrases they use to describe their day-to-day job responsibilities. Using key terms when describing your lab experience is more likely to draw the eye of an industry recruiter. Plus, with electronic applications being the norm these days, many organizations use software programs to search for designated keywords. So getting the vocabulary right is a must if you want to make it through the first screening!

Once you've learned your industry's language, you can work on couching your professional experience in that new vocabulary. Things you should think about are what job title you're seeking (how do you want to represent yourself within the vocabulary of your target career?), appropriately describing your skill set, and reframing previous work experience in terms that industry recruiters will understand. We'll address this more in Chapter 16 when we discuss job applications.

FINDING A BALANCE

"OK," you might say, "all your advice is great, but how do I make it work for *me*?" We know that pursuing your degree and training is difficult and time consuming, and adding more obligations on top of that could be a recipe for disaster. Yes, it *could* be, but it all depends on how you go about it.

Finding a balance between academic commitments and career-related pursuits is the key to staying sane during this process.

While I can't give you a definitive rule book on how to find balance in your life, consider the following tips to help you manage your many competing obligations:

- *Keep an organized schedule*: Outline your commitments for each day and specify time slots for each commitment. Make sure to designate time for more independent—but equally important—activities such as writing manuscripts or your thesis. Visually charting out your schedule is an easy way for you to see where the gaps are that could allow you a few hours to volunteer or work on an independent consulting job, for example.
- *Plot out the stages of your academic career long-term*: This especially applies if you're currently completing your degree. Each degree program has several phases or stages that you go through as a graduate student. Familiarize

yourself with each phase and the requirements of that phase. It's likely that there are certain stages in the program that allow for a little more flexibility in your schedule. Take advantage of those times to try to fit in career-related opportunities such as a short internship or fellowship. Take advantage of existing tools to help plot your long-term plans. For example, as mentioned several times in this book, there is a great tool in the book, *The Professor Is In*, called the 5 year plan. It is simply a grid with the 12 months across the top and 5 years down the left side. You fill in the months with big deadlines and career goals for 5 years at a time. It is a very powerful planning tool, check it out!

- *Know the policies*: Familiarize yourself with the policies of your program, position, or institution. Do they allow outside employment or not? How much vacation time do you get each term or year? Try to work *within* these policies to avoid undue stress by putting yourself in a situation that could compromise your academic career. If you get 1 or 2 weeks off, see if there's a career-related opportunity that would fit into that window. If you need to avoid other paid employment, then volunteer work, informal workshops, or online trainings are excellent options to help you gain that needed career-related knowledge and experience.

- *Create a support network*: Hopefully, your family and friends will be understanding and supportive of what you're trying to accomplish with this balancing act. They are your immediate support network. Try to look further, though, and seek out individuals at the university who are supportive of your career goals. This will be easier for some than others, and it also depends on the prevailing mentality in your particular institution about careers outside of academia. Feel out your PIs, supervisors, mentors, and colleagues to see who identifies with your alternative career aspirations. Some people might be much more open-minded than you would expect. Having a partner on the "inside," so to speak, can be incredibly helpful as you attempt to navigate this oftentimes challenging path.

- *Be realistic*: I've said this before, but let us reiterate it one more time. *You* know yourself and how much you can handle. If a part-time employment opportunity or internship is more than you can take on at the moment, then don't pursue it. Seek out alternatives that require less of a time commitment. Working as a contributing writer on your own time instead of pursuing an AAAS fellowship might be a better fit for now.

The bottom line is to *know when to say no*. This applies both to your academic and career-related involvement. If your PI or supervisor asks you a favor that extends far beyond the outlined responsibilities of your position, don't be afraid to decline. On the other hand, if you're asked to come in for your internship on a day that you weren't scheduled, you might have to say no to that also. Make sure that you are meeting all requirements of each respective position, but also be assertive when you're asked to exceed those requirements. Being an advocate for yourself now is the best way to prepare for selling yourself once you get to the job market.

What Current Graduate Programs Are Doing to Support Nonacademic Career Preparation

While graduate programs have been relatively slow to respond to the reality of the changing job market, some schools have begun to develop programs and resources designed to assist graduate students and postdocs with preparing for a nonacademic career. These schools are on the right track:

University of California, San Diego—Gradvantage

http://grad.ucsd.edu/gradlife/gradvantage/index.html

This initiative combines various on-campus professional development and career preparation opportunities for PhDs and postdocs. This includes a certificate program in Leadership and Teamwork and a Communication Skill Development Workshop, which were developed based on input from local industry leaders regarding weak areas in recent PhD graduates. The school's Career Nights also bring in speakers from a wide range of organizations to share their insight with students.

Georgia Tech Graduate Cooperative Education Program

http://www.gradcoop.gatech.edu/

Sponsored by Georgia Tech's Center for Career Discovery and Development, this certificate program offers current graduate students opportunities to work with leaders in industry and government related to their discipline. Since the co-op works in cooperation with one's degree program, participating students are given approval to work for a semester at a time on full- or part-time work assignments related to their research interests.

University of California San Francisco Graduate Student Internships for Career Exploration (GSICE)

http://gsice.ucsf.edu/home

GSICE is a program that specifically targets graduate students in basic and bio-medical fields who have interests in careers outside of academia. The internships are structured to be full-time 3-month assignments that can occur during a regular academic period or once the student has graduated.

Case Study

Sarah Martin was the 2015–16 science policy fellow with the American Society for Biochemistry and Molecular Biology (ASBMB). Before becoming the fellow, she attended the University of Kentucky earning her bachelor of science in animal sciences, her master of science in animal nutrition and her doctorate in biochemistry. Here is her story, in her own words, of how she filled in knowledge and experience gaps to obtain her policy fellowship.

I knew as early as my second year of graduate school that I didn't want to pursue a postdoc, I didn't want to stay at the bench and I never had a knack for teaching. I used the "my Individual Development Plan" from Science Careers to try to explore potential career paths. My number one career recommendation was science policy. I've always been interested in politics, I was really concerned about the funding climate for biomedical research in the United States and my greatest

Continued

Case Study—cont'd

personal talent is communication of complex scientific concepts to both specialist and nonspecialist audiences. To learn more about science policy, I applied to be a part of the ASBMB Hill Day and was selected to attend. I flew to Washington, DC, received training on how to communicate with legislators and learned the federal budget basics. After a day at the capitol advocating for science, I knew I wanted to pursue science policy for my career.

In order to gain more policy experience, I became a member of my university's graduate student congress. My experience with the congress allowed me to improve my communication skills because the organization is made up of graduate students from every department and college. The interdisciplinary nature of the group helped me to learn to communicate with diverse groups with unique interests. My primary commitment in the congress was to advocate on behalf of graduate students in campus matters. In the time I served on the congress, I helped establish an open line of communication with the president and provost of my university by hosting an annual event in which we discussed issues pertinent to graduate students. This experience helped me to become comfortable communicating with high level officials. I developed, organized, and implemented a successful panel discussion series that examined graduate issues with topics such as "Making Cents of Your PhD: A Financial Workshop," "Careers Outside Academia: Panel Discussion," "Careers Inside Academia." Though none of those topics were necessarily related to science policy, the experience of planning a panel discussion is useful for work in the field. While on the graduate student congress, I worked in collaboration with our state government relations office to develop a graduate student hill day in our state capitol to showcase to our legislators the cutting-edge research performed at our university. All of these opportunities gave me real world science policy experience that I could point to in my applications.

When I was ready to apply to science policy fellowships, the most important resource for me was current and recent fellows. I found that many fellows would be willing to look over my resume or cover letter and give me valuable feedback on my application. I also took time to meet with the state and federal government relations officers at my university and learn about the issues on which they were working. Most scientific societies have public affairs committees. I was a student member of a couple scientific societies and took advantage of those memberships to get to know more senior scientists who were also passionate about science policy issues.

Making the transition to science policy is exciting but you have to be familiar with the field. While in graduate school, I started reading political news outlets to become well versed in current affairs. I started out by reading the news for 10–20 min every day in between experiments and built my knowledge base. Beyond subject matter familiarity, it is important to start to develop opinions about science policy issues as you will most certainly be asked during your interviews. In fact, it is great to start using these opinions and perspectives to start practicing your nontechnical writing skills. I wrote some pieces about science policy for my personal blog, but I would recommend trying to publish an op-ed in a local magazine or your university newspaper.

Case Study—cont'd

Science policy fellowships are very competitive, so don't be afraid to take time away from the bench during graduate school to develop skills you will need to be a successful applicant. Volunteering with graduate student congress and for ASBMB's Hill Day allowed me to gain relevant experience I highlighted during the fellowship application process and helped to show my commitment to science policy as a career path. But much of the work necessary to overcome knowledge gaps to move into science policy can be done while you are literally still at the bench: reading about politics, making connections with government relations officers, and writing about science policy for your blog can all be done in between experiments or during long incubation steps. I'm the proof!

Case Study

Vidhya Nair, MD, MA, is a Postdoctoral Researcher at the University of Texas Southwestern Medical Center. Here is her insight, in her own words, into using a networking opportunity to gain valuable work experience through an internship in a career area of interest.

I had been working in academia as a postdoctoral researcher for about 4 years when I decided to join the regional chapter of a global nonprofit biotechnology organization called BioNorthTX. Since our institution is a sponsor member, all the graduate students and postdocs were invited to the events and meetings. The Dallas area is not known for being a biotech hub, so the inaugural meeting of BioNorthTX was a great place for trainees to be introduced to a large group of science professionals working in both academic and industrial settings in Texas. It was during this meeting that I met the cofounder and CEO of the pharmaceutical firm that I later interned for.

As a scientist, inherently known as a rather antisocial group, I was hesitant to approach the professionals at the BioNorthTX event and was nervous about discussing both their work and mine, as well as my interest in working and interning in industrial firms. The extra nudge from a career mentor definitely helped me in overcoming this hesitation and got me to talk to these people, who were actually very approachable and welcoming to all of my questions and inquiries. Once I started interacting with them, I realized it was much easier than I expected and all I had to do was express my genuine interest in their work.

I later got in touch with the CEO of the above-mentioned pharmaceutical company and after discussion, decided to do a monthlong internship with the firm. This internship had to be done in conjunction with my full-time postdoc, a consideration the CEO was very understanding of. We decided that I would work on site for 3–4 h for the first 2 weeks, after which I would work partially from home/remotely. It was not easy doing an internship on top of my full-time job, especially for the first 2 weeks since I had to travel to be onsite. To make matters worse, the office was in downtown Dallas, where parking is almost impossible and I got two parking tickets in 2 weeks.

Continued

Case Study—cont'd

However, the work was very interesting and different from my research. It involved learning about different pharmaceutical industries and the clinical trials they run, from which I learned a great deal. By the end of the month, I was able to deliver what I had promised in terms of the work I had to do for my internship, which was personally very satisfying. I also kept my postdoc mentor informed about the internship I was doing and made sure my lab work was done promptly. This experience definitely benefited me not only as an actual industry experience to put on my resume, but also as a learning experience working in a research environment outside academia. I believe the addition of this experience to my resume helped me get a job interview with a major consulting firm a few months following my internship. Although I did not get the job, the internship experience greatly strengthened my resume and made the consulting firm notice me.

To conclude, networking is very important and just some small effort on my part to make a new contact not only helped me get an industry experience, but also led to the opportunity to interview with one of the biggest global strategic consulting firms. I am glad I took the opportunity to do the internship and I strongly advise others to network and accept opportunities when they are presented to you because you never know what might come out of it.

Case Study

Robin Frink is a Scientific/Medical Writer for Cardinal Health, formerly a postdoctoral fellow in cancer biology at the University of Texas Southwestern Medical Center. Here she relays her experience in participating in two internships during her postdoctoral training.

I was able to obtain and undertake two internships during my postdoctoral training, and both were phenomenal learning opportunities. The first was with a family foundation investment office, which invests in biotech and healthcare start-ups. The second was with a regional biomedical/biotech organization.

The family office internship was a formal program with an application and interview process. I learned about the opportunity while attending a career talk sponsored by my graduate school. The internship was an incredible experience. Applying for and accepting the internship position was also a convenient way to bring up the "I don't want to stay in academia" conversation with my PI and show that I was exploring alternative options. The internship itself was intended to be an educational experience and not one which led to a job. The time commitment was 6–10 hours per week with most of the work completed at home—ideal circumstances for a postdoc. Through this internship, I became aware of many different career options.

My internship with the regional biomedical/biotech organization was quite serendipitous. The organization was less than 6 months old and I happened to meet one of the cofounders at a networking lunch. She mentioned she was overwhelmed with the workload because it was run strictly by volunteers, so I asked if I could help in any way. The actual work was basic administrative work—taking minutes at meetings, running registration at events, internet searches to expand their database (of course on my resume/CV these tasks are listed as "documenting key organizational milestones,

---

Case Study—cont'd

facilitating networking events, and project management"). However, the value of this internship was not in the actual work. It was in the networking, observing, and learning I was able to do while doing that basic administrative work. I was invited to attend all of the Executive Committee meetings and the inaugural, as well as subsequent Board of Directors meetings. I now know, on a first-name basis, the CEOs and VPs of 10 different life science companies. Because I was invited to listen to the Executive Committee meetings, I was able to witness firsthand the board meeting process—from the preparation to the execution and delivery. I was able to observe an organization grow from a few members to over 100 and be involved in key decisions which led to the growth. The internship was an incredible learning opportunity!

Internships are great for more than just learning about a particular career choice. During both internships I learned what I enjoy doing and, just as important, I learned things I don't enjoy doing. While I'm still in a discovery mode about my next career move, both of these internship opportunities helped narrow down my choices for my next direction. Internships are great for self-discovery.

I fully appreciate that internships are not always readily available as well as finding the time to dedicate to one, while completing a postdoc, is a challenge. However, if you are committed, you can find something that works for you. I am a mother to three young children, so I have limited "free time." Both internships had minimal time commitment and the majority of the work was done from home, so these opportunities were a good fit for my circumstances. I obtained my second internship strictly by chance. Always keep your eyes and ears open for opportunities. You never know when someone might need a helping hand and what it could turn into.

REFERENCES

1. Cole J. What's more important: qualifications or experience? *Total Jobs* February 17, 2014. http://www.totaljobs.com/insidejob/whats-more-important-qualifications-or-experience/.
2. Career Development Opportunities at NCI. http://www.cancer.gov/grants-training/training/at-nci.
3. NCI Health Communications Internship Program. https://hcip.nci.nih.gov/hcip/index.html.
4. Gewin V. Making the move into science policy. *Nature* March 2003;**422**. http://www.nature.com/naturejobs/science/articles/10.1038/nj6930-452a.
5. Deveau D.J. Reframing doctoral skills: articulating academic experience for the nonacademic workplace; April 26, 2013. *DanielleJDeveau.ca*, http://daniellejdeveau.ca/blog/wp-content/uploads/2013/04/reframing-doctoral-skills-for-the-private-sector.pdf.

TO LEARN MORE…

Check out these additional resources for help overcoming your gaps in career-related knowledge and experience:

Janssen K, Sever R, editors. *Career options for biomedical scientists*. Cold Spring Harbor Laboratory Press; October 31, 2014. http://www.amazon.com/Career-Options-Biomedical-Scientists-Janssen/dp/1936113724.

This book provides a view and description of many of the different career paths individuals with PhDs can pursue and thrive in. Personal accounts from individuals within various careers are included.

Basalla S, Debelius M. *"So what are you going to do with that?": finding careers outside academia.* 3rd ed. University of Chicago Press; December 26, 2014. http://www.amazon.com/What-Are-You-Going-That/dp/0226038823.

An excellent guide for PhDs and MAs in the sciences who are planning to seek a career outside of higher education. Written by two PhDs who have made the transition to the private sector themselves, it is full of practical insight, including concrete tips on things like converting a CV to a resume and preparing for the job interview.

Nelson MR. *Navigating the path to industry: a hiring manager's advice for academics looking for a job in industry.* Annorlunda Books; September 10, 2014. http://www.amazon.com/Navigating-Path-Industry-Managers-Academics-ebook/dp/B00NABNFVW/ref=sr_1_1?s=books&ie=UTF8&qid=1443071105&sr=1-1&keywords=navigating+the+path+to+industry.

This brief, informative guide is written by a hiring manager from the biotechnology industry. It provides practical insider advice for new PhDs on the essentials of launching a successful industry job search.

The Versatile PhD's PhD Career Finder. https://versatilephd.com/phd-career-finder/.

This dynamic online tool sponsored by the folks at The Versatile PhD—an excellent resource in itself—lists potential careers for PhDs from any discipline. Aside from providing a basic description of the career or industry, it offers tips on how to get your foot in the door and information on advancement opportunities. It also provides a list of disciplines that are best suited for the career, as well as actual resumes and biographies of PhDs who have established a successful career in the industry. Although you have to join for access to the resumes and biographies, membership is free and offers you access to a whole network of nonacademic PhDs.

Vault. http://www.vault.com/.

Vault provides a variety of resources that are aimed at giving professionals and students an added advantage to career development, job searches, and the job application process. You can search for internships, browse company profiles, and gain access to valuable information on how to perfect your job application and nail your interview.

Chapter 10

Transferable Skills: How to Describe What You Really Know

Nathan L. Vanderford

Chapter Outline

**What Is a Transferable Skill,
Anyway?**   **107**
Skills Employers Really Want   **107**
**Recognizing Your Transferable
Skills**   **109**
  Finding the Hidden Skills in
  Your Academic Profile   109
  Analyzing Your Work, Sports,
  and Leadership Profile   110
  Garnering Feedback From
  Nonacademics   111

  Assessment Instruments   112
  Accomplishment Statements   114
Look Beyond the Obvious   **115**
References   **117**
**For More Information About
Identifying and Developing
Transferable Skills, Check Out
the Following Additional
Resources**   **118**

Chapter Takeaways:

- Think beyond your label—Years of academic life have pushed you to fine-tune a statement regarding your research interests that is short and to the point. It often starts with "I am a doctoral student in…" To hone your transferable skills, or the skills that are valued in research as well as other career areas, you have to break away from thinking about yourself in those terms.
- Prove that you can do the job even when you do not have direct job experience— You will do this by learning to think broadly and comprehensively about your transferable skills.
- Know how to identify your transferable skills—For everything that you have achieved in your life, there is an accompanying set of skills that will add value to you as a job applicant. Know how to describe them.
- Know how to portray your transferable skills in industry terms—There are phrases that resonate with key industries and organizations in their search for new recruits. Identify the correct terms to be understood in your chosen career field.

What do you say when employers ask: "What experience do you have?" Learn how to translate your academic achievements into skillsets that organizations want.

ReSearch. http://dx.doi.org/10.1016/B978-0-12-804297-7.00010-0
105

If you've already started putting labels on yourself as an academic, that's perfectly understandable. It's a global trend, actually. You've simply been swept into the cultural current of trying to please those who want their information in bite-sized, easy-to-digest pieces. On everything from a dating site to a job site to a professional networking site, you're likely to pull out the label that is closest to how you want to portray yourself at that moment. At job fairs and networking events, that label becomes, "I am a master's student in…" or "I am a doctoral student studying…."

One of the hardest things to do in life as you reach past your familiar academic world into a new, perhaps more corporate, governmental, or nonprofit one is to drop your comfortable labels and push to describe yourself differently. This is also a crucial step toward achieving the success that you want in life.

In this chapter, you'll find the resources to change the way you think about yourself. In the process, you'll learn how to discard labels and find ways to tell the world what makes you unique and valuable. You'll learn to break down what you know into a series of skills that can be applied to each unique situation in which you find yourself.

In a nutshell, you will discover what your "transferable skills" are. These are the skills that transfer you from your academic world, your volunteer world, your leisure world, and your work world into what is needed by your target employer or industry/field. This chapter is not about describing yourself in terms of *what* you have achieved, but about *how* you got to where you are now and all the skillsets that you picked up along the way.

Vitae columnist Dr. Elizabeth Keenan,[1] an academic turned realtor and writer, writes about the difficulties she faced when moving from one world to the other. In an article called "PhD's Do Have Transferable Skills," she reminds masters and doctoral students that they have many desirable skills beyond teaching and concentrating thoroughly on one topic for a long time. But she also acknowledges that it's difficult to figure out how to use your skills in a different career outside of the university walls. Harder still is making your skills obvious to the person who might hire you.

Keenan confessed that when she first started looking for a nonacademic job, she was frozen with fear that she would be doomed forever to horrible, menial jobs like the kind she had held to support her academic studies. "In one of my few, non-panicky moments, I had an epiphany. My jobs didn't matter, my *skills* did. I knew that I had skills that people would find useful—I just had to make them relevant to another career."

By altering your perception about what labels fit you, you will find that you DO have a variety of skills that are portable and move freely from one work environment to another. For example, you cannot possibly complete a doctoral or a master's degree without acquiring the skills of doing research, of writing in-depth reports, of organizing and planning work over a period of many months—and even years—of being both a team leader and a team member on occasion, of writing and giving presentations, and of thinking logically and strategically.

WHAT IS A TRANSFERABLE SKILL, ANYWAY?

As stated above, these are the skills that you acquire in the course of your academic studies, your work life, your volunteer world, and your personal interests and hobbies that are applicable in a new employment setting are known as transferable skills.

Essentially, when you see a job that you would like to apply for, you should be able to figure out if the skills you have acquired in your many years of study would line up well with the position you are seeking. This process might seem relatively easy at first: just making lists of the skills needed and the skills you have, and ticking off the boxes to see if there are sufficient matches to apply for the position.

But when you sit down to actually identify your transferable skills for the first time, it doesn't usually go that smoothly.

Why does this task prove so daunting? It comes down to the fact that, despite all the great knowledge you've accumulated in your graduate and postgraduate studies, you've likely never heard the word "skill" used in the classroom or lab.

In an article entitled "The #Alt-Ac Job Search 101: Identifying and Describing Transferable Skills,"[2] published online on *Hook & Eye,* readers are reminded that students in graduate programs rarely if ever hear the word "skill." This is primarily because all the outcomes for graduate courses are "knowledge-based, not skill based." In graduate school, you learn new *fields*, not new *skillsets*. Except in rare cases, students are never made aware that the new knowledge they are gathering through their studies or related graduate work is the foundation for a highly transferable skill.

If graduate students are lucky enough to find themselves engaged in a program where the word "skill" is used, it's usually in the context of a skill—grant writing, for example—that will help them achieve tenure in an academic facility, not a career in a different professional environment.

The end result? While scholars like yourself may have some experience in at least recognizing a skill, they still don't have the expertise to apply that skill to careers in other sectors outside of academia.

This problem can be solved—that's what we'll achieve in this chapter. First, let's take a look at the most wanted skills in the professional worlds beyond academia. Then, I'll walk you through an exercise to determine if you have matching skills and how to recognize them.

SKILLS EMPLOYERS REALLY WANT

To determine what skills employers currently demand most from their new hires, we turn to the National Association of Colleges and Employees (NACE), the leading source of information on the employment of the college educated in the United States. According to respondents to NACE's *Job Outlook 2015* survey,[3] employers seek individuals who can communicate effectively and work successfully with others; 77% want candidates with leadership skills and the skills to work in a team structure.

Next on the list of priorities for employers surveyed by NACE are applicants with "written communication skills," "problem-solving skills," "strong work ethics," and "analytical/quantitative skills." A total of 67.5% of respondents wanted new hires to have technical skills, and 67% wanted excellence in verbal communication skills.

In descending order, the top skills and attributes sought in addition to those already mentioned included initiative, computer skills, flexibility/adaptability, interpersonal skills (relating well to others), detail-oriented, organizational ability, strategic planning skills, friendly outgoing personality, entrepreneurial skills (risk taker), tactfulness, and creativity. Other skills that would place one candidate ahead of the other included having held a leadership position; their major (if it was relevant to a particular industry), a high GPA (3.0 or above); involvement in extracurricular activities such as clubs, sports, and student government; the school attended; volunteer work; fluency in a foreign language; and experience studying abroad.

But what about Asia, Australia, Europe, and the rest of the globe? What kind of skills will workers around the world need in the next 5 years? In their "Future Work Skills 2020 Report," the Institute for the Future (IFTF),[4] a nonprofit research organization, cited 10 crucial skills that workers of the future will need. These include the following:

- **Sense making**: The ability to make sense of what is being expressed at the deepest level.
- **Social intelligence**: The ability to connect to coworkers and clients deeply and directly to sense the reactions and interactions they want.
- **Novel and adaptive thinking**: The ability to come up with solutions and solve problems beyond standard rules or protocols.
- **Cross-cultural competency**: The ability to function effectively in cultural settings different from your own.
- **Computational thinking**: The ability to translate a large quantity of facts into abstract ideas and to comprehend data-based reasoning.
- **New media literacy**: The ability to critically assess and develop content using new forms of media to effectively persuade others. This includes everything from running a successful Facebook campaign to keeping a discussion alive on Twitter.
- **Transdisciplinarity**: The ability to grasp ideas across many disciplines.
- **Design mindset**: The ability to develop work processes and tasks to create a desired result.
- **Cognitive load management**: The ability to filter information to ascertain what is most important and to use many different tools and processes to make the most of your cognitive functioning.
- **Virtual collaboration**: The ability to work productively and lead engagement as part of a virtual team.

In other words, the new transferable skills that your future employers will be seeking will go far beyond the traditional skillsets that we're currently familiar with. The authors of the IFTF report suggest that to be successful in the decade from 2010 to 2020, you will have to be forward thinking and capable of navigating your way through a shifting landscape of organizational forms and essential skills. Not only that, but you will also be required to frequently reassess the skills you have and quickly apply them to new situations.

The IFTF's conclusion emphasizes the importance of this chapter's topic. Being able to identify your transferable skills and apply them to current hiring practices is only going to become more invaluable as the work world continues to evolve over the coming years and decades.

RECOGNIZING YOUR TRANSFERABLE SKILLS

There are five effective tools for learning how to recognize your transferable skills. These include the following:

1. Analysis of your academic profile
2. Analysis of your work, sports, and leadership profile
3. Garnering feedback from nonacademics
4. Assessment tools such as SkillScan or the Myers–Briggs-type indicator
5. Accomplishment statements created prior to compiling your resume

Finding the Hidden Skills in Your Academic Profile

Activity: To make the most out of this suggestion, start with a pen and a blank sheet of paper (you can also do this using a word processor if you prefer). Draw a line down the center. On the left side, write "My Experience in Academia." On the right side, write "Corporate Skill Translation."

Let's explore a few examples of potential experiences you may be able to apply to your skills list.

One such situation is applying for financial aid. Perhaps the whole under-graduate, master's, or doctoral experience for you started with an urgent search for scholarships/stipend or applications for a student loan. To apply for these, you had to sell yourself as a trustworthy person of value who would use the provider's money wisely. Basically, you were asking them to invest in you and to believe that what you had to offer was better than those trying to secure the same goal. If you had also applied for student loans, you may have had to present a detailed budget to illustrate how much money you needed to borrow and how you planned to pay it back once you completed your education. Your documentation of this experience would look something like this:

Your left notation could read: Applied for scholarships/stipends and student loans.

Your right notation could read: Experience in writing persuasive proposals, budgeting, and completing government forms.

Once you began your studies, chances are that you had to begin researching, reading, and writing papers (and eventually your dissertation). You had to learn how to use the academic library, online library databases, and other related resources. You had to learn to write clearly and persuasively to support your point of view, edit and proofread your work, manage your time effectively so your projects were completed on deadline, and deliver a polished document with the proper references and citations. You can break these down into a host of transferable skills:

Your left notation could read: Researching and writing complex, technical documents.

Your right notation will be considerably longer and could include: Research skills in public, academic, and virtual library systems; reference management; article writing experience; editing skills; proofreading skills; excellence in time management and handling multiple projects simultaneously and; delivery of professional and well-documented scholarly work.

Now you have a better idea of how this process works. Another example: If you tutored other students or gave presentations on your area of expertise to a group, you could add "experience in one-on-one training and group education; excellent communication skills; skilled in public presentations, design, and PowerPoint; analytical skills; and experience translating complex scientific data into everyday terms."

The best way to approach this exercise is to think about all the actions you've performed over the years in terms of the skills they represent. As you complete a few notations, you'll see that the process gets easier and easier.

At the end of this exercise, you will discover that while there may not be a lot of jobs being posted for individuals with master's or doctorates in biology, there may be hundreds of potential employers looking for people who "have the ability to operate in high-pressure situations," "have excellent organizational skills," and are "able to translate complex data into every day, understandable terms." Your transferable skills will open up a whole host of opportunities for you as you enter the job market.

Analyzing Your Work, Sports, and Leadership Profile

In every experience that you enjoy, there is some element of learning—some skill that you emerge with or some ability that you raise to a new level. Part-time jobs to support your academic career, participation in university sports programs, and time spent honing your leadership skills in student government or through a business fraternity or career-related professional association all contribute to your profile of transferable skills.

Because all of these things are so different, it may seem overwhelming at first to determine how your many and varied experiences can be funneled into one comprehensive list of transferable skills. One way to do this analysis of your work, sports, and leadership profile is to think in terms of management skillsets frequently requested in job postings for management positions.

The Office of Career Services at Princeton University[5] suggests breaking down your skills into four key categories and citing examples of how the skill relates to your experience. Below these skills are described with mock examples to spark your own ideas as to how these fit into your life:

- Interpersonal Skills—This refers to such things as cooperating with others (participation in a team that built a house for Habitat for Humanity), responding to concerns (serving as dorm student supervisor), motivating people (captain of a sports team), assisting others (volunteer work to teach immigrant students English), resolving conflicts (serving as a representative in the graduate student association), and being a team player (sports teams).
- Organizational Skills—This skillset has to do with follow-through (securing corporate sponsors for a business fraternity networking event), multitasking (continuing to work in the laboratory while writing your dissertation), setting and attaining goals (consistently achieving a 3.0 GPA or higher), meeting deadlines (ensuring all assignments were delivered on time), planning (taking the concept of your dissertation and breaking it down into manageable tasks), and time management (working while simultaneously managing a heavy course load).
- Leadership Skills—There are many areas of part-time work and extracurricular or sports participation that push you to develop leadership skills. Look for ways that you demonstrated decision making (university or departmental newspaper); evaluating (taking complex research data and determining what it really means); managing and supervising (overseeing an undergraduate in the lab); initiating (developing a new program to aid students that continues to operate after you leave); delegating, motivating others, and team building (being a leader in a trainee-led group or organization in your department or within your university); and problem solving and planning (organizing a trainee symposium).
- Communication skills—Few things get done without excellent communication skills. Take a couple of minutes to go over all verbal and writing interactions you've had in your sports, leadership, or work experience. Look for examples to illustrate advising (recommending a training program to your department), explaining (teaching children how to use a microscope), persuading or selling (getting corporate sponsors for a symposium), public speaking (delivering a presentation/poster at a conference), articulating and presenting (soliciting support for your point of view in a student organization), instructing and training (teaching your lab technique to a new lab member), and writing and editing (reports, letters, email campaign materials, papers, and your dissertation).

Garnering Feedback From Nonacademics

As a master's or doctoral student, you don't function in isolation. Within your circle of family and friends, you likely know lots of people in the business or government spheres who understand what their employers are looking for when it comes to hiring. Those in your inner circle also see things in you that strangers would not because they know you well and they understand how you react to life's challenges and rewards. So, when you're trying to draw up the most comprehensive list of your transferable skills possible, it makes sense to call on your personal army of family and friends to solicit their feedback on what skills you possess outside of your academic achievements.

Activity: Why not ask them in person or via email to advise you of three skills they believe you possess that would make you a good hire in any position that you're seeking? Many of the attributes they'll list for you can find new definition as transferable skills.

For example, several of your friends may cite your empathy and communicativeness as a skill. Others may remark on your artistic talents when creating images on canvas and through a camera lens. Still others may call you their go-to coach or praise you for your great ability to solve problems. They may talk about your endless flow of great ideas, your skills as a good listener, or your ability to persuade others to follow you.

It's inevitable with this kind of exercise that certain attributes will rise to the surface as they're repeatedly mentioned by different sources. That repetition of certain attributes from different friends and family is sufficient evidence for inclusion on your list of transferable skills. Try to use their feedback to think about genuine examples that you can use to illustrate those skills or attributes.

Assessment Instruments

To describe your transferable skills in the most accurate and persuasive way possible, you need to know what skills you have and what skills employers want—I've already covered that. But to be most effective in putting your skillset together, it also helps a great deal to know and understand your own strengths and weaknesses. That way, you can focus on your strengths when articulating your skillsets and find ways to demonstrate those traits as skillful actions.

Chapter 8 can provide you with more details on different types of self-assessment tools available. One that is widely used in industries and organizations around the world, and discussed in Chapter 8, is the Myers–Briggstype indicator (MBTI). If a classmate describes herself as an ESTP (Extraverted Sensing Thinking Perceiving), for example, you know right away that she has taken the assessment and is summarizing her findings. In fact, taking an assessment of this type can be both a fun and an enlightening exercise—especially if you take it with a group of friends or colleagues and then share your results.

The MBTI, developed by Isabel Myers and her mother Katherine Briggs, is based on philosopher Carl Jung's theory of personality types. Myers and Briggs believed that if they could build an indicator to help people understand themselves, those people could land in occupations that were most compatible with their personal psychological preferences, thus leading to more fulfilling careers and, in turn, happier lives.

When you take the MBTI, your preferences will be categorized as one of 16 different types of personality. There are no good or bad results, and there are no winners or losers. In fact, the authors stressed from the beginning that all personality types are equal and each one has value, and is necessary for balance—both in general populations and within individual personalities. Your MBTI results are not compared with those of other people; that isn't the point. The assessment is simply a vehicle for getting to know yourself better and to be able to use that information to find work areas where you will thrive.

Having such self-knowledge can help you to start identifying and promoting the transferable skills that most closely match your personality. Let's take a look at the different categories in the MBTI that make up someone's personality:

The (E) is for Extraversion and the (I) for Introversion, both referring to how you relate and respond to your world. The E's are inclined to turn outward, to favor action, and to thrive on their interactions with people. The I's are more inward turning and focused on their own thoughts, and need to be alone to restore their energy.

The (S) is for Sensing and the (N) for Intuition, both referring to how you secure information in your world. If you are in the Sensing category, you pay a lot of attention to the real world around you and your hands-on experiences in learning new skills. If you are in the Intuition category, you are more likely to be an expert at analyzing data and forming conclusions based on patterns and impressions. You are more of an abstract thinker.

The (T) is for Thinking and the (F) for Feeling and these categories have to do with how you make your decisions once you have secured your information. The Thinking person is heavy on the side of facts and objectivity; the Feeling person leans toward emotions and feelings.

The final scale is about how you deal with the outside world and how you live your life. The (J) is for Judging and the (P) is for Perceiving. The J's want structure and solid decision-making in their lives. The P's are more flexible and adaptable, and open to whatever opportunity comes along.

All personality combinations can be summed up in four-letter codes that reflect these personality scales.

In the United States alone each year, about two million people, many of them college graduates take this test to learn a little more about themselves. It is best to take the official MBTI and have your results verified and interpreted by a licensed professional who can guide you to determining your true MBTI type. You may find versions of the MBTI online but they will usually be in the style of the MBTI and may not be completely accurate or comprehensive. Nonetheless, many people find the MBTI useful in gaining a little self-knowledge regardless of how the assessment is administered. To take the online official MBTI, go to www.myersbriggstests.com.[6]

If you have access to a university career center, you may wish to work with a career counselor and undertake another highly valuable self-directed assessment tool called SkillScan. This is a card-sort activity for identifying 60 of your transferable skills within six major skill categories, along with opportunity to evaluate your proficiency at various skills and, most importantly for graduate students, the chance to visualize and determine what skills you might possess but **do not wish to use** in future work. This is an important point to consider, especially since this chapter focuses on how you can transfer skills from science and academia into other fields. Through use of self-assessment tools, you get the chance to reflect on both what you want to use in a career, and what you do not want to take with you on your career journey. SkillScan can be completed with a traditional deck of cards or an online version, www.skillscan.com but is primarily available through career counselors.

Accomplishment Statements

Activity: Another exercise to clarify your transferable skills involves writing accomplishment statements. Employers are eager to know that you bring value to their business, as the experts at The Career Center at San Jose State University[7] recognize. They explain that, when you are able to demonstrate what you *did* (i.e., your accomplishments), as opposed to just citing a skill, it's extremely effective.

Every accomplishment statement moves naturally through three stages:

1. You must identify a problem you encountered in your academic or work life and illustrate the severity of its nature.
2. You must outline the specific method you used to solve the problem.
3. You must provide a follow-up detail on whether or not the problem was solved and the longer term results, if known.

Look especially for problems that involved creating efficiencies of money or time or of increased sales or revenue. Is the system you established still in place? Demonstrating concrete results is always a plus.

The Career Center at San Jose suggests that you use the acronym S.T.A.R. (Situation, Task, Action, and Result) to create your accomplishment statements, and in Chapter 16 we also recommend using the S.T.A.R. method to prepare answers for interview questions. Whatever method you use to put your statements together, be sure to use action verbs throughout your outline. Be specific and as detailed as possible about what you did.

In recounting the action or series of actions you performed to solve the problem, talk in terms of the identifiable skills I have been mentioning in this chapter. The result is really the most important part of your accomplishment statement. When you can give exact statistics, you add a lot of weight to your statement.

If you're having trouble thinking about situations from your work or academic life that would qualify as accomplishment statements, ask yourself about times in either environment when you felt proud of or satisfied with a project. Did you ever take responsibility for arranging to get something done that you knew was necessary? Are you leaving any lasting legacies as you prepare to leave academia?

What kinds of special projects have you worked on? What was your dissertation about? Did you break any records in your sports career or win any awards in your extracurricular activities? Did you win any academic honors? Considering past experiences in these terms will help you recognize what activities stand out as accomplishments that occurred as a result of your skillset and can be transferred to industry terms.

Here are a couple of sample accomplishment statements:

"Managed graduate student symposium, overseeing a team of fellow trainee organizers and full program development."

"Organized and led a cross-functional team to develop and conduct a science outreach program to the local public school system."

While discovering how past skills can apply to new situations, remember to be broad reaching in your approach. Once you have your accomplishment statements down, you'll be ready to incorporate abbreviated descriptions into your resume. We'll talk about that more in Chapter 16.

LOOK BEYOND THE OBVIOUS

Remember to take this process one step further when you're compiling your list of transferable skills. *Look beyond the obvious* and try to find some unique skills that will intrigue your potential employer and help you stand out from the pack. Being able to present yourself with creativity and intelligence will make your package of skills even more appealing to your ideal employer.

Quick Guide to Translating Your Academic Accomplishments Into Industry Skills

To identify your transferable skills and highlight them in all your job interviews, resumes, and cover letters, experts at the University of Michigan's Career Center[8] suggest you categorize your skills into six key categories.

These are analysis and problem solving, interpersonal and leadership, project management and organization, research and information management, self-management and work habits, and written and oral communication.

For a quick guide, here are four ways to match your academic skills to those categories:

Analysis and Problem Solving
- Skilled at identifying problems and discerning likely causes
- Expert at investigating problems and forming independent conclusions
- Well versed in finding patterns in a large quantity of data
- Experienced in developing protocols to resolve conflict

Interpersonal and Leadership Skills
- Facilitator of discussions
- Mentor to peers and employees

Continued

Quick Guide to Translating Your Academic Accomplishments Into Industry Skills—cont'd

- Experienced motivator of teams and individuals
- Capable of moving effectively through bureaucratic work cultures
  Project Management and Organization
- Capable of prioritizing work to meet deadlines
- Able to be flexible to changing organizational priorities
- Experienced in creating realistic timelines for projects
- Effective in project management from start to finish
  Research and Information Management
- Expert at creating and analyzing surveys
- Ability to organize and comprehend large amounts of data
- Effective at discerning appropriate information sources for problem solving
- Research skills in both traditional and virtual libraries
  Self-Management and Work Habits
- Capable of meeting deadlines
- Able to work creatively under pressure
- Disciplined to work without constant supervision
- Able to absorb new information quickly and design appropriate solutions
  Written and Oral Communications
- Skilled at preparing professional grant proposals and other technical documents
- Experienced with designing effective PowerPoint presentations
- Ability to write clearly and concisely about complex topics
- Strong editing and proofreading skills

Additionally, an international research skills perspective is available using Vitae's Researcher Development Framework. Collecting data from characteristics of the United Kingdom researchers over a number of years, this framework provides description of 4 domains and 12 subdomains of knowledge, qualities, skills, intellectual abilities, techniques, and research professional standards which researchers possess. There are over 60 descriptors within the framework. This resource can be found online at: https://www.vitae.ac.uk/vitae-publications/rdf-related/researcher-development-framework-rdf-vitae.pdf/view.

Case Study

Lily Raines, PhD, is a global projects manager in the Office of International Activities at the American Chemical Society. She completed her PhD in biochemistry, cellular, and molecular biology at the Johns Hopkins University School of Medicine. In her current position she manages programs for science students and for professional chemists.

I changed my career course late in graduate school. I originally planned to be a professor at a primarily undergraduate institution. As such, I actively pursued teaching opportunities early in graduate school. I started off as a tutor for an underprivileged high school student, then was a teaching assistant for medical

Case Study—cont'd

students, and finally was a course director for a class titled "Effective Science Communication." Even after I decided that route was not for me, I assessed the skills I developed and was able to parlay my teaching, communication, and interpersonal skills to my ultimately successful job application.

I decided that I no longer wanted to be a professor around my fourth year of graduate school, but was otherwise unsure of what I wanted to do. I became highly involved with a science outreach group as a hobby, both because I enjoyed this work and because I think it is important, and ended up organizing a successful science café series and a number of science communication workshops. I had to manage my time well to keep up with my lab responsibilities, but was able to use this as a "break" while also developing skills useful for various careers. I did not seriously consider science outreach a viable full-time career option at the time.

When the opportunity to take an internship in science outreach at the American Society for Biochemistry and Molecular Biology (ASBMB) came up, I leapt at the chance. I was able to get a leave of absence granted from my NIH (National Institutes of Health) F31, and my advisor and I were able to schedule my internship with the ASBMB to be minimally disruptive to my experiments. This internship, in addition to teaching me many useful skills and giving me an understanding of science outreach as a career, introduced me to an amazing network of scientists and communicators who were incredibly helpful as I was looking for jobs and working on my resume. Under their guidance I won a travel award to attend a conference I helped organize, and then expanded my network even further.

Ultimately, I was offered a position at the American Chemical Society in their Office of International Activities. As of this writing I am coordinating science outreach programs abroad and I will often travel internationally, which is a rare position and one I am exceedingly happy in. Although science outreach is a small field, it is growing. I was very lucky, but as Louis Pasteur said "fortune favors the prepared mind."[3] You can still prepare yourself to be as competitive as possible, even if you start later in your graduate career.

REFERENCES

1. Keenan E. *PhD's do have transferable skills, Part 1.* Vitae; July 17, 2015. https://chroniclevitae.com/news/1068-ph-d-s-do-have-transferable-skills-part-1.
2. Hook&Eye. *The #Alt-Ac job search 101: identifying and describing transferable skills.* March 12, 2015. http://www.hookandeye.ca/2015/03/the-alt-ac-job-search-101-identifying.html.
3. National Association of Colleges and Employees. *Job Outlook 2015: the candidate skills/qualities employers want, the influence of attributes.* November 2, 2014. www.naceweb.org/surveys/job-outlook.aspx.
4. Institute for the Future. *Future work skills 2020 report.* 2011. www.iftf.org/futureworkskills.
5. Princeton University Career Services. "Transferable skills." http://careerservices.princeton.edu/undergraduate-students/resumes-letters-online-profiles/resumes/transferable-skills.
6. The Myers & Briggs Foundation. "MBTI basics." www.myersbriggs.org.

7. San Jose State University Career Center. "Accomplishment statements." http://www.sjsu.edu/careercenter/students/find-a-job-internship/resumes-cover-letters/accomplishment-statements/.
8. The Career Center, University of Michigan. "PhD transferable skills." https://careercenter.umich.edu/article/phd-transferable-skills.

FOR MORE INFORMATION ABOUT IDENTIFYING AND DEVELOPING TRANSFERABLE SKILLS, CHECK OUT THE FOLLOWING ADDITIONAL RESOURCES

Denicolo P, Reeves J, editors. *Developing transferable skills: Enhancing your research and employment potential (success in research).* SAGE Publications Ltd.; January 7, 2014. http://www.amazon.com/Developing-Transferable-Skills-Enhancing-Employment-ebook/dp/B00HU8VK0O/ref=sr_1_1?s=books&ie=UTF8&qid=1445099687&sr=1-1&keywords=transferable+skills.

Designed especially for those PhD students who want to make the move from academic to corporate research, this easy-to-comprehend book is also perfect for postgraduate students who want to move into roles as private sector researchers or supervisors/managers of research facilities. Denicolo is a chartered psychologist and Reeves is a veteran skills trainer for researchers.

Pellegrino JW, Hilton ML, et al., editors. *Education for life and work: developing transferable knowledge and skills in the 21st century.* National Academies Press; August 29, 2014. http://www.amazon.com/Education-Life-Work-Developing-Transferable-ebook/dp/B00N5ONYZ0/ref=sr_1_2?s=books&ie=UTF8&qid=1445099687&sr=1-2&keywords=transferable+skills.

This thoughtful book focuses on the important skillsets needed to develop deeper learning and higher order thinking. It's aimed at aiding postgraduate students in honing both the skills needed for academic careers as well as careers within business and industry.

Transferable Academic Skills Kit: University Foundation Study

Fava-Verde A, Griffiths P, Manning A, et al., editors. *Course book.* Garnet Education; July 21, 2009. http://www.amazon.com/Transferable-Academic-Skills-Kit-University/dp/1859645364/ref=sr_1_8?s=books&ie=UTF8&qid=1445099687&sr=1-8&keywords=transferable+skills.

This is a flexible learning research study designed to cultivate the critical transferable skills that facilitate students' success in their academic studies. The series of exercises gives students the tools needed to create a set of skills that can be used within a broad range of contexts both inside and outside of academia.

Chapter 11

The "Me Brand": Tips for Successful Personal Branding

Nathan L. Vanderford

Chapter Outline

What Is Branding, Anyway?	121	Personal Blog	131
Figuring Out Your Four W's	121	Science Blogging	132
Beginning to Build Your Brand	124	Bringing All Aspects of Your	
Your Resume	125	Brand Together	133
Cover Letter	126	Wrapping Up Your Branding	
Letters of Reference	126	Efforts	133
Elevator Speech	127	References	137
LinkedIn	128	To learn more about personal	
Facebook	130	branding, here are four additional	
Twitter	130	resources to broaden your brand	138
Personal Website	130		

Chapter Takeaways:

- Your personal "me brand" highlights your four w's: **who** you are, **what** impact you want to make, **where** you want to be, and the **work** you want.
- Central to crafting your brand is to define your four w's including developing a personal mission statement.
- Building your brand involves a variety of strategies that range from traditional resume design to a more modern active presence on key social media platforms. In today's digital age, managing how your brand is portrayed online is critically important.
- Managing your social media use is key to maintaining your brand image.
- An elevator speech is a vital component of "advertising" and "selling" your brand.

What's the secret to finding engaging work in your field of study? Creating a personal brand that will bring recruiters to your door!

When it comes to finding purposeful work in today's volatile job market, there's only one thing you can know for certain: the old rules are just that—old. If you plan to start your job search by sending out resumes and knocking on

ReSearch. http://dx.doi.org/10.1016/B978-0-12-804297-7.00011-2

doors as your studies come to an end, you'll be miles behind clever colleagues who have already turned themselves into hot commodities by building strong personal brands. While you're busy trying to secure an appointment with an organization's recruiter, your employer of choice will have already begun courting your colleague—someone who has invested the time to establish his or her expertise and credibility in the industry.

YOU can be that person who is actively sought out by recruiters if you start to work on your own brand now.

The new rule of the job-seeking game is this: *the day you step foot onto a university campus is the day you enter the labor market*. No matter what level of education you're seeking, this rule applies. You must be poised and ready to leap at opportunities that come your way from then until the day you retire from active employment. That means that you must build yourself into a strong brand and continue to develop it every day of your working life.

But what if you haven't yet started a focused effort to build your brand? The good news is that it's not the end of the world! All you need to remember is that *career development is a lifelong process*. No matter what point you're at in your career—undergraduate studies, graduate school, postdoctoral research, or beyond—you can commit yourself to being actively involved in the process from today forward. That's what we're here to teach you.

In this chapter, I'll cover the basics of personal branding to help you take the reins of the career development process. I'll walk you through the essential steps to create your own "me brand" to help you prepare for your ideal career— or to improve your career advancement opportunities within your chosen career.

Rest assured that you CAN take off and soar even though you're facing a labor market that has its share of turbulence and uncertainty. According to the *World Employment and Social Outlook: Trends 2015*[1] report published by the International Labour Organization, in 2014 there were 74 million people under the age of 24 seeking employment around the world. "The world economy continues to expand at rates well below the trends that preceded the advent of the global crisis of 2008 and is unable to close the significant employment and social gaps that have emerged," the report states. In other words, employment conditions are strained and competition is fierce.

We know it can be tough out there with those employment gaps being troublesome for current and future job seekers like you. Often we can find ourselves worrying about mounting student debt and the possibility of finding employment. But we are here to tell you that if you are intentional about planning your career, you can lessen this burden significantly.

Personal branding starts with a belief that you can become what you want to be. That's why it's important not to get caught up in doomsday reports. Yes, there are economic problems and jobs are not plentiful. But there are also signs of improvement. United States employers will hire 9.6% more college graduates in 2015 than in the previous year, according to the National Association of Colleges and Employers. And in Europe and Japan, unemployment rates are steadily falling.

Plus, employment rates remain higher for college graduates at any level than for those at lower education levels. In fact, at least within the United States, an average of 98% of the total population of PhDs is employed at any given time. That means that you've already done one thing right: seek a higher education. All that remains is to continue on your path and to incorporate branding as a priority along the way.

In the end, there is only one important statistic: *you*. As one individual, you need one job. You can get that job by building up your personal brand using both traditional and nontraditional techniques (covered in this chapter) in an innovative way that makes the world of potential employers notice you.

WHAT IS BRANDING, ANYWAY?

Finding the career you want is ultimately all about selling yourself as the best candidate for the job. It could also involve persuading investors to back your research or buy shares in your entrepreneurial enterprise. As is the case with any product, selling something is easier when you have an established, credible brand. And, it is important to realize that no matter what career path you are pursuing (Yes, even an academic one!), having a strong, positive "me brand" is critical to your short- and long-term success. After reading this chapter, you will have the tools you need to start building your own brand NOW.

The idea of having a personal brand dates back to 1997 when the business management expert and bestselling author Tom Peters[2] coined the concept in an article in the August/September edition of *Fast Company* magazine. He explained that in order to obtain whatever we want in life, we have to be able to convince people that we are a qualified and credible choice. "It's time for me – and you – to take a lesson from the big brands, a lesson that's true for anyone who's interested in what it takes to stand out and prosper in the new world of work," Peters wrote. "Start today."

As Peters emphasized, creating a personal brand is especially important for job seekers. Why? Because the old method of career advancement—starting low in a menial position and working your way up the career ladder—just doesn't exist anymore. "It's over. No more vertical. No more ladder. That's not the way careers work anymore. Linearity is out. A career is now a checkerboard. Or even a maze. It's full of moves that go sideways, forward, slide on the diagonal, even go backward when that makes sense. (It often does.)"

In this new world of work, instead of a single upward climb, a career should be regarded as a collection of different projects that enable you to grow professionally—learn new skills, gain expertise in different areas, broaden your professional network, and constantly improve and revamp your "me brand." Let's get started!

FIGURING OUT YOUR FOUR W'S

Ultimately, your brand as a job seeker comes down to four w's: **Who** you are, **What** impact you want to make, **Where** you want to be, and the **Work** you want. Once you've determined these things, you can make use of available vehicles (traditional and virtual) to drive you to your destination.

Who you are: Most of us spend our lives trying to figure out exactly who we are and what will make us happy in life, so it may seem like a massive task to try to discern this immediately to begin the branding process. One way to work through this is to create a personal mission statement about yourself, defining who you are in terms of the world you want to serve.

Drafting a personal mission statement:

1. First, think about what you know now and what you are learning. Think about what you've accomplished so far and what you hope to accomplish. Do you already have a specialization and are you happy with it? Are there other aspects of life sciences or other areas of study that intrigue you?

2. Think about your emotional appeal as well as your academic and practical skills. Write down how your friends, family, and colleagues would describe you. How would you describe yourself? What joy would other people take in having you on their team? Once you do this, ask others to critically and honestly evaluate you using these same questions and then compare your analysis with theirs. Work to reconcile any differences. For example, if others perceive you as "the grumpy curmudgeon" or "the latte-clutching mad scientist," then you will want to work to build a more professional brand.

3. After recording all of these impressions, try to sum them up into a descriptive phrase no longer than a tweet of 140 characters. Let's look at corporate brands for some inspiration. Nike brands itself as "authentic athletic performance." Disney brands itself as "family fun." An individual in the life sciences might be an "adventure-loving food scientist," or "visionary breast cancer research scholar," or "innovative hybrid-plant scientist in training."

4. Once your personal mission statement is drafted, it should convey a clear message about what you're interested in and your personal strengths, as well as hinting at your future goals. Your statement should pique their interest by indicating to potential employers that you are different from your colleagues. Keep in mind that if you use words like "visionary" or "innovative," you will need to be able to give examples to substantiate your claims. As long as you can show that you did at least one thing out of the ordinary, though, then it's fair game. If you have not done one thing outside the box, I encourage you to do so in the near future. Living life occasionally outside the box is often a key to career success.

The important thing is not to limit yourself to one job title or confine yourself to one job description. Keep your brand open enough that it will grow with you. Pay particular attention to determining the special qualities or skills you have that distinguish you from your competitors. For example, think of how forceful my brand sounds when it is written as: "Faculty administrator with interests in operations management, cancer research, and career development" compared to "Faculty working in administration."

What is also important to remember is that you're not just selling yourself, you're selling your background, experience, and education—in essence, everything that determines your potential for success. Considering this, your brand may change over time as you gain experience and expertise.

What impact you want to make: What impact do you want to make in the professional world? This question extends far beyond the specific type of job you want at the moment and gets back to the original question of who you are. What concrete results do you want to produce over the course of your career? Would you like to boast a lengthy bibliography of publications in life sciences education? Do you want to contribute to new innovations in biomedical equipment? Do you want to effect environmental policy change? Having an idea of your long-term goals will prove invaluable as you begin to lay out a path for yourself in the professional world.

Keep in mind that your long-term impact isn't something to fret over too much at the moment. It should simply help guide you as you make decisions throughout your professional career. Remember, this is a lifelong process, so it's important to take it one step at a time.

Where you want to be: The third "w" relates to your personal life. Aside from your professional aspirations, what are your personal goals or plans for the next 5 years? Is starting a family on the horizon? If so, will you need a more flexible schedule or nontraditional work arrangement? Would you like to set down roots in a certain location or are you interested in traveling and living in different places around the world? What kind of lifestyle appeals to you? One that is fast-paced and unpredictable, or something that provides more stability? Keeping your personal goals in mind is extremely important as you begin to define the type of work that you want.

The work you want: The personal mission statement that you created is an excellent first step in helping you narrow down and define the type of work that you want. Review your statement, as well as your thoughts regarding what you want to make and where you want to be. Next, think about the following questions to help you further define your ideal career:

- Have you already identified an area of further study or research that intrigues you?
- Do you work best individually or in a team?
- What type of environment are you most comfortable in (academic, research-oriented, corporate, government, etc.)?
- Do you want to establish yourself as a consultant, a communicator, or a practitioner in a particular field?
- Do you want to use your skills to run your own business?
- Are you willing to travel in the course of your work or relocate to other places?

As you reflect on these questions, what relevant career options come to mind? Take the time to do some online research to determine what career(s) your specific interests and preferences align with. For example, you can use *Science Careers myIDP*[3] tool for this, although there are several tools available.

Also, talk to multiple mentors and/or colleagues and pick their brains about what they think would be a good fit for you. Are you more suited to a research position at a large pharmaceutical company, or a leadership role in a governmental organization? Or might work at a small biomedical start-up or a life sciences publishing house be more suitable to you?

Your career choice may also be influenced by which industries are currently doing the most hiring. According to WorkplaceTrends.com, the hottest industries for 2015 were health care, engineering, consulting, and accounting. Others with great potential for growth are semiconductors and software development. Are the skills and knowledge you've acquired (or are in the process of acquiring) applicable to any of these industries? As a scientist, you may be surprised to find that many of your skills are transferrable to career fields that you might not have mentioned. Think about this when you read about transferrable skills in Chapter 10.

BEGINNING TO BUILD YOUR BRAND

Once you know what your personal brand is, shift your focus to getting your brand out there. You can accomplish this in person through traditional networking avenues or virtually through your presence on social media or by establishing personal blogs or guest blogging for others. I recommend that you combine both in-person and electronic methods of branding for the best results.

From the start, realize that you can't do everything! You're better off identifying basic points of brand promotion and sticking to them rather than trying to do everything at once.

At the very least, you need the following:

- **An excellent resume** that reads less like a list of your job experiences and academic qualifications and more like a marketing brochure of your skills and accomplishments.
- **An excellent cover letter** that can be customized for each specific job application.
- **Letters of reference** that you will begin collecting from professors, supervisors, project chairs, and community leaders.
- **An elevator speech** for use when you're networking in person. This brief speech allows you to quickly introduce yourself and explain who you are, what you do now, and what you hope to do in the future.
- **A LinkedIn profile** that presents your skills and accomplishments in a professional manner.
- **A Facebook profile** that is devoid of pictures of your party days and instead depicts your professional image.
- **A Twitter account** with a nice balance of tweets showing your personal and professional interests and knowledge.
- **An online website** that contains all of the content in this list and is linked to your LinkedIn, Facebook, and Twitter profiles, as well as to any research papers or articles you've written.

If you've already assembled the items above, you can add to them:

- **A personal blog** designed to establish you as an authority in your field.
- **A collection of links to guest blog postings** you've written for others in your field of expertise.
- **A science blog** focused on your area of interest can be added, especially if you have aspirations to be a science communicator.

YOUR RESUME

From this point forward, lists are for groceries and things you need to accomplish. They are not for use on your resume to cite the litany of places you have worked, the tasks that you completed there, and the dates of your entry and departure at all those stations in your life. Instead, your resume should now become a brochure for your personal brand. The image you present here should be consistent with your 4 w's: who you are, what you want to make, where you want to be, and the work that you want.

A strategic resume should not just list your skills, but it should rather bring them to life by illustrating how having those skills led to concrete results and improvements in your area of responsibility. How were you able to enhance the quality of life for the people around you at the time? Remember that, as a science scholar, the kind of work that you will do for the rest of your life will impact how people live, regardless of which field you select.

Personal branding through your resume:

- Include some version of your personal mission statement as your "Objective" at the top of your resume.
- If possible, only include professional experiences that are directly relevant to your desired job or area of study. This allows you more space to elaborate on each experience.
- If your work experience in the field is sparse, then try to fill it in with other types of experience: internships, volunteering, shadowing, etc. The final option, if absolutely necessary, is to include work experiences that are not directly relevant, but that highlight the relevant skills that you gained from them.
- Instead of simply listing job responsibilities under each experience, list concrete achievements and highlight the skills and actions you used to reach them.
- Include all of the important projects that you have worked on, and take credit for the accomplishments that can reasonably be credited to you.
- Cite any research work that has been published in peer-reviewed journals, and summarize it concisely.
- When you mention volunteer work, illustrate how it helped you learn new skills relevant to your field, or how it contributed to advancing your field in some way.

By reading your resume, the potential employer should know who you are and what kind of work you want to do and are capable of doing. They will also be able to gain some insight into the value that you place on yourself. We will cover aspects of successful job applications in Chapter 16.

COVER LETTER

Your cover letter should contain the essence of your personal brand in terms of what motivates you and the kind of work you're seeking. While the core of your cover letter may remain the same, each one needs to be customized to the specific position for which you're applying.

General structure for your "me brand" cover letter:

- State the position you're applying for.
- Give a brief version of your personal mission statement, including your main interests, and illustrate how they relate to the organization or position in question.
- Mention some specific information about the organization to demonstrate your knowledge. A good way to prepare for this is to read the last five news releases from that organization, and then reference that information in the letter.
- Discuss a couple highlights of your relevant experience. Pick just one or two projects and illustrate your skills by giving a specific example of how you executed a plan that helped a previous employer achieve their goals.
- Conclude with a statement that summarizes your brand while emphasizing how you could contribute to the organization.

Just as you have your personal brand, make sure that you're aware of the intended employer's brand and that you make some reference to it in your letter. Try to keep the letter as concise as possible, preferably no longer than one page.

LETTERS OF REFERENCE

Busy people often say they will send you a letter of reference but they forget or don't get it done when you need it. That's a fact of life. They are not being mean-spirited; it's just that people like professors, company presidents, and community leaders often have so many demands that unless they have devised a system for things like recommendation letters, they can get easily forgotten.

That's why it's perfectly acceptable to draft half a dozen letters about yourself that point out your expertise in a particular area and carry them with you as a class, project, or work term is ending. Armed with these drafts, approach the person you want a reference from and ask them if they would consider writing you a letter of reference for your (specific skill) in (specific area or subject) as exhibited in the recently completed project or work term. If they say yes, ask if they have time to write it or if it would be more convenient for you to furnish a draft that they might review and sign if they feel comfortable. More likely than not, they'll answer that they'd like the draft. Produce it immediately. Most individuals will give it a quick read, perhaps make a few tweaks and then quickly return it to you.

While requesting your letter, make sure to ask your reference if it is acceptable for you to use the letter in your online profile. That way, you can post their recommendation as a testimonial on your personal website or social media pages.

You may find those who prefer to write their own letters, which is wonderful—it usually means they have some really nice things to say about you! However, most people will respect the efficiency of your process and you will end up with far more reference letters than your colleagues if you adopt this practice. Start now and you will soon amass a large number of them, which will come in extremely handy when that new job application arises.

Always ask if they would be willing to write you a STRONG letter of reference. Because in the event that you are asking for a letter to be submitted that you will not be able to review, such as for an application for a fellowship or graduate program, you will want to ensure that your letters are the best that they can be.

ELEVATOR SPEECH

Your elevator speech is the way you introduce yourself at networking events, at ice-breaking sessions before conferences, and to potential employers and supporters throughout your career. Continually honing your elevator speech is an important part of the lifelong process of career development and advancement. True to its name, this speech should be short enough to be delivered in 20–30s—the amount of time a short elevator ride normally takes. Imagine that you happened to step into an elevator to see the CEO of your dream organization standing there: you need to be prepared to make the most of the short time you have him or her as your captive audience! Seriously, these things really do happen.

Teresa: I have been told by one of my mentors that you should expect to be in the elevator one day with the President of the Institution, so what would you say? For many years as a trainee I never saw the guy, except for in pictures of course. Now I share a building with him and still to this day remember the first time that we got on the elevator together and rode the longest four floors of my life. But you better bet that I was prepared with my elevator pitch.

Natalie: I have several friends who work in different roles at Google, and they all have those jobs because they sat next to a Google executive on a plane.

Nathan: I once landed a job because my elevator pitch included a mention of my hometown and it just so happened that despite being several hundred miles from my location at the time, the hiring manager graduated from the same high school as me but 20 years earlier.

The point here is that whether in an elevator, on an airplane, in line at the coffee shop, or applying for a job, you need to be ready with a good elevator pitch.

Your elevator speech should convey the essence of your personal brand and highlight what makes you unique in a way that is easily and quickly understandable to the person hearing it. It should be short and well practiced so that it rolls off your tongue without a moment's hesitation.

By analyzing some of the best elevator speeches out there, we noted that the second word opening the speech is always a verb. If you can make it an action verb that grabs your audience's attention, it will set you apart from just about everyone else. The Expressions of Excellence website[4] has samples of some great elevator speeches for a variety of different professions that can help get your creative juices flowing. The Postdoc Way[5] also offers specific insight into preparing a scientific elevator speech.

As an example, instead of Teresa just saying to the president in the elevator "I am working in this building as a part of the graduate school and I hope to expand my focus to help all trainees," which is the whole truth, think how much more intrigued the listener would be if she said: "I'm working to keep our graduate trainees engaged in career planning," or "I'm determining the needs of our graduate trainees in the area of career planning and developing novel programs to meet those needs."

So, here is what she said to the President:

"Hello, my name is Teresa Evans and I am a recent graduate of the Biomedical Science PhD program here at the Health Science Center. I am currently working to build innovative programs for the career development of our graduate trainees, both students and postdoctoral fellows, within the graduate school. As you know many of our trainees will not purse an academic position and if they do the competition is steep for these limited positions. My goal is to provide trainees with all the necessary tools they will need in order to succeed in their chosen field."

If you deliver your creative elevator speech with confidence and a smile, your listener will want to know more. Once you're finished, stop and let the other person respond. This gives your listener a chance to keep the conversation going by asking you a follow-up question or by commenting on your speech in some way. The longer you can keep the conversation going, the better. If appropriate, ask to exchange contact information with the individual.

Remember that there is no one-size-fits-all elevator speech. Create two or three. The one you'd use with a colleague at a professional seminar is not the same one you'd use with the lead researcher at the company picnic. Also, I suggest using your cell phone and recording yourself. I know this sounds scary but we all have a very valuable tool that we carry in our pockets. We are crazy to not use it to practice and improve our communication skills and delivery of our message.

LINKEDIN

People often think of LinkedIn as their online resume. However, LinkedIn is much more than a static platform through which to display your professional experience. The key to using it successfully is recognizing how *dynamic* it is. LinkedIn provides an invaluable snapshot of your actual accomplishments through the measuring sticks of recommendations and endorsements from your connections to substantiate each of your skills and professional experience. Plus, it's an excellent online networking tool that allows you to easily connect with others in your field and slowly expand your professional network.

Taking full advantage of LinkedIn:

- Be as thorough as possible when building your profile. Fill in as much information in each category as is relevant and appropriate to your experience. Make sure that all information that you include will reflect positively on your brand.
- Display your personal branding message prominently (this should be a version of your personal mission statement). It will probably fit best in the "Summary" section.
- Do some research on the most common keywords used in your field or profession of interest. Include those keywords in your profile to ensure that anyone looking for recruits in the field can easily find you. The "Skills" area is one of the most important keyword sources in your profile, so build it out as extensively as possible. This is not the time to be modest! Another important aspect of the LinkedIn search algorithm is the first word of your job title. So, writing your title as "Neuroscience Researcher" is more powerful than simply "Postdoctoral Fellow."
- Ask for recommendations and endorsements from colleagues and associates. The great thing about LinkedIn is that it's reciprocal, so people likely won't mind writing you a brief recommendation if you write them one. The more you have, the better. Just make sure that you always request them from individuals who you know have a positive opinion of you. Keep in mind that this recommendation may vary between job sectors. Your strategy for how you approach this may be different if your career path is in academics versus industry or the government sector, etc.
- Add your in-person connections. Make an effort to collect people's business cards whenever you attend an event or meet a potential connection. When you get home, use the information on their business card to connect with them on LinkedIn. Or, better yet, download the LinkedIn smart phone application and connect with them immediately through the app.
- Stay active. LinkedIn allows you to write updates (brief and informal) and posts (longer and more formal—almost like blog posts) that will be posted to your profile and visible to all of your connections on their homepage. Share what you've been up to—whether it's a brief update about the seminar you just attended, or a link to your most recent blog article.
- If you're a business owner, create a company page for your business. This allows you to link your personal profile to your company, letting potential associates and recruiters learn more about your organization. The company page allows you to post updates, as well as information on services and career opportunities.

- Keep your profile updated. Set a monthly reminder to check and see if there's anything you can add.
- If you have a personal blog or website, be sure to link it to your profile.

FACEBOOK

Having an effective personal brand means creating consistency across your social media profile. Even though many people keep their Facebook presence as their personal social networking tool, it is still important to make sure that your Facebook site maintains the professional image that you want to portray. Sure, you can still share personal photos from your fun weekend trip or a recent family outing, but keep them appropriate. A good rule of thumb is, don't post anything you wouldn't feel comfortable showing to the company president or college dean. That goes for photos, but also for status updates about political or social issues that are particularly controversial.

There are many other types of Facebook posts that are perfectly acceptable and will help build your brand:

- Talk about a project you're working on.
- Post a picture from a volunteer effort that you found rewarding.
- Promote a special lecture or seminar in your field.
- Mention a great book you just finished reading.
- Reference a speaker you just heard who inspired you.
- Link to an interesting article in your area of study.
- Share an inspirational quote.

It's also important to go through your previous Facebook entries and get rid of any public posts that portray you in an unprofessional light. There are several helpful online resources that walk you through how to permanently delete photos or posts from Facebook.[6,7]

TWITTER

The same rules apply here as they do for Facebook. Twitter is a great way to follow and connect with like-minded individuals in your field from around the world. So, connect with these people and engage in professional conversations. Share interesting links and information through your Twitter feed that show your range of personal and professional interests. Retweet and favorite others' tweets frequently to build a connection to other Twitter users and to further highlight your areas of interest in your on feed.

PERSONAL WEBSITE

The central idea for creating and maintaining a personal website is simple: it makes you easily searchable online and provides people with your up-to-date contact information. Having your own website helps you control the content that comes up when someone performs a Google search for your name. If possible, try to get a domain that contains your full name, as that will make it even easier for people to find you.

Free online websites can be created using such platforms as WordPress, Tumblr, and Blogger. While some of these are marketed as blogging platforms, they offer most of the same capabilities needed for a straightforward informational website like the one that you want to create. You can compile a simple website in a single evening with the content that you've already assembled through the steps outlined in this chapter.

Basic items to include on your website:

- Your resume (make sure that it's downloadable as a PDF).
- Your elevator speech to introduce yourself (this could be used as a "Bio" or "About Me" page).
- Links to your LinkedIn, Facebook, and Twitter profiles, as well as any other social media accounts like Pinterest or Instagram.
- Testimonials (the letters of reference that individuals have agreed can be used on your site).
- A link to your personal blog, if you have one. You can also choose to embed a blog into your website to keep them linked together. However, having a separate personal blog will help bring more traffic to your website.
- Links to publications or other online guest blog posts or articles you've written.
- Keywords that recruiters would commonly use to search for people in your field.
- A photo gallery with pictures of yourself that lend authenticity to your brand. For example, post pictures of your work in the lab listed on your resume, or a selfie with someone well known in your field.
- Your current contact information. This generally means your email address, although you can post your phone number if you feel comfortable.

Your website does not need to be extensive. In fact, the simpler it is, the better. Make sure that it is easy for someone to navigate and that your contact information is readily accessible.

PERSONAL BLOG

There is no better way to establish yourself as a fresh and innovative voice on a particular subject than to launch your own personal blog. A personal blog differs from a website in that it is a log of your thoughts or ideas presented in different regular posts (daily, weekly, or monthly). Blogs tend to be more informal in style than online magazine or newspaper articles, and they give you an open platform to exhibit your knowledge and expertise in a unique and creative way. As your blog gains more followers, it can help you build your reputation as an authority in your field. You can build a blog free on platforms like WordPress or Tumblr, or you can create it through your website.

When it comes to branding through personal blogging, the standard rule of "write what you know" applies. To use it as a tool to a great career, your blog's focus should be on your area of study and expertise. Try to create a blog of informed opinion about something that is happening in the world at large as it relates to your field.

Potential approaches to your personal blog:

- Discuss the potential you see in new developments in your field.
- Report on new studies that have been published in peer-reviewed journals.
- Translate the life sciences concepts you're studying or researching into language the everyday reader can comprehend.
- Document your experience in the lab or at the worksite to give people a sense of your everyday process.
- Share your scientific perspective on relevant news topics like new climate change legislation, etc.

People are fascinated by science, but sometimes they become frustrated by the use of unfamiliar terms and jargon. By translating science to everyday language, you can perform a valuable service and grow your readership. Your blog also helps establish you as a serious professional, and someone who is interested, thoughtful, and engaged in their field. In other words, you become the kind of employee everyone wants to hire.

How to extend your reach:

- The secret to attracting readers is to ensure that every blog is helpful to readers. Give without expecting in return, and you will be amazed at the way readers respond.
- Read the blogs of others in your field and comment on their posts, referring them to a post you wrote about the same subject or a related topic (include the link).
- Offer to guest blog for other bloggers or websites in your area of expertise.
- If a colleague writes a great blog and you know your readers will be as impressed as you are, ask for permission to link to it on your site or to run it as a guest blog on your site.
- Post links to your blog articles on your social media accounts, especially LinkedIn and Twitter.

In the blogging world, the operative word is *share*. By giving of yourself and your knowledge, you will build yourself up as someone who people want to get to know better and potentially work with. As you get started on your blog, read a lot. Find other blogs in your field or on related topics of interest and identify what you like about them. Then work on emulating those things in your own blog.

Science Blogging

There is a special demand for the confirmed science blogger, and this is a field where you can establish yourself as an expert in your field. In certain cases, you may even be able to turn your science blog into a career stepping-stone as a full-fledged science writer. You can launch your science blog as a solo enterprise, or you can become a contributor to a group science blog. You might start by contributing to an informal wiki or discussion board in your field, and work your way up to a more established blog with a larger following. You can choose to blog regularly or just guest blog occasionally to start building up your reputation. For guidance on the world of science blogging, check out the Science of Blogging website.[8]

BRINGING ALL ASPECTS OF YOUR BRAND TOGETHER

Effective personal branding to secure the job of your dreams works best when you ensure that every piece of information in circulation about you reflects precisely the brand that you've identified for yourself. Make sure that this information contributes to your goal of becoming known as an authority or innovative thinker in your field.

Keep in mind that all of the aforementioned items work together to create your brand. That means that a breakdown in just one area could tarnish your entire reputation and be reflected in other areas. For example, a serious LinkedIn profile can be torpedoed by an endless array of Facebook or Twitter photos and postings that show inappropriate or immature behavior; a simple Google search along these lines will point you to several examples of how such behavior has turned out bad. In another scenario, your perfect resume will become less effective if you meet the company president at a networking event and have no elevator speech prepared to present yourself as someone who could fit into their company.

One word of advice as you become engaged in the branding process: *be realistic and honest about where you are in your career path*. If you're a life sciences undergraduate student, it makes more sense to portray yourself as being "interested in" a field as opposed to being "an expert" in the field. If you have more years under your belt in your chosen area of specialization, then you have a right to claim expertise. Just make sure that whatever claims you make can be justified if challenged.

A key component to the branding process is that you need to understand that it must be a continuous effort and that your brand may change slightly over time as you gain more experience and expertise. So, it is important to constantly be surveying your banding strategies and tweaking your statements.

WRAPPING UP YOUR BRANDING EFFORTS

There are many other social media platforms that I haven't touched on in detail here, such as Instagram and Pinterest. Consider exploring their potential to enhance your "me brand" even more. Instagram is a great platform for more visually oriented people and Pinterest can help showcase certain skills like science illustration or photography, scientific modeling or simulation, or lab work. If used right, all social media platforms can attract recruiters to your door.

As you complete each level of your personal branding efforts, begin a new social media campaign. Just be cautious about spreading yourself too thin. It's better to have a great blog and LinkedIn profile and nothing else than to be everywhere but have no substance on any single platform.

As I've shown in this chapter, building your personal brand is possible for any scholar at any stage in their career. The sooner you get started, the more impact you'll have in your field and the more control you'll have over your career advancement process. What are you waiting for?

Case Study

Zen Faulkes, PhD, is a full professor in the Department of Biology at The University of Texas Rio Grande Valley. Dr. Faulkes is an active scientist, blogger, and social media strategist. Here is his insight, in his own words, into personal branding.

I started developing my personal brand as a working scientist when I started blogging in 2003, although I didn't have the concept of "branding" in my head consciously at that time. I began blogging because author Neil Gaiman was doing it, so it must be cool. I loved how he "pulled back the curtain" on his writing process and career. I wanted to do something similar, but for science instead of fiction writing.

I wanted to declare publically, "I want to talk to you." To me, that was part of being a public intellectual. That phrase—"public intellectual"—can sound pretentious and stuffy, but I haven't found a better one that captures the sense of wanting to take academic research to the streets. My notions of what a professor could be were shaped by scientists like Stephen Jay Gould and David Suzuki: people who wrote stuff for the public, who were not afraid to put in the time to be seen by the public, and who people would specifically come out to see. My dad used to joke that he thought I should have David Suzuki's job.

My first lesson in building a brand was that it takes time and effort. It took years to build an audience for my first blog. At one point, I made a conscious decision to see if I could get noticed by blogging. I decided to get serious about blogging and see how far I could push it. I managed to write more posts per year than there were days of the year a few times.

As I continued blogging, new social media tools opened up. When I started, there was no Facebook. There was no Twitter. I decided to use Facebook more for personal stuff and used Twitter more for my professional stuff. I created accounts for these new sites as they sprung up. Some took off and were useful. Twitter became my most important professional resource by a wide margin. Others have folded or are things I visit rarely. But I decided to invest some time in each, because there was no way to tell in advance which would turn out to be important to me.

My second lesson in branding was that people care about a brand because of what it can do for them. My first blog was very inward looking for a long time and had few readers. That changed when a website was created that promoted blog posts about journal articles. My posts that were aggregated on that site got more traffic, so I started writing more of them. I started to think of the blog less of a personal journal and more of a resource for others.

My third lesson in branding was brands should be readily identifiable. One of the advantages I have in developing a personal brand online is that I have a weird name. There are not many people with either my given or family name, particularly in science. I had always joked with students that I went to graduate school

Case Study—cont'd

so that I could be called Doctor Zen, and sound like the villain from a bad kung fu movie. "Doctor Zen" was a short, memorable name for social media, which became my Twitter handle and home page name.

One of the smartest things I ever did was to expand my blogging by starting new, highly focused, "niche" blogs. People who wanted to use just that resource could go directly to those blogs and not have to search through all the other unrelated material. People like to know what they're getting.

All three of these lessons came together in what has, to date, been my most successful online project by far: a blog devoted to poster presentations. First, I had to invest time in building it. I started it by writing one post a week. It took months before it got its first recommendation (for which I will be forever grateful). Second, it was a resource to help other people. The blog was often critical, but I think people realized that the criticism was genuinely meant to improve the poster and wasn't coming from a place of meanness. Third, the blog had very clear marching orders: it was about how to make better posters to present at academic conferences. People could tell their friends or students, "If you're going to make a poster, go read this poster blog."

I've focused on the professional advantages of developing a personal brand, but it's also been personally rewarding. Thanks to social media, I've gotten to know a lot of people who do very cool research. Online conversations are real conversations, and the voice people use online is usually very close to the voice they have in person. It's fun to see people's quirks and hobbies outside of their professional work.

Everything has its price, and the most obvious cost for me may have been missed opportunities. Time spent blogging was time that could have been spent writing something that might have been more readily recognized as the stuff a working scientist is supposed to do: write an academic paper or a grant proposal.

But on balance, I am convinced I would have achieved much less professionally if I hadn't invested the effort in creating an online presence and personal brand. I can trace the origin of several papers back to connections I made on social media. I've been invited to give presentations. I've been quoted some of the best known scientific journals in the world, where my original research has never appeared. I've been interviewed on national media.

It's always an uphill road to those sorts of achievements in academia, but some of those roads are steeper than others. I didn't have some advantages that might have made those achievements easier. For instance, my university was not well known, due to its location and history. When I went to conferences, people would ask what university I worked at. After I would tell people, I got very used to the follow-up question being, "Where's that?" Similarly, my research is not on topics that regularly receive media coverage.

Once, I was asked to appear on a national radio show. I was acutely aware that my appearance on the show was only possible because of the years I spent "wasting time on the Internet." If it hadn't been for that, there is no way that I would have been asked to talk to these media outlets. Because news organizations don't think, "Let's call up researchers from a university that we haven't heard of and ask them what they think." Social media can act as a leveler and can give voice to people who might not normally have one.

Case Study

Jamie Vernon, PhD is the director of science communications and publications at Sigma Xi, The Scientific Research Society and editor-in-chief of American Scientist magazine. Since earning his doctorate in cell and molecular biology at The University of Texas at Austin, he has successfully transitioned from the research track to a professional career in science communication. His multistep career conversion includes a teaching position at American University, a Cancer Research Training Award (CRTA) postdoctoral appointment at the National Cancer Institute, an American Association for the Advancement of Science (AAAS) Science and Technology Policy Fellowship, and an Oak Ridge Institute for Science and Education (ORISE) Fellowship at the US Department of Energy. Here is his story, in his own words, about the personal branding effort that transformed him from a bench scientist into a leader in science policy and communication.

The voice on the other end of the phone said, "We've been looking for someone to speak on science communication, and we were given your name." I instantly realized that my hard work was paying off. I'd spent countless hours connecting on social media, networking at cocktail parties, and speaking at conferences to earn some much-needed recognition. I was far from a communications expert, but the arduous process of rebranding myself from researcher to communicator was well underway.

The phone call was a turning point in my pursuit of a career in science communication. Early in the process, I learned that the most critical aspect of building a personal brand was to establish a clear and obtainable goal. My task was to recast my expertise as a research scientist into an asset for communicating science. Fortunately, I had been unwittingly preparing for this career change my entire life.

Despite having a natural inclination toward art and literature at an early age, I developed an unshakeable affinity for science and decided to pursue a career in biology. I balanced my interests in high school by enrolling in art classes and joining science clubs. As an undergraduate student studying zoology, I used my elective credits to register for literature and writing courses. By the time I reached graduate school, I began to entertain the notion of doing something other than academic research with my PhD.

Even after publishing a few scientific papers and filing my first biotechnology patent, I decided to reconnect with my passion for writing. I had heard about the growing field of science communication and decided to pivot in that direction. I created a Twitter account, set up a website, and started a blog. I embraced a burgeoning interest in science policy and joined Scientists and Engineers for America, a Washington, DC-based organization focused on communicating science in the policy arena.

I sought out colleagues with similar interests and collaborated with them to gain a foothold in the world of science communication and policy. Where opportunities didn't exist, I created them. I started *Science in the Pub*, an outreach event that connected scientists with local residents. To raise awareness about the organization, I learned the basics of marketing and promotions. I designed event posters and sent press releases to local publications and news outlets. Eventually, I became known for my efforts to introduce science communication and policy to students and faculty on campus.

While continuing to navigate a traditional research career path, I established a personal brand as a communicator of science policy. I leveraged social media platforms to connect with emerging and established science communicators. I shared their work; they generously reciprocated.

Case Study—cont'd

At that time, converting "virtual" acquaintances into real–world interactions was a novelty. I attended local gatherings of Twitter users, called "tweetups," and science communication conferences, such as ScienceOnline, to meet others in the field. Many of them became close friends and collaborators. We often discussed science and promoted policy positions online. These relationships proved to be the most fruitful of all my efforts, leading to writing and speaking engagements.

As my network became more distinguished, I worked harder to professionalize both my work and my attitude. I voraciously consumed literature on science communication. I studied the intersection of science policy, communication, and journalism. I reached out to thought leaders and connected with influential communicators. Together we helped shape the future of science communication through conferences and publications. I took on projects of greater significance, including blogging about policy for Discover magazine, becoming an AAAS Science and Technology Policy Fellow, and working with a federal interagency group focused on climate communications at the US Global Change Research Program.

Throughout this period of professional growth, I wanted others to appreciate my commitment to the craft as well as my understanding of the underlying principles. I shared my thoughts and experiences through personal blog posts and on my social media accounts. I maintained an up-to-date LinkedIn profile to inform potential colleagues and employers about my interests and accomplishments. The cumulative effect was a personal brand that advanced my pursuit of a career in science policy and communication.

When I received the call from a major university inviting me to lead a workshop about science communication, I had already invested hundreds of hours to redefine myself. Despite managing a full-time research career along the way, I had successfully fashioned a parallel path toward science communication. Ultimately, my blogging efforts, use of social media, speaking engagements, and personal networking led me to Sigma Xi, where I continue to build a brand that I hope will lead to new and exciting opportunities in science policy and communication.

REFERENCES

1. *World employment and social outlook – trends.* International Labour Organization; 2015. http://www.ilo.org/wcmsp5/groups/public/---dgreports/---dcomm/---publ/documents/publication/wcms_337070.pdf.
2. Peters T. The brand called you. *Fast Company Magazine* August 31, 1997. http://www.fastcompany.com/28905/brand-called-you.
3. http://myidp.sciencecareers.org/.
4. Harrison C. Sample elevator speeches. *Expressions of Excellence.* http://www.expressionsofexcellence.com/sample_elevator.html.
5. Uyen. *Elevator pitches for scientists: what, when, where and how.* August 18, 2013. http://thepostdocway.com/content/elevator-pitches-scientists-what-when-where-and-how.
6. WikiHow. How to delete photos from facebook. http://www.wikihow.com/Delete-Photos-from-Facebook.

7. Golbeck J. I decided to delete all my facebook activity. *Slate* January 1, 2014. http://www.slate.com/articles/technology/future_tense/2014/01/facebook_cleansing_how_to_delete_all_of_your_account_activity.html.

8. http://scienceofblogging.com/.

TO LEARN MORE ABOUT PERSONAL BRANDING, HERE ARE FOUR ADDITIONAL RESOURCES TO BROADEN YOUR BRAND:

The Tipping Point: How Little Things Can Make a Big Difference by Malcolm Gladwell, Back Bay Books (January 7, 2002) http://www.amazon.com/The-Tipping-Point-Little-Difference/dp/0316346624.

This is a great read for anyone who wonders who they as one small individual can have an impact with their personal brand in this world. It is a classic book that gives real insight into how messages can be spread around the world effectively. In the book, Gladwell focuses on the tipping point, which is that moment of critical mass when a single action or reaction can change the course of your life.

Unconscious Branding: How Neuroscience Can Empower (and Inspire) Marketing by Douglas Van Praet, Palgrave Macmillan, November 13, 2012. http://www.amazon.com/Unconscious-Branding-Neuroscience-Empower-Marketing/dp/0230341799.

Your personal brand may be all about you, but if you want to know how it could impact other people, this is the book. It goes beyond the why of behavior change and asks how. Van Praet's approach is to apply science and divide the brain into seven codified actionable steps to behavior change when he considers how to brand things. It offers a unique perspective on branding.

The New Rules of Marketing and PR by David Meerman Scott, Your Coach-In-A-Box; Una Upd Re edition (July 1, 2009) http://www.amazon.com/The-New-Rules-Marketing-Podcasting/dp/1596592907.

What's great about this book is that it challenges all your assumptions. Meerman Scott, who also wrote Marketing the Moon and Marketing Lessons from the Grateful Dead, is a wake-up call to anyone who thinks marketing and personal branding are just a question of following the procedure. It reminds us that people want to hire and do business with other people, not procedures, and encourages us to focus on connecting and interacting with people for true success.

Branding Basics for Small Business, 2nd Edition: How to Create an Irresistible Brand on Any Budget by Maria Ross, NorLightsPress.com; 2nd edition (April 1, 2014) http://www.amazon.com/Branding-Basics-Small-Business-Edition/dp/1935254871.

If you envision setting up your own business or working as an independent consultant, this book is essential. Ross teaches you how to develop your core promise, your personality, and your reason for being and how to combine all three to create large numbers of loyal followers.

Chapter 12

Building Your Professional Network

Natalie Lundsteen

Chapter Outline

Networking 140
Don't Assume Networking Is
Only for Scientists Seeking a
Career Beyond the Bench 141
Every Minute Spent Building Your
Network Is Time Well Spent 141
How Do You Network Effectively? 141
Informational Interviewing 144
How Do You Find People for
Informational Interviews? 144
Conducting a Successful
Informational Interview 145
Above All, DO NOT ASK FOR
A JOB 146
Maintaining Your Network 147
Building Your Network: Putting
It All Together 148
An Unexpected Connection,
Thank You Twitter! 148
Sample Informational
Interview Email Request 149
Reference 153
Networking Resources 153

Chapter Takeaways:

- Building a professional network is necessary throughout your career, not just when you are starting to explore possible career paths
- Effective networking is about finding and sharing information
- Opportunities come from people—in all industries and occupations
- Even introverts can network!
- Informational interviews are the best way to learn about careers (and possibly find a job as a bonus)
- Maintaining your relationships is an important part of networking

Establishing connections and communicating effectively is critical for success in all careers—both inside and outside of academia. This does not always come naturally for many scientists, so it's important to *learn, develop, and practice* your

ReSearch. http://dx.doi.org/10.1016/B978-0-12-804297-7.00012-4

communication and interaction skills so that you can improve your ability to make connections with other professionals.

In this chapter, you will find information regarding the following:

- Networking: Learn how to understand and practice relationship building with colleagues and others for the purposes of research and career development in multiple career fields.
- Informational interviewing: These interviews are a gateway tool to building connections. Defined broadly as "informal meetings with professionals," the goal of an informational interview is to understand aspects of different career paths and environments.

NETWORKING

Networking is a way to advance your career, by making contacts with current and future colleagues. It's also an activity that allows you to learn things about careers you may not learn any other way. If you don't like the word "networking," (we know many people cringe at the word), then instead we encourage you to think of networking as *a career research activity in which people are your primary source*.

The formal (Merriam-Webster dictionary) definition of *networking* describes "the exchange of information or services among individuals, groups, or institutions; *specifically*: the cultivation of productive relationships for employment or business."

Building productive relationships is critical for **all scientists**, no matter your career goals. Networking is an excellent way to find potential postdoc mentors, disseminate your research findings, meet people related to your career field of interest, search for potential job openings, and meet new colleagues.

However, let's go back to those of you who cringed at the first mention of the term "networking" and helped you start reframing your view of this important career activity. Have you ever asked someone in another lab for a reagent or helped another scientist find a solution to a problem? Have you given a fellow scientist advice on a topic you are very familiar with? Then you have already engaged in networking. The act of networking doesn't have to be a formal request and often happens naturally in work groups. Networking is simply sharing information or resources that you have or knowing who might have the information or resources you don't. You might need to think of networking as expanding your work group, rather than building something new! Think about other ways you have networked in life—maybe with your acquaintances, such as looking for an apartment to sublet or getting advice on great restaurants in a new city.

Asking questions of individuals you know to learn more about a topic is rarely seen as intrusive or self-serving. So try thinking about career networking in the same way. Are your friends irritated when you confess you don't know anything about scuba diving in Belize, but you know they have taken a few trips there and you'd love their advice? Probably not. Most likely, they are thrilled to be asked to talk about something they enjoy. You often have limited information on a topic, and there are people you know who are happy to share their knowledge. When you are job searching, you may have very limited information about career paths, companies, or specific job responsibilities. Therefore, in career-related networking you can ask experts in the industry or career you are interested in to share some of their knowledge. When you are career networking, you may be in more of the "asker" role to obtain knowledge and advice related to your career goals. But the people who are offering you advice and information are usually very pleased to be asked (just like your friends who told you about the great restaurants they found on vacation).

DON'T ASSUME NETWORKING IS ONLY FOR SCIENTISTS SEEKING A CAREER BEYOND THE BENCH

Did you know that to secure tenure at many universities, tenure committees ask for a list of references, who then are asked for additional references to vouch for your abilities as an impactful researcher? A primary goal of networking is to get to know people, but it also is important to make yourself known. Networking can be done in person (for example, during a coffee meet up or at conferences) or virtually (through social media or email). But no matter the avenue, scientists must continuously network throughout their careers. Getting comfortable with networking early in your career is essential. Fundamentally, networking is important to ensure that we are propelling science forward through the sharing of our ideas and collaboration with others.

EVERY MINUTE SPENT BUILDING YOUR NETWORK IS TIME WELL SPENT

No matter where your science career takes you, whether it is into industry, advocacy, or academia, you will appreciate knowing people both in your specialized field and outside of it. Your career probably will not take a linear path, so you might end up moving from one sector to another or making a geographic change. Having a wide circle of contacts is beneficial both in an immediate sense and in the "long run." Every conversation you have or connection you make is valuable, particularly when you are starting your career and gathering knowledge and information about potential career paths. Connections you make when you are exploring different career options will remain valuable resources should you ever want to change your career direction or even call on an expert in another field someday.

HOW DO YOU NETWORK EFFECTIVELY?

An effective instance of networking can be as simple as a conversation with a colleague in another lab or you might have to breach your comfort zone to make yourself stand out by interacting with someone barely known to you. Reaching out to others from diverse career backgrounds can be beneficial both when seeking new information, as well as when transitioning to different jobs. Below are some tips and resources to help you become a more effective networker:

Break away from your circle of friends/colleagues

- Make a concerted effort to converse with strangers. You can practice this in "low-threat" settings outside of science, such as when you are in line at the supermarket, or, when attending a seminar, simply saying hello and introducing yourself to the person seated next to you. Breaking away from familiar colleagues is especially important at scientific conferences or meetings. For current students or postdocs, striking up a conversation with a fellow trainee at any event is a fairly low-risk networking move that will give you practice!
- Rehearse a few conversation starters. For example, ask "what are you researching?" If you're meeting someone specific, perhaps a prestigious researcher in your field, familiarize yourself with his/her research and open with "I was reading your most recent publication, and I am very interested in…" This is flattering for the person you are meeting, and it illustrates your interest and breadth of knowledge.
- Want to open conversation with someone outside of research? Do background research on that person or their company using LinkedIn or doing a Web search on the individual. Compose a list of questions you would ask that person. Connect with this person via email or LinkedIn, and ask your questions or suggest a meeting. What's the worst that can happen? They either don't respond or they don't want to meet. People are busy, and while many would love to help you, they might just not have the time—so don't take it personally. Read on for how to take this leap.

Put yourself out there

- Attending meetings and conferences are arguably the best modes to enhance your network. The most beneficial approach to "force" yourself to network at meetings/conferences is to *attend the conference by yourself or only with your mentor.* If other lab members attend the same conference, they can become a crutch that may hinder your opportunities to meet others because you will tend to engage mostly with them. If you do attend a conference with a large group of people you know, use the comfort and safety of having a familiar group present to give you courage to break away at a session or event to meet others, if only for a short time. Attending with your mentor can be beneficial because he/she can introduce you to his/her colleagues to help expand your network.
- Use social media, such as LinkedIn, to contact people whose careers you are interested in exploring. (Chapter 11 has more information on using social media in your career search.)
- Join campus organizations to promote yourself, meet others, and get first dibs on speaker lunches and opportunities for one-on-one interaction with outside visitors. Leadership roles in organizations lead to even more opportunity for meeting campus visitors.

- Attend seminars (scientific or career related), lunches, and other events that expose you to other professionals. Toastmasters International, a national nonprofit organization with chapters in nearly every city, is another great way to meet others and improve your communication skills. In Toastmasters, local clubs of professional people meet regularly to practice their public speaking and develop leadership skills. Attending a Toastmasters meeting just once might be the jump start you need to understand the importance of networking and to see how friendly and supportive strangers can be. Toastmasters meetings are usually held over lunchtime so you can make time to get away from the lab.
- If you find yourself continuously stuck in the lab, then make use of social media to reach out to others. But there really is no substitute for face-to-face interactions to build your network.

Practice makes perfect

- Seminars and workshops on networking are fine to learn what networking is, and to start getting comfortable with the idea of connecting, BUT lectures, articles, and websites won't help you build your own network. You absolutely must get out there and take action! Some examples of this kind of action include public speaking or playing a sport—theory is fine, but **practice is essential.**
- Gain networking practice simply by immersing yourself in events that foster making connections with others. A few simple actions you can take: speak up in lab meeting or ask questions at work-in-progress seminars. Think of yourself as taking "baby steps" if you are truly paralyzed by the idea of talking to someone you don't know. Don't start with huge networking events if you are not yet a skilled networker. Try and find venues or environments that are less intimidating—a panel discussion or a dinner. Or, if you have no choice but to attend a large event, go early when the crowd is smaller and people are waiting for their friends to arrive (and if it's an event with alcohol, perhaps attendees are less tipsy). You can also attend networking events with a buddy so you have an "anchor" to return to in the room if you need to.
- Another good practice is to **perfect your** "elevator speech" when you get the question: "what do you do?" Every scientist must be able to adjust that answer to the person asking. Is it another scientist, a researcher from a different discipline, a friend from college who works in accounting, or a family member? The way you respond will differ depending on your audience, but no matter who or where, you will want to sound articulate and confident. Preparing a few sentences now will help you when you need those sentences most!
- One of the best resources we have found for learning more about networking basics is Alaina Levine's book *Networking for Nerds*. Read it if you really don't like networking (or read it if you do, and want some new ideas). As a physicist, Alaina is familiar with how many scientists think and act. She has experienced the types of typical networking situations where scientists may find themselves, such as scientific conferences, and she definitely understands the types of people who might find the concept of networking difficult to imagine or undertake. Her advice is encouraging, and the book is an engaging read.

INFORMATIONAL INTERVIEWING

Informational interviews (or informational "chats," as they are referred to in the United Kingdom) are *informal* conversations that are useful for obtaining information about a particular career. **They are not job interviews**. Informational interviews are arranged by you, with someone you would like to learn more about, and are an excellent source for learning about the duties of certain professionals, future job prospects, what skills are required for the job, what a work environment is like, and whether a specific career fits your values.

Setting up and undertaking informational interviews will help expand your network and open more doors for you, as well as give you some conversation practice in a professional setting outside of the lab. It is not uncommon for scientists to be invited for job interviews stemming from an informational interview connection, whether it is at the same company as the person you met with or through a connection from that interviewee.

HOW DO YOU FIND PEOPLE FOR INFORMATIONAL INTERVIEWS?

There are many places to find individuals for an informational interview, but first you need to think about what your overall goal is. Is the goal to learn more about a particular industry, for example, research and development in a pharmaceutical company? Would you like to make connections within a specific organization? Or is the goal perhaps to build your network in a new city as a young professional? Once you have chosen what the goal is, then you can search the following for potential candidates who you feel could shed a light on the particular topic you are working to investigate or goal you are trying to achieve. Here are some ideas on where you can find individuals to talk to:

- Laboratory and university alumni: Alumni might not be on the top of your list but they should be! You are already connected to these individuals simply by sharing in an experience (the place you studied or trained), and you might find that there are literally thousands of interesting people to talk to. Reach out to both alumni who you know **and** those who you do not, who might be engaged in an area of interest to you. Be sure to investigate alumni databases from all universities that you have attended or programs that you have been a part of. Postdocs—remember that you should be considered an alumnus/alumna of any institution where you trained.
- LinkedIn: One way to find alumni is through LinkedIn. Search for institutions you have attended to see demographic information on all alumni with LinkedIn profiles. LinkedIn can also be used to find individuals in a field of interest through groups and posts.
- Professional societies and organizations: Most of these organizations have a public list of members, but further, they also have committees that are focused on career and professional development. Be sure to know the resources offered by your scientific (and other) societies and take advantage of them.

- Friends and family: Finally, do not underestimate the value of the relationships you have with your friends and family. Often, you can be surprised by the "I know someone who knows someone" routine.

Once you have identified someone about whom you would like to learn more, there is an "art" to asking people to meet with you for an informational chat. Successful informational interviewing is all about diplomacy and not being pushy. Be polite, respectful, and concise in how you communicate. A personal email, rather than a LinkedIn message, is ideal, because many busy people don't regularly check LinkedIn messages. However, it is not always possible to find a direct email address (although there are tricks to this such as phoning the main reception of an organization to ask for email addresses or deducing the email "protocol" of an organization using Internet research skills). If you are not able to find a personal email address, you can include an abbreviated version of an informational interview request in a LinkedIn message.

When you do email a request to meet, make sure your request states that you would like either a brief phone call or brief in-person meeting and that you want advice or to learn more about a particular topic. A great email subject heading for an informational interview request might be something like: "Boston U alumna seeking advice on careers at Sanofi." (Quick Latin lesson: "alumni" refers to a group, alumnus is a singular male graduate, and alumna is a singular female graduate.)

Be clear in your message that you can be flexible in the timing and location of that meeting; make it very easy for the person you are contacting to say "yes, sure, I can spare 15 min, especially if I don't have to leave my office." Do not suggest specific timings or dates, other than to say you are available for most of the month of August or something similarly agreeable-sounding. Let the person whose advice you are requesting set the time and place that is easiest. Although you can make suggestions—meeting for coffee is always an acceptable suggestion for an informational chat venue. Furthermore, if you find someone on Twitter you are interested in meeting, it is good to try to share a meaningful conversation with him or her via message before requesting to speak. A sample informational interview request email can be found at the end of this chapter.

After you have made contact and agreed to a mutually convenient meeting time and place, prepare for the informational interview by learning as much as possible about the person you will be meeting, and get ready to ask questions about their background, current work, and perhaps even future plans.

CONDUCTING A SUCCESSFUL INFORMATIONAL INTERVIEW

Research the person you will be interviewing

- You should know their title and the company or organization at which they work. You will learn about their background education and other aspects of their career preparation during the interview.

Act polite and professional

- This person is doing you a favor, so be gracious and kind. Be as flexible as you can in your availability to meet. Buy the person a coffee (or at least offer to do so). Dress in a professional manner. Business casual should suffice. Shorts, flip-flops, or pajama pants are not ok—especially if you have the opportunity to visit your interviewee's workplace.

Prepare a list of questions for the interviewee

- Don't ask any question to which you can find the answer yourself. Be sure to look at the LinkedIn profile of the person you are meeting, or find any other publicly available information about the person. If you would like, you can share the list of questions you have prepared ahead of your meeting with the person you are meeting—but generally it is best to have an informal free-flowing conversation in an informational interview.

Consider asking/discussing the following:

- What does a typical day look like for you?
- What skills are required for your position, and what skills are preferred?
- What is your background education, and how did this influence your ability to land your job?
- How do you describe the environment of your workplace?
- Is there room for promotion at your company/in your position?
- How can I make myself a competitive candidate for a position like yours?
- Do you like this work, this company, and/or this field?

Respect their time

- Be very respectful of the time of the person you are meeting with. Ask for 15–20 min, and make sure you give the person an opportunity to end the meeting at the agreed-on time. If your interviewee wants to continue speaking, graciously take the opportunity. Another thing to be aware of is keeping the tone of the informational interview pleasant. Do not hammer your interviewee with a barrage of questions—let him or her lead the discussion.

ABOVE ALL, DO NOT ASK FOR A JOB

If you are actively job searching at the time you are informational interviewing, you can mention that but do not elaborate. It makes people feel very pressured and also manipulated if they feel your primary motivation for meeting them is merely a "means to an end" and is not the request you made to get to know that individual. Consider how it would feel if an undergraduate student contacted you and asked to speak about your experiences obtaining a science PhD at your university. You would probably be flattered and willing to give advice. But if that student started asking you questions about application statistics, admissions requirements, and tips for getting admitted, you would most likely be very annoyed and would not want to continue the conversation. The same holds true for job seekers having a talk with someone currently working in a company of interest. Be cool—you may even learn in the informational interview that it's not even a great place to work! Or, you might learn about an opening that has not yet been advertised that might well be a perfect fit for you.

However, if you do have an interest in the organization your informational interviewee works for, you could submit an online application and get your details into the HR system (this generally only works for very large companies). You can do this before the informational meeting, or after—it really depends on the situation. Always have your CV and/or resume completed and ready to go when you informational interview, in case your interviewee asks you to send it after your meeting (and do send your documents electronically as well as give a hard copy—that way he or she can easily forward your materials).

For those of you who are truly overwhelmed at the idea of meeting with a stranger, the best way to increase your comfort level is to start by conducting informational chats with individuals closer to home. Practice informational interviewing with a friend, or with a collaborator or faculty member who is not a direct supervisor. Sometimes having a direct introduction can make it easier to start informational interviewing. It is definitely hard to reach out to people you don't know, but look at it this way: someone who doesn't want to talk to you will probably just delete your email request and you don't have to worry about them anymore. Most professionals **will** take the time to be generous and respond to you. Adam Grant, author of *Give and Take*,[1] has researched interactions and human nature in his book, an excellent resource for learning about your own interactive style. *Give and Take* is also a great "primer" for understanding how and why people might or might not offer to help you. If you are an introvert, this will give you courage. If you are an extrovert, it's good to be reminded that not everyone loves personal interactions.

After an informational meeting, show your gratitude. Say thanks, but then compose an email, or better yet, a handwritten note thanking your interviewee again for his/her time. It is also a good time to connect with your interviewee after an informational meeting if you have not done so already. Use LinkedIn, Twitter, or other professional social media sites to stay connected. Feel free to provide your social media information (as well as email if the person doesn't already have it) in your thank you note.

MAINTAINING YOUR NETWORK

One of the greatest things about informational interviewing can be finding a job lead. But there are other benefits to building your network! What many people neglect to realize is that all the efforts made in talking to people about what they do and how they ended up in their current post will lead to connections you can take with you throughout your career. You may eventually start working in a totally different field from some of the individuals with whom you had informational chats at the start of your career exploration. That's great—you now have contacts and expertise in areas outside of your own, should you ever need advice or help on a topic. Or, you may end up with a job in the very same field as some of your contacts and already have a group of people to support you as you start your career in their company or industry.

If nothing else, make sure to keep your network updated when you get a new job or change roles. Sites such as LinkedIn are the easiest way to do this, but if someone was particularly helpful to you during your informational interviews, don't forget to let them know that, and send an email to say "I have a great job now and I couldn't have gotten this far without your advice and expertise." You may even end up being in a position to help that person somewhere down the line. Networking never stops, it is a constant ebb and flow of connections!

Informational interviewing is the single most helpful tool for researching careers and making connections that can lead to jobs. Opportunities come from people, and the knowledge you will gain from talking to people will lead you to opportunities, some of which you might never have known about otherwise. It may seem scary to reach out to strangers for advice (in fact, it may also feel awkward to ask people you know!), but push yourself out of your comfort zone for this. The positive results from making connections in informational interviews will lead to incredible career knowledge and professional relationships.

BUILDING YOUR NETWORK: PUTTING IT ALL TOGETHER

Advice encouraging network-building is everywhere, not just in this chapter, and there's good reason for it. Without a network of people to support you, your career won't move quickly (or may not move at all). People allow opportunities to occur. Every job needs a person to make a decision about who gets that job. Every interview happens between people (one of whom gets to choose who gets the job!). Almost every career involves interactions with people. So get started as early as possible on building your network and never stop building!

An Unexpected Connection, Thank You Twitter!

Teresa Evans, PhD

I have spent a large portion of my career sharing with fellow scientists the importance of communicating science and self-branding via social media. I began using Twitter regularly in my last year of graduate school. Over the last 2 years I have built my Twitter following to over 200 people and am constantly working to master the art of communication in this form. I do, however, have one outstanding success story. Following the exchange of five or so Tweets regarding an article on an NIH policy, I asked the person I was Tweeting with if they would be willing to continue our conversation off-line, via phone, as it seemed that we had a lot in common. The individual gladly agreed and following a

15-min phone call we had established the collaboration that is now in part this book. I met Dr. Nathan Vanderford, coauthor on this book, on Twitter and for that I must say, "Thank you Twitter!"

Sample Informational Interview Email Request

Dear Dr. Smith,

I am a 2014 University of Pittsburgh graduate and a current graduate student at the University of Michigan. I will soon be finishing my PhD in Cancer Biology, and I'm interested in pursuing a career in medical affairs.

I found you on LinkedIn as a U of Pittsburgh alum working at Pharmaco, and I asked Dr. Susan Taylor (U of Pittsburgh's Dean of Alumni Affairs) to get your email address from the alumni database. I'm contacting you because I am interested in learning more about your career path in medical/regulatory affairs and global health outcomes at Pharmaco. If you have some time in the next month, I would love the opportunity to talk with you. Perhaps we can set up a time for a phone call. My schedule is flexible and I promise not to take up more than 15 min of your time.

I'm looking forward to hearing back from you. Thank you so much for your time and help!

Sincerely,

Your Name

University of Michigan

PhD Candidate

Laboratory of Your PI

Case Study

Confessions of a science networking convert

By Róisín McMahon, PhD

Róisín McMahon is an early career researcher, biochemist, and protein enthusiast. She is currently a senior research officer at The University of Queensland, Brisbane, Australia. Her research interests are characterizing and targeting bacterial proteins to develop new antimicrobial drugs. She has a PhD in structural biology from the University of Oxford.

"Oh, I hate networking. I can't do it. It's awful." This was once the narrative of my inner monologue whenever the dreaded word "networking" arose. This dogmatic voice was usually also accompanied by an assumption that networking was something that, frankly, just didn't apply to me. I am an academic research scientist, not an investment banker. Networking was not for me, I misguidedly thought. It is for people in business attire who work in the private sector.

Now I am delighted to say that I network. I am good at it. I even enjoy it! And it has not only proved highly appropriate in my research career but also of great benefit. My Damascene conversion was at a conference when I came to recognize that despite my fervent aversion to the practice of networking, I was in fact already doing it.

Continued

Case Study—cont'd

Are you, too, a networker in denial? Try substituting the term "networking" for "collaborating," "socializing at a conference," "talking to new people," or "asking a peer about their research interests" and you, too, may be forced to admit that you are already networking as well. If you aren't doing it, perhaps it suddenly doesn't sound so heinous? Networking isn't about gauchely thrusting your business card on an internationally renowned professor at a conference dinner, breaking into exclusive cliques, brash self-promotion, or whatever else encompasses your specific imagined nightmare networking scenario. Practically, it is about talking to people. Crucially, it is about asking questions and truly listening to the answers. This light bulb moment revolutionized my relationship with networking. Maybe "I don't know how to network," but I definitely know how to talk to people. So now I talk to people, and in doing so have become a card-carrying (literally—see below) network convert. Here are the five insights that have accompanied and enabled my new life as a networker.

Networking at Work

Networking doesn't just happen "somewhere else." You don't have to go to a conference or a formal event. Let it happen on your doorstep. I work in a research institute that employs several hundred people. By serving (networking) on internal committees I have met and worked alongside peers and senior staff with whom I doubt I would have otherwise spoken. Interacting (networking) in this way helps to build a local profile and may be of great direct benefit when you need an external referee or are going for promotion. Personally, the most significant outcome of undertaking service roles at work has been building connections (networks) with my fellow early career researchers. The resulting friendships (networks) and contacts (networks) that I have forged with peers in this way have been invaluable professionally and personally as I navigate the various trials and joys of academia.

Indirect Benefits

The impact of networking may not be immediately evident and may be impossible to trace back to a specific event. Similarly, one cannot predict what, if anything will come of any given networking effort. Accept this, be honest and professional in all of your interactions, and remain open to new opportunities wherever they may present themselves.

The Power of Pact-Making

A number of years ago I struck a deal with myself: if a professional networking opportunity arose and I heard my inner voice chirp "I can't do that…," then I *had* to do it. That was the very simple rule. Whether it was a one-on-one meeting with an invited professor, introducing myself to a speaker at a conference, or self-nominating for a seminar, if I as much as entertained a thought that I couldn't do it, I immediately said "yes." Inevitably, I could always execute the task at hand, and I learned quickly that the worst that could happen was a socially awkward 20-min conversation (which has not yet proved life-threatening).

Scientists Are People Too

On more than one occasion I have watched helplessly as a single-minded networker has doggedly interrogated a visiting professor at lunch, lambasting them

Case Study—cont'd

with their entire academic CV, and asking for a job before the arrival of coffee. When networking, be mindful of your audience and afford them normal social courtesy. Effective networking is a two-way conversation rather than a self-serving transaction. Play nice.

Business Cards Are Old-Fashioned but Effective

In the modern digital era, handing someone a printed card with your contact details feels anachronistic and quaint, but it is still the least obtrusive way to provide this information to a new person, particularly if multiple people are vying for their attention. Add your Twitter handle to the card to contemporize the experience to some extent.

I like networking. I can do it. It's actually alright. I have rerecorded my inner voice, and when it threatens to revolt, I remind it of all the positive experiences and professional benefits that networking has yielded: the new collaboration that resulted directly from dinner with a visiting seminar speaker; the real-life introductions and conversations at conferences that started on Twitter; the opportunity to talk with senior staff across the university because of internal service roles, as well as less directly tangible benefits such as seminar invitations or during grant reviews. Networking is for you. So print yourself a set of business cards, power up your Twitter handle, get out there, and start talking.

Case Study

The Power of Networking: This Book

  By Alaina G. Levine

  President, Quantum Success Solutions

  Author, *Networking for Nerds: Find, Access and Land Hidden Game-Changing Career Opportunities Everywhere*

  I was delighted and honored when the authors asked me to contribute to their book. I knew immediately that I would focus my essay on networking, a subject about which I am very passionate. I am a huge fan of networking, in part because I have seen it work wonders on my own career and take me to places, people, projects, and positions I never imagined or even knew existed. In many cases, networking has even enabled me to create my own career opportunities! In fact, my first book, which was published in 2015, is entitled "Networking for Nerds: Find, Access and Land Hidden Game-Changing Career Opportunities Everywhere" and is a direct result of networking—I met and developed a partnership with a colleague at Wiley Publishing who ended up securing my contract.

  But what exactly is "networking"? The concept of networking is often misunderstood as a dirty deed, erroneously referred to as "schmoozing," in which one aspires to "get" something from the other party. Nothing could be further from the truth. In fact, networking is the most honorable endeavor you can pursue because it is all about how you can help the other party. The definition of networking, very simply, is a spectrum of activities that aims for a *win–win alliance* where both parties provide each other value in different forms and fashion over time and ends

Continued

Case Study—cont'd

only when one or both of you drop dead. Networking is only and entirely about adding value, providing new solutions, and helping the other person prosper. But the true beauty of networking is that the more you aim to give, the more you gain from the relationship.

You should know that networking is one of the most important tools you possess in your job search and career development toolbox. It provides you with new sources of inspiration, ideas, and innovation, and thus it is a requirement for any profession. But for industries and fields that rely heavily on collaboration, such as science and engineering research and development, networking's value is especially clear. How can you expect to advance your scholarship if you don't have a constant influx of new colleagues who can provide insight to enable you to solve problems in novel ways? The answer of course is that you can't. You have to network to move your field forward.

Networking is also a necessity for professional advancement. Part of the reason behind this is because networking is the only way to gain access to hidden opportunities. I estimate that about 90% of jobs are hidden, meaning they are not advertised, or if they are, they are offered up first "under the table" to people who are already known by the individual decision makers and their counterparts. Hiring someone is always a gamble, so if I already know you because we have been networking and I have gotten a sense of your skills, attitude, abilities, and experience, I am always going to pursue you first. I am going to tell you about unadvertised positions, or I might even magically fashion a job or other career-related opportunity out of thin air because I can see how you would add value to my team, and I want to grab you before the competition does.

If I examine my life, I can easily see a pattern in which I looked for and seized as many opportunities as I could, pursuing opportunity after opportunity, each of which led to the next. And the thread that weaves all of these together has been networking. Networking helped me build and expand my company, Quantum Success Solutions, and it facilitated my bliss and success. I am where I am today because of win–win alliances I have crafted with multiple leaders throughout my existence.

One of those leaders is one of the authors of this book, Natalie Lundsteen. I first made the acquaintance of Natalie in 2013. I was writing an article for *Science Magazine* about how postdocs can market their value. I had announced my need for sources for this piece via a website called Help a Reporter Out (HARO) and Natalie responded to my HARO request. At the time, she was working for MIT. We had a great interview and she gave me some terrific quotes. But beyond that, something clicked. I could tell she was passionate, talented, and energetic. She had extensive expertise in career development, particularly for PhD students and postdocs, and was a consummate professional. It was clear that our interests and personalities aligned and we began emailing each other every now and then to discuss ideas for collaboration.

Since then Natalie has helped me in myriad ways. She introduced me to associates, which have led to fascinating conversations and fruitful partnerships. She has promoted my book, even writing about it for *Inside HigherEd* and purchasing

---

Case Study—cont'd
_____

multiple copies to give out when she speaks. As I write this, I am on my way to give a keynote at the inaugural career conference at the University of Texas at Arlington, a gig I got because Natalie on her own referred me to the meeting organizers.

With all of these activities that Natalie engaged in, she did so to assist me, as she could. She wasn't in it to "get" something out of it. She is a natural connector—she takes pleasure in bringing people together and offering new avenues for growth. But behold the magnificence of networking! Because Natalie has done what she can to assist me, I am eager to assist her. I want to enable her triumph just as much as she wants to enable mine. So together, we have built a true mutually beneficial partnership, and I can't wait to see where it goes next.

REFERENCE

1. Grant A. *Give and take: why helping others drives our success*. Penguin Books; 2013.

NETWORKING RESOURCES

1. Elevator pitches for scientists: what, when, where and how. www.thepostdocway.com.
2. Networking tips for scientists – the psychology behind connecting. www.thecheekyscientist. com.
3. Minshew, K. 2016. The 15-minute method to writing an unforgettable elevator speech. www. themuse.com.
4. Levine A. *Networking for nerds*. Wiley; 2015.
5. Toastmasters International. www.toastmasters.org.
6. Van Noorden R. Online collaboration: Scientists and the social network. *Nature* 15 August, 2014;**512**:7513.

Networking for Introverts Resources

1. Susan Cain's 'Quiet Revolution' website—a great resource for introverts. Includes multiple articles and resources for those who get their energy from solitude and find interacting with others exhausting.
2. TED talk video: interview with award winning author of *Quiet: The Power of Introverts in a World That Can't Stop Talking*, Susan Cain. Tips start at about 8 min 30 s.
3. Zack D. *Networking for people who hate networking*. 2010 (Interactive book).

Informational Interviewing Resources

1. Gould J. From start to finish: a guide to informational interviewing. 2015. naturejobs.com.
2. Herman L. 9 Questions you have about coffee meetings but were too afraid to ask. 2016. muse. com – how to arrange a meeting with a professional you've never met.
3. Informational Interviews, NIH OITE. Extensive list of questions to ask. https://www.training. nih.gov/assets/Informational_Interviews.pdf.

Chapter 13

Create Balance in Your Life and Career

Teresa M. Evans

Chapter Outline

Knowing Your "End"	156	Learn to Speed Read and Write	160
What's Your One Thing?	157	References	163
Get a Dog	158		

Chapter Takeaways:

- Start at the End: Think about where you want to go in life to plan the steps you need to get there.
- Keep your focus by always being mindful of what your one true mission is.
- There are many ways to set goals, but be mindful of what yours are and have a plan to achieve them.
- Find a way to gauge and monitor your time management skills, whether that be getting a pet or finding a friend or family member to keep you accountable.
- Do not be a workaholic but rather a high performer.
- Hone the skills you use most, such as reading and writing, to free up time for other things.
- Embrace modern technology to manage your time and life.

Time stays long enough for those who use it.—Leonardo Da Vinci

Managing your time really means managing your life. Before you can plan a journey it is first most important to know what your destination is. Ernest Hemingway is credited with saying, "It's good to have an end to journey toward; but it is the journey that matters, in the end." We (the authors) are aware that those who are most likely to read this book are those who are unsure about their career destination. We want to remind you that your destination is only the "end" and that what really matters is crafting the journey. Planning your journey can take on many different meanings and forms. In this chapter, we will focus on tools, tips, and tricks to ensure that you are making the most out of your time and getting the most out of your journey.

ReSearch. http://dx.doi.org/10.1016/B978-0-12-804297-7.00013-6

KNOWING YOUR "END"

This book focuses on one end or destination, a career choice, or job placement. However, Hemingway speaks of another end all together, your final "life" destination. Yes that's right; to plan your days you must think about when those days end. *Living Forward*, a book by Michael Hyatt and Daniel Harkavy, is devoted to helping individuals plan not just their careers, but also their lives.[1] When I set out to write this chapter I did not outline a chapter that would begin with life planning, but it became clear to me after reading *Living Forward* that I must include this invaluable trick. This book was different from the pile of others that I purchased off the Amazon top 10 charts on Time Management. After spending hours learning how to manage my days, it was refreshing to think about how to manage the big picture. Personal experience has taught me that a well-managed life can result in much more efficiently managed daily tasks.

Creating a life plan is like creating a business plan. It is a living document that will include many pieces. Fundamentally, this document will answer the following questions: (1) How do you want to be remembered? (2) What matters most to you?, and (3) How to get from here to where you want to go? Now you might be thinking, "I already have a good work–life balance." Well, I'm here to tell you that this is not an effort in pursuit of work–life balance but a means to effectively lead yourself to the life that you want. Creating a life plan will guide you to make choices, as multiple opportunities are set before you. If you know your end goal, your life plan, you can choose the opportunities that best align.

Here's how to get started:

1. **Know your current location.** It is important to know where we are in relation to where we wish to be. This means being honest with yourself and accepting your current reality in every area of your being. To do this, the authors of *Living Forward* suggest you ask this question of yourself, "How would I like to be remembered?" (See activity below)
2. **Figure out where you want to go.** Be empowered to visualize what your ideal future looks like. Think about what kind of health you want to be in? What kind of marriage you want to be a part of? What do you want to put time into each day?
3. **Start moving toward your "end" destination.** Once you have a plan and know where you want to go every day begin to take action. Your plan then becomes a platform to move you a step closer toward that goal. This process requires that you thoroughly know your wants and desires and commit to attaining them.

Activity: Write your own eulogy. This activity is described in *Living Forward*, and for it to be effective you must take this exercise very seriously. Think through each of your loved ones or groups that you interact with… how do you want them to remember you, and what do you want them to say about you? I have to say that I did this exercise myself and found it very eye opening to realize what I find most valuable. This activity will help you to center your thoughts when your life becomes unbalanced. You will have a clear view of what your priorities in life are.

Activity: Write a personal mission statement. This activity is taken from Stephen Covey's, *7 Habits of Highly Effective People* .[2] Where the Habit #2 is to "Begin with the End in Mind." A personal mission statement is designed to outline what you want to be and do.

WHAT'S YOUR ONE THING?

If you are what you repeatedly do, then achievement isn't an action you take but a habit you forge into your life.—Aristotle

Now that we have discussed the importance of planning your life we can now begin to think about planning your career. This following comes from the world of entrepreneurship and a book titled, *The One Thing,* by Gary Keller who is the chairman of the board and cofounder of Keller Williams Realty, Inc., the largest real estate company in the world.[3] It does not take a rocket scientist to deduce that this book is about finding the one thing that you will focus all your efforts on, as the key to being most productive is to stay focused! Think about those around you who completed their experiments and wrote their dissertation or thesis in a record amount of time. What do they all have in common? I would bet that they all were highly focused and knew what their one thing was. Their one thing was not to do side experiments but to focus on the work needed to get their degree and stay away from all other detractors. In an environment with unlimited options and distractors, we often lose sight of where we put our attention and focus. Those around you who complete their degrees early or seem to get to where they want to go more efficiently are those who build their research plan (in a narrow sense), and lives (in the broader sense), not around novelty and breadth, but around meaning and depth.

Research by Phillippa Lally, a health psychology researcher at University College London published in the *European Journal of Social Psychology*, shows that on average, it takes more than 2 months before a new behavior/habit becomes automatic—66 days to be exact.[4] And depending on what habit you are trying to form, the person, and the circumstances, the time can vary greatly—anywhere from 18 days to 254 days exactly.[4] What I take from this is not that it takes a long time to change behaviors, but rather that we need to be intentional about how we spend our time and STAY FOCUSED if we choose to make staying on task a habit.

I often meet with students who for one reason or another have found themselves changing research labs well into their graduate careers. They express concerns about how long they will be in school or about what will happen if they are forced to start from the beginning again. What they are often surprised to hear is that I too changed labs well into my degree, and yes, I still finished in 5 years. "How did you do it?" I am often asked. After reading this far you should not be surprised to hear my answer, I did it by staying focused and knowing that my one thing was to finish my degree. I finished, and 3 first-author papers later, am here checking a box off my "bucket list" writing this book. You too can accomplish such goals!

Activity:

1. Find a sticky note
2. Find a pen
3. Write on the note your One Thing
4. Hang the note somewhere you will see it every day
5. Stay Focused!

The most efficient graduate students and postdoctoral fellows have a strategy for each day that they are in training. This includes not only planning each experiment in the lab but also planning how each activity they take time for will impact their career and by default will result in a line on their CV. Yes, I am encouraging you to make decisions about what you do based on what can help to build your CV or resume and in turn build your career. Your goal should be to add at least two new CV lines per year… if not more! This can only be accomplished with a good plan and staying focused. I recently reviewed, *The Professor is In*, and found one thing *very* valuable. That is a template for a 5-year plan.[5] We should all have one! No matter the stage of your career. You can find an example by visiting The Professor is In website.

Further, this would not be a chapter about creating balance if I did not mention SMART goals. So here is a brief description.

SMART goal setting goes as follows:

1. Specific: make sure that your goal is not too broad such as: "Get my PhD," but rather is more specific such as: "Publish paper on the effects of BDNF on neurogenesis."
2. Measureable: set milestones for your goal that will allow you to determine if you have accomplished it.
3. Attainable: do not set a goal that is too big for the time you have allowed yourself.
4. Realistic: Think about the realities of the work you do, for example, and be honest with yourself about if the goal can be attained.
5. Timely: Do not give yourself too much time to achieve the goal.

GET A DOG

So, I bought a dog. After transitioning from my graduate student life into a full-time academic position, I began to realize just how easily one can fall into a routine of work, work, work, and more work. I saw so many of my colleagues falling victim to a workaholic lifestyle. Further, I realized how as academically trained professionals we find ourselves filling our calendars with meetings, and over time these meetings steal our lives away. This all changed when I got a dog.

If a dog is not for you, maybe it's too much of a commitment or you are allergic, that is okay. Get a fish. I have a colleague who told me that one day she came home and found that her fish was dead. This is when she knew it was time to change her lifestyle. Her life had become so busy, and she had become so distracted that she could not even keep her fish alive. In this way, the fish served as a litmus paper for her life. Having someone or something in your life that depends on you is a key to maintaining a work–life balance. How this manifests in each of our lives is unique, but I encourage you to find your own litmus paper, whether that be in a spouse, friend, or fish.

My dog not only helps to keep me centered and balanced but also she serves as a constant reminder that life is more than just work. She forces me to come home at a decent hour to let her out, she helps me to exercise more as I must walk or run her, oh, and most importantly she reminds me that even in the darkest of days there is love in the world and I too have a soft side. So, if my N of one is not enough to convince you of the power of owning a pet, several studies have shown just that. For example, owning a pet can reduce stress, particularly dog ownership has been shown to be effective in improving one's health.[6,7]

It might seem counterintuitive to suggest managing time by adding more responsibilities to your plate, but in general, having other commitments is a great thing. You will find that the more responsibilities you have, the more you must learn to prioritize your time and get things done within the allocated times you set for yourself. Otherwise, we fall prey to the illusion that "we have all day to do this" at which point we procrastinate and/or fail to be productive. Just ask anyone who has children; they too understand this concept very well.

Another reason to get a pet is to avoid the pressures to become what in academia many of us would call ourselves: a workaholic. You should know that workaholics are not what hiring committees are looking for. They are looking for high performers. What's the difference? See the table below and strive to be a high performer, with or without a dog:

Workaholic	High Performer	Comments
Let others determine their value	Know their own value	As trainees we often find our value in our mentors views of us. I suggest that you know your own value and except that first.
Values performance based on hours worked	Values performance based on efficiency or getting things done	The lab environment often feels like you must be on 110% all the time. If you plan and are more organized you will find yourself drifting into the 100% at the right time category. Be strategic!
Are reactive	Take initiative	Do not just jump at any opportunity. Think about it before reacting. Further, if you plan you will be able to take initiative rather than always having to react to your surroundings. You will be in control of your plan.
Are busy	Do business	This is something that we can all fall into. You need to work toward efficiency so that when you are busy it is because business is being conducted and only that.

LEARN TO SPEED READ AND WRITE

Finding career and life balance is not just about managing the time you have but making more time out of what you currently are not using efficiently. One way to do this is to read and write effortlessly. The first step in solving a problem is admitting that you have one. As scientists we are all capable of going to the literature and learning new things. I encourage you to dive into the literature on speed reading and learn *now* how to master this skill. You will find that once you do you have more time than you realized tied up in tasks such as reading the literature. There are several ways to read more quickly so here are a few resources to get you started:

Huffington Post, Tim Ferriss on Speed Reading: http://www.huffingtonpost.com/tim-ferriss/speed-reading_b_5317784.html

Speed Reading Lounge How-To: http://www.speedreadinglounge.com/how-to-speed-read

Once you master speed reading you will have time left over to do other things and accomplish other tasks, all while staying current on the literature and learning new skills.

The same is true for writing. You must acknowledge that you could be a more efficient writer first and then seek help in honing this skill. If your goal is to pursue a career that will require a lot of writing, the only way to ensure that you will succeed and that you will make the most of your time is to hone this craft. Some of us are natural writers and others must work at this skill, but I assure you that the time is worth it. In searching for resources to guide our readers in this section, I came across the memoir of Steven King, titled "On Writing."[8] I did not have to read far to realize that this was the exact reference that I needed. Below is an excerpt from the second forward of the book:

> *This is a short book because most books about writing are filled with bullshit. Fiction writers, present company included, don't understand very much about what they do—not why it works when it's good, not why it doesn't when it's bad. I figured the shorter the book, the less the bullshit.*
>
> *One notable exception to the bullshit rule is The Elements of Style, by William Strunk Jr. and E. B. White. There is little or no detectable bullshit in that book. (Of course it's short; at eighty-five pages it's much shorter than this one.) I'll tell you right now that every aspiring writer should read The Elements of Style. Rule 17 in the chapter titled Principles of Composition is "Omit needless words." I will try to do that here.*

To follow the guidelines of Steven King, I will keep this brief, as all scientific and nonscientific writing should be. The memoir is a great read and has some very to-the-point guidelines for how to become a more effective writer. Get it and read it! (by the way I found the whole book online, just search for it). In the meantime here are a few of his tips:

- Watch TV less. Read as much as possible.
- Be ready to fail and to take criticism (this is ever true in science).

- Write for the joy of writing.
- Do the hardest things to write first.

In summary, we are all on our own unique journey that can sometimes lead us down very busy and taxing paths. When you find yourself struggling to keep up, remember that with some thoughtful changes to your own behaviors and goals, you can achieve balance in your career and life. Use the tips in this chapter as a starting point and work toward finding your own protocols for achieving balance and your career and life goals.

Case Study

Guillermo Vela is the founder and CEO of Nebulab (www.nebulab.io), a San Antonio–based software company building data management software for scientists. Guillermo is a current Career Advisory Council Member for the Graduate School of Biomedical Sciences at the University of Texas Health Science Center in San Antonio, as well as an active Board Member for San Antonio Science and the Chamber Orchestra of San Antonio. Guillermo is also an advisor to Hecate OncoSolutions, a biotech company focused on developing a new drug targeting peripheral nerve tumors, and winner of its category in The Neuro Startup Challenge—an international competition aiming to commercialize NIH-owned innovations through early startup ventures.

Previously, Guillermo worked as a brain cancer and stem cell researcher for the Department of Neurosurgery at Johns Hopkins. Guillermo received his Bachelor of Arts and his Masters in Biotechnology from the Johns Hopkins University.

With ample experiences in entrepreneurship and biotechnology Guillermo shares his insights on unique tech and tools of the trade for managing our time and career.

In 1981, IBM introduced the world to the IBM 3380. It was the first hard drive to break the 1 GB barrier, offering a total of 2.52 GB of storage with each GB (adjusted for inflation) costing roughly $800,000. The IBM 3380 was about the size of a washing machine. It weighed over 500 pounds, and at the time, it was the future of computing.

By comparison, today's smartphones offer up to 128 GB of storage for a few hundred dollars. They weigh just a few ounces and are 100,000 times more powerful. It's easy to marvel at what we've accomplished in 35 years, yet this was predicted as far back as 1965, when Gordon Moore famously predicted this would happen, later known as "Moore's Law."

What seems more difficult to predict, however, is how technology changes us. Technology has now infiltrated virtually every aspect of our daily lives, but this is still a very recent phenomenon. A giant social experiment is just unfolding, and we are all the subjects. While we wait to see the aftermath, I'd like to offer some do's and don'ts of technology, especially as it relates to our time and attention span.

Let's start with the smartphone. What makes this beautiful feat of engineering so unique is how quickly it became an extension of ourselves. It brought access and convenience to our hands, and with it came subtle but profound changes in our everyday experiences. The way we use maps, hail ride services, order food, or interact with others is radically different from how we used to just 10 years ago. Today, even finding a date is just a screen swipe away.

Continued

Case Study—cont'd

And while smartphones brought unprecedented simplicity into our lives, our continual reliance on them is morphing technological adoption into technological addiction—with side effects. This is also no accident, for the apps we interact with on a daily basis are purposely built to play on our neurobiology. News feeds and red notifications are there to stimulate our brain's reward system. They make it too easy to indulge our natural desire for distractions, and this is precisely what makes technology so addictive. Google's former Design Ethicist, Tristan Harris, provides some excellent insights on this issue.

As we are conditioned to seek out and expect instant gratification by apps, this same expectation begins to spill into other aspects of our lives. It's the difference between skimming a *BuzzFeed* article while waiting in line and dedicating 20 min of deep reading to a thoughtful piece by *The Economist*. The former is like junk food for the brain. It's quick and pleasurable to digest but ultimately void of any real substance. The latter is vastly more filling, but how many of us would actually have—or frankly make—the time for it?

Of course, technology can also be a wonderful asset. The key is to know when and how to rely on it, and this usually starts with good habits. As an example, I recommend spending around 20 min each night to plan your next day. This involves outlining what you need to accomplish, what you would like to accomplish, and what commitments you cannot miss (e.g., doctor's appointment). Then, estimate how much time each would require and allocate a time slot to it. This is precisely where the principles discussed under SMART goals kick in. In other words, you need to be realistic about what task you can accomplish in a given day, and how much time you would need to accomplish them. This will allow you to assess how quickly you can accomplish set tasks, and whether adjustments are necessary, such as giving yourself more time to accomplish a task, or by figuring out how to be more efficient.

The goal is to create good habits, and then use technology to support them. For example, it's vital that I have access to my schedule at all times so that I can see how I'm doing on time and what's coming next. This would be difficult to accomplish if I was relying on a paper notebook. Instead, I rely on apps that I can access across all my devices. Which apps to use is a matter of personal preference, but I recommend apps that require as little steps as possible to access and input information. Native apps already built in Apple's, Google's, and Microsoft's operating systems are functional enough and constantly improving. A recent favorite of mine is the iOS and Mac app, Doo. It boasts a beautiful design, but more importantly, it's easy enough for me to set and view daily reminders on all my devices. Other popular apps I recommend are Trello and Evernote. And, if you want to get fancy, you can even incorporate apps such as IFTTT (If This Then That) or Zapier to streamline tasks and other apps. For example, through IFTTT, you could have a new event automatically added to your Google Calendar whenever you create a card in Trello.

When working on tasks, it's important to avoid the temptation to multitask, especially during tasks that require deep concentration. This only enforces our brain's desire to work on perfunctory tasks, and this diminishes our ability to concentrate. It's equally important to limit or eliminate to the many distractions provided by technology during such times.

Case Study—cont'd

One way to limit such distractions is by simply deleting the apps you find most addicting from your phone. If you're regularly checking Facebook or Instagram, simply delete them. This won't delete your accounts, but it will help reeducate your brain to not seek them out on your phone, while also limiting the amount of time you spend on social networks. Conversely, if you usually feel the urge to check your social networks when you're working on your computer, allow yourself to only check social networks through your phone, and purposefully keep your phone away when you need to get work done on your computer.

When used properly, technology can also help you achieve goals that might otherwise be very difficult to achieve. For example, I set a personal goal of reading one book per month for 2016. But I also knew that at the moment, it would be difficult for me to allocate the amount of time necessary to accomplish this, so I turned to audio books as my solution. To be clear, I would much rather read paper books, but audio books allow me to take advantage of time spent on everyday tasks such as driving to work or doing laundry. In the past 5 months, I've finished five books totaling 44 h of audio. In other words, by using apps, such as Audible, I was able to reuse 44 h spent on chores and daily routines for my goal.

In short, apps are a wonderful asset when applied to good habits and time management skills, but they can also be a source of distraction. Our overreliance on technology can strip our everyday experiences of depth or deliberation, while the appropriate use of technology can instead enhance them.

REFERENCES

1. Hyatt M, Harkavy D. *Living forward: a proven plan to stop drifting and get the life you want.* Grand Rapids: Michigan: Baker Publishing Group; 2016.
2. Covey S. *7 Habits of highly effective people.* Franklin Covey Co; 2015.
3. Keller G. *The one thing: the surprisingly simple truth behind extraordinary results.* Austin: Texas: Bard Press; 2012.
4. Lally P, Van Jaarsveld C, Potts H, Wardle J. How are habits formed: modeling habit formation in the real world. *European Journal of Social Psychology* 2009;**40**(6):998–1009.
5. Kelsky K. *The professor is in: the essential guide to turning your Ph.D. into a job.* Three Rivers Press; 2015.
6. Allen K, Shykoff B, Izzo J. Pet ownership, but not ACE inhibitor therapy, blunts home blood pressure responses to mental stress. *Hypertenstion* 2001;**38**:815–20.
7. Friedmann E, Thomas S. Pet ownership, social support, and one-year survival after acute myocardial infarction in the Cardiac Arrhythmia Suppression Trial (CAST). *The American Journal of Cardiology* 1995;**76**(17):1213–7.
8. King S. *On writing: a memoir of the craft.* New York: Scribner; 2000. New York.

Chapter 14

The Art of Communication

Teresa M. Evans

Chapter Outline

Would You Consider Yourself Confident? **166**
Are You Thoughtful in Your Communications? **166**
  Oral Communication 167
    Introductions 167
    Presentations 168
    Communication and Mentoring 171
  Verbal Communication 172

  Written Communication 173
    Email Communications 173
    Thank You Notes 175
Communication Struggles: Overcoming International Barriers **176**
Personal Communication Success Story **177**
References **178**
Places to go for help **178**

Chapter Takeaways:

- Be confident and thoughtful when communicating in any form.
- Not all introductions are the same; prepare many versions and practice them.
- There are tricks to the trade when presenting: consider telling a story, planning your slides, and practicing your presence.
- Mentoring is a skill required for all career fields. The key to a strong mentoring relationship is communication, specifically communication of expectations.
- Slow down before pushing send on an email to avoid mistakes.
- Write thank you notes with a pen and mail them with a stamp!
- There are skills one must practice to master a new language as well as to communicate effectively with someone who does not speak your language fluently.

There is no argument that communication is fundamental to a successful career journey. With strong communication skills, you will find that pursuing the career of your choice will be so much easier. The art of communication is a skill to be mastered just like any other art form. You must take time to perfect your skills in both the verbal and written forms. This chapter will introduce you to essential communication skills for both oral communications and written communications and techniques to perfect them.

ReSearch. http://dx.doi.org/10.1016/B978-0-12-804297-7.00014-8

By visualizing the individuals at the helm of the career field you are interested in, you can see that it is clear that strong communication skills are key to excelling in one's career.

Activity: I would like to start with a few basic concepts [Answer the questions below and then ask a friend (honest friend) to answer the questions about yourself as well]:

WOULD YOU CONSIDER YOURSELF CONFIDENT?

If yes, could you be overconfident? Overconfidence can result in the lack of preparation as well as potentially an off-putting exchange or communication.
If no, how could you work to be more confident? The first step to being a strong communicator is to convince those that you communicate with to believe in you and listen to what you are saying. To be convincing, you must believe in yourself and that what you have to offer has value. This is confidence.

Ways to feel more confident:

1. Practice a power pose—You need to find a pose that makes you feel strong or confident and position yourself that way before you start to communicate. For example, if you are sitting down you can simply stand up before presenting; alternatively you could sit with your arm spread out over the seat next to you. Making yourself appear as big as possible will indicate power to your audience and help you to feel more confident.
2. Introduce someone else—It is much easier to promote someone you know rather than to promote yourself. So, to break the ice and help yourself to feel more confident, first introduce your colleague.
3. Think about what you have to offer in advance, this could be simply showing interest in what the other person has to say—list 2–3 keywords that you want someone to remember about you when they meet you. Then strategize about how to get that message across.

ARE YOU THOUGHTFUL IN YOUR COMMUNICATIONS?

If yes, what do you think about? Also, do not overthink what you are going to say. Often we can fall into the pattern of memorizing what we are going to say and this will cause us to sound less confident when we present or communicate.
If no, the idea of walking into a room and giving a flawless presentation without thinking about what you are going to say first is a BAD idea. Slow down and think about what you wish to say before you say it as you do not want to appear unprepared or give a bad first impression.

Things to think about before communications:

1. Who is your audience?
2. What might get them interested in what you have to say?
3. How can you make a strong impression?

We will go over how to answer these and other questions throughout this chapter. First, let's discuss the most common form of communication—oral communications.

Oral Communication

Introductions

One such form of oral communication not so often practiced in science is the formal introduction. A great introduction can leave a lasting impact, good or bad. You must spend time thinking about what you want your impression to be and how you will get it across in many different settings. Practice these intros and be ready at any time to execute them.

Length Matters

Sometimes you have less than 60 s to introduce yourself. This type of introduction is very different than what is commonly referred to as an "elevator speech" (thoroughly described in the Branding chapter), which is longer. A quick introduction is often needed at networking events, as well as in a boardroom setting. In brief, a short intro requires you to stand and state your name and job or business. When presenting to executives or committees, as we often do in academia, you might state your name, role, department, and location. Although these sound like easy lists of things that you can recite without much effort, people often stumble, fumble, and mumble through these introductions as anxiety sets in. This type of lack of preparation will result in the wasting of a valuable opportunity to make a good impression. To avoid this, remind yourself the following guidelines when giving a short introduction:

1. Prepare. What will you say? Think about what matters to the audience whom you will be coming into contact with in advance. A short introduction at a conference networking event will be much different from that at a high school science fair, for example.
2. Practice. You must practice all forms of communication, but in this case be sure to practice out loud. Even if it is out loud to yourself. Do not hesitate to record yourself and play it back to yourself. Listen for filler words such as I guess, um, I mean, kinda, like really. You should also practice in front of a mirror to be sure that you remember to smile.
3. Communicate self-confidence. If you do not project confidence, then how can the audience be confident about what you are saying? (See below to learn how.)
4. Focus. Pay attention to the person to whom you are introducing yourself to. Listen to the other person's introduction and comments.
5. Business cards. Give your business card if asked or ask permission to give it (and receive the other person's card respectfully).

Introducing Others

The unique thing here is that I am not just talking about introducing yourself to someone who you wish to know but more importantly introducing your colleagues to someone who **they** might want to know. If you can master the ability to introduce your colleagues in a strong and confident manner, you will have colleagues for life. For example, you are at a conference and a scientist in your field who you have always admired walks up to your poster at the same time that your mentor does. What do you do? Well, I would suggest that you MAKE THE INTRODUCTION. "Hello Dr. Smith, this is my mentor Dr. Jones. Dr. Jones this is Dr. Smith, one of the leading neuroscientists in the field of dementia. His work has been instrumental in moving this area of research forward and not only that, he is also an outstanding mentor to his trainees." It would be flattering to hear this said about you, right? Would you forget this young trainee? Of course you wouldn't. And that, my friend, is how you leave a lasting impression.

Presentations

As scientists, one of our staple career tasks is presenting our work. If any of you chose to be a scientist because you did not want to have to present... well, you are in the wrong profession. The best scientists and professionals for that matter can give a presentation that leaves a lasting impression. Can you remember the last three presentations you went to within your department... or outside of it for that matter? If so, what do you remember about them? Do you remember the specifics of the graphs that were shown, the color of the slides, or even the name of the presenter? I would bet that one thing that the presentations that you can remember have in common is that they all told a story, or took you on a journey of some kind. In the case of a scientific presentation, was it a journey to a discovery? Or maybe a story of a patient or disease state and the clear relevance of the research?

The book, *Talk Like TED,* lists nine things that make up amazing presentations like those given by TED presenters:

1. **Tell a story**

   Some of the best presentations in the world are centered around a common theme or story. We are trained as scientists to have the standard background slide or slides that provide a context for our research and that is supposed to get the audience engaged. But I am not sure that this is always a success. Think about your last presentation. How did you begin? Dementia is bad; stroke is the third leading cause of death and disability worldwide; Ebola is a growing threat affecting millions of lives... Let's take the first example and rethink how we might tell it as a story. Rather than giving a list of statistics could you provide the same information but within a personal context, "As the granddaughter of a man who suffered from dementia, I can personally share that Alzheimer disease affects the family and the patient. As our elderly population grows, our society is in growing need of a treatment for this debilitating and life-altering disease." More powerful?

    Activity: Think about your area of work and decide how you might tell a story, it could be a personal one or a story about the journey toward discovery.

2. **Use images and plan your slides**

A powerful image speaks a thousand words. We all know what it is like to be in a presentation where the slides are filled with words and the presenter just reads straight from the slides… if this is you, it's time to make a lasting change. PowerPoint can be a powerful tool for good or for evil. If you wish to be a super hero whose power is making great slide presentations, listen up!

- *Use pictures or illustrations whenever possible.* There are times when I use only illustrations in my presentations. I have found that these presentations allow me to focus on the story I wish to tell and help me to relax in front of the audience. You need to find what works for you.
- *Keep slides brief.* Keep the bullet points to no more than 3–4 per slide. The words for each bullet point should not exceed two lines, one line is best. You do not want to read from the slide anyway so the words should be much less than what you plan to say.
- *Choose a font carefully.* The size and style of the font both matter. You can also use colored font to emphasize but be mindful that your audience might include individuals who are color blind (no yellow and green or red and green, for example).
- *Motion should be used sparingly.* For those of you whose research includes complex pathways or protocols, it is quite tempting to work your magic using animations. Although it feels like doing magic to make your proteins appear and disappear from the page just as they might in the cell, I suggest you do this with caution. As long as these great effects are used properly, they can really help to clarify your point…, but alternatively they can distract from your story. Proceed with caution.

3. **Plan your delivery**

There are several ways to prepare and plan for a presentation, and I am here to say that there is no one size fits all. Many individuals will use note cards or some form thereof to outline their talk and guide them as they present. Some will strictly memorize their "lines" prior to the big day. I myself will strive to practice my story/presentation until I can say it with ease and without the aide of my slide presentation. It is not my goal to memorize the words that I am going to say but more importantly it is my goal to memorize what the order is of my slides and the key point to each. In this way, every time that I give the talk it might be a little different than the last but I do not miss my intended points. You should strive to practice in whatever way will result in you giving the most relaxed and natural presentation possible. This is one step toward convincing your audience that you are confident. Dr. Jean-luc

Doumont is a world-acclaimed expert on scientific communication with over 20 years of experience lecturing and giving workshops in these areas (if you get the chance don't miss out on seeing him speak). When looking for more information about any of the topics discussed in this chapter, turn to some of his resources, one such resource is the Scientific Communication Topic Room through Scitable by natureEDUCATION.[2]

4. **Show confidence**

It is crucial that your audience knows that you are confident in what you are sharing with them. This is integrally related to the success of your presentation as well as the impression that you will leave. Here are a few ways to show confidence:

- *Think about your voice and how you sound.* Speak loudly, slowly, and clearly enough to be heard and understood. Watch out for filler words (i.e., um, uh, like, however).
- *Smiles matter.* Smiling helps you look relaxed, and communicates warmth and sincerity.
- *Make eye contact.* If you don't have time to look at everyone pick a few key people.
- *Posture is important.* Stand up straight, shoulders back, head up, weight evenly distributed on both feet. If seated, sit up straight, keep your hands on the table and your feet firmly on the ground. Remember to shake hands (that you have practiced) firmly while making eye contact and smiling.

5. **Command the room/stage**

I was recently invited to a meeting where we were taught how to "COMMAND A ROOM." You must watch the TED Talk by psychologist Amy Cuddy who discusses the importance of posture and how it shapes the impression you share with others.[1] Your body language is worth a thousand words. Learn how to control it and how to command a room. Nick Morgan, the president and founder of Public Words, a communications consulting firm and author of *Power Cues: The Subtle Science of Leading Groups, Persuading Others, and Maximizing Your Personal Impact*, provides a few tips on this subject for the Harvard Business Review.[3] Nick tells his readers to be aware of their unconscious cues such as, when you enter a room have good posture, keep your eyes up, and move confidently. He makes the point that we are always signaling about our intentions and feelings to others and others are always signaling to us. Furthermore, he states that we are often not aware of the signals that we are giving to others. So be mindful of not just what you say verbally but how you might be perceived without saying a word.

Activity: Record yourself giving your presentation using your cell phone or other device. Now once recorded, you must watch the video back and take notes. Pay attention to the above items and list all of the things that you would like to improve. Repeat this process a few times, as well as show the video to a few colleagues and ask for their input. This might sound like a crazy thing to do but I speak from experience, there is not a single more powerful way to improve your presentation skills than seeing how you present yourself.

Communication and Mentoring

Another differing form of verbal communication is that which occurs between a mentor and a mentee. As a trainee in the sciences, you have been exposed to both being the mentee as well as the mentor. A key element to a mentoring relationship is strong communication. Furthermore, the success of science and many professions for that matter is teamwork. For a team to strive, effective communication among team members is key to attaining an exceptional end product.

For the sake of this section please put on your mentor cap. Think about a situation in which you have served as a mentor, for example, to an undergraduate in the lab, to a graduate student who is looking to you as a postdoc to guide them.

As a mentor you must strive to establish a rapport with your mentees. This requires effective interpersonal communication skills consisting of nonverbal and verbal sharing of information between two people. This is a two-way interaction, a conversation if you will. Just like when giving a presentation, body language tells those with whom we are communicating a great deal of what we are thinking and feeling. We can all recall that moment, in our mentor's office, when we received the shoulder shrug that changed our outlook on our dissertation topic and made us rethink our entire existence… Word to the wise, be mindful of the power of your shoulder shrugs.

Nonverbal Communication

Nonverbal communication makes up a significant portion of all human communication. We share both positive and negative feelings or emotions via nonverbal communication. As a mentor we must be mindful of these forms of communication and that they can have a significant impact on our relationship with our mentees. Furthermore, as mentees we need to realize that our mentors might not always be aware of their nonverbal communications. Once we educate ourselves about what to look for we can more accurately decipher the thoughts of the other person in our mentor–mentee relationship, as well as put forth the proper image of ourselves.

Examples of nonverbal communication included:

- Positive body language:
  - Direct eye contact
  - Nodding/other affirmation
  - Pleasant demeanor
- Negative body language:
  - Obscuring face
  - Crossing arms
  - Wagging fingers

Verbal Communication

The first communications you should have with a new member of your team or your mentee is an introduction. You should introduce this person not only to yourself, but also to the work environment and other team members. Furthermore, you can discuss with the mentee your expectations. Discussion of expectations is one of the most important pieces to a mentee–mentor relationship. If these are clear then you can avoid misunderstandings in the future. I knew of a mentor who kept a log of the "rules" of her lab. This log of lab rules became infamous around the university as this lab grew in size and in prestige. The log included all the things you would expect: notify the primary investigator when you will not be in lab, keep your bench clean, mark all your samples clearly, and use a lab notebook. But also included were some things that might not be expected, such as detailed instructions on the process of making orders, on the steps to take before requesting a vacation, or authorship requirements in the lab. The mentor stated once that this was a living, breathing document that was updated as issues in the lab arose in an effort to make sure that no one was not informed. Is this the right way to communicate with a team? Maybe and maybe not. But I include this description of how one set of expectations was conveyed to a lab team as just one example of the level of detail to which this kind of communication can go.

If you find yourself in a mentoring relationship where the expectations are not clearly defined by the mentor, I encourage you to start the conversation and to start it sooner than later. Simply ask the questions, in a one-on-one meeting, that will help to define what is expected of your work and your professional interactions. Often, the mentor might not have thought through these questions before, so be prepared to allow them time to think them through. Some questions you might ask are as follows:

How often should we meet to discuss data and my career plan?
How do you prefer that I communicate with you, by email or in person?
What is the lab policy on vacation time?
What is the lab policy on authorship?

It is important to set a standard of verbal communication that does not remove the two-way conversation. You do not want to communicate solely by email or simply by saying, "It's in the handbook." These types of communication prevent the ability to listen to what the mentee, or mentor, is saying and create an open environment to share. When having conversations with a mentee or even with a mentor you need to work to communicate attentiveness.

Below are a few key points to help promote effective verbal communication:

- Active listening
  - What the mentee is really saying versus what you are going to say next!
- Communicate attentiveness
  - Verbal follow-up
  - Nonverbal cues

- Reflective listening/paraphrasing
  - Verbally reflect back what the mentee just said
    - Helps mentee feel understood

Activity: How might you answer the below questions, if they are asked of you by your mentee? (Think about a mentee you currently have or have had in the past when answering.)

- What are the responsibilities of team members?
- What are the proper channels of communication I should use?
- What are the work hours?
- What are your goals and expectations for our relationship; for my project?

As you think through these questions also think about how your answers to them might change as the mentee changes. If you are a team leader and your best team member asks these questions, will you respond the same as your most junior team member, for example?

In summary, as a mentor it should be your goal to maintain a positive and productive relationship with your mentee. To do so you must be mindful of your communications and be sure to keep work on the relationship at all times. This requires that you maintain ongoing communications as well as a shared understanding of what each person expects. There are several tools in the academic/scientific setting that are often used by mentors and mentees to facilitate these discussions. Here are two examples:

- Individual development plans: These come in many forms, online or written, but the purpose is to think through not only the short term goals but also the long term goals and expectations. These should be shared and updated often.
- Mentor–mentee compact: For example, American Association of Medical Colleges (AAMC) compact between postdoctoral appointees and their mentors that clearly defines the expectations of the postdoctoral fellow and the mentor. This document can serve as a contract between a mentor and a fellow. (https://www.aamc.org/initiatives/research/postdoccompact/)

Written Communication

In this section, we will discuss written communications. Many of these tips and skills I have learned throughout my career and will share with you my personal stories of how I learned them. Additionally, know that these skills will apply to all written materials, scientific and nonscientific.

Email Communications

Everyone Needs a "Slow Down" Post-it Note

During the first few weeks of my new job, following my PhD graduation, I sent many an email. More emails than I had ever sent before. Transitioning from graduate student to academic administrator meant, along with many things, that

I would now spend a lot of my time requesting and scheduling meetings. In part because of this, my days were spent in large part sending emails. As I worked to keep up with the flood that was in my inbox, I began to realize that I was sending emails faster than I could read and reread them. As if my realization of this was not enough, my mentor and colleague, who is often a recipient of these emails, noticed my haste as well. She would highlight my misspelling, typo, sentence fragments, etc., and then return the sent email to me with the subject line "SLOW DOWN."

This soon became my mantra. I would repeat to myself, prior to hitting send, those two words and then reread what I wrote looking for these easy-to-make mistakes. Why do you think this was such a priority? Well, this is because it is these little mistakes that can leave a lasting impression with the recipient of your emails, whether that be an executive at a company or a chairman of a department. Hastily sent emails, with simply made mistakes, indicate to a reader that you are disorganized, not thoughtful or just plan a mess. So, to serve as a constant reminder I encourage each of you to do as I did and slap a Post-it note on your computer monitor that reads, SLOW DOWN! This is my constant reminder of the importance of being mindful of what I am doing… especially in my emails. Oh and in case you have not figured it out yet… emails last forever and there are no take backs once the sent button is pushed. So send each message with care.

Now you might be wondering, how do I make sure that I am sending the best email or letter possible? Well, this is something that I was lucky to learn how to do before graduate school and here is where I learned and the tips to help you master this skill.

How to Master the Power of a Strong Email or Letter

As an undergraduate student, I did not realize the power I had been given when I was taught to write a strong letter/email. I had a wonderful professor and mentor who guided me through my graduate school application process among other things. This process included teaching me how to craft a strong and compelling email or letter. Here are some tips I learned from her that have been priceless throughout my career:

- Begin with Dear and always use the formal version of a person's name if this is the first or formal correspondence, i.e., Dr. Smith.
  - Do not use only the first name until the individual has said that it is okay or you are of equal experience to the person you are corresponding with. Even then, I often err on the side of using their title for the first email.
- When closing say something like, "Thank you in advance for your support." You want to thank them before they have a chance to not do what you have asked.
- Reread to ensure that you are clear and concise throughout.

- Include a beginning, middle, and an end:
    - Beginning: This is the introduction. You need to briefly introduce who you are and the reason for the email.
    - Middle: This is where you include the meat of the email. What are the details of why you are contacting this person.
    - End: This is the conclusion. You need to summarize what you have told them in the email and also include a final statement of your ask (e.g., would you be available to meet in the coming week to discuss your career path?).

For all of the emails that you send, it is also strongly encouraged that you have someone read them over, especially as you are learning. My mentors have been instrumental proofreaders of my writing, which has taught me so much about how to navigate these tasks in my career. If you do not have access to a great writing mentor, look to your university writing center (if there is one) for handouts or guides to email communication, along with this article from InsideHigherEd.[4]

Thank You Notes

Now, I am well aware that the age of the written letter is potentially behind us, but I am a firm believer that there is still a place for a thoughtfully written note of thanks.

Jimmy Fallon says, "It's Friday, and Friday is the day that I catch up on things and WRITE my thank you notes." These are words of wisdom. Jimmy does not type his thank you notes, he writes them. I encourage you to do the same. Get some cards, fancy or plain, and keep them in your desk along with some stamps. Yes, I said stamps. You know those things that you buy at the... wait for it... post office. A handwritten note is something that will make a lasting impression! As I hope you are beginning to appreciate, all forms of communication are about formulating an impression of yourself for others and you want to put together the best impression possible. A handwritten thank you note is just icing on the impression cake. These can be very simple such as:

Thank you for your time today.

I greatly appreciate your insights and continued guidance as I purse my career goals.

Best,
Teresa.

Activity: Make a written communication goal for the next month. It might include things such as having your emails read by a mentor at least twice a week, buying thank you notes and sending them out to connections you have made at a conference, or simply drafting a letter you might send after an informational interview and requesting feedback from a colleague.

COMMUNICATION STRUGGLES: OVERCOMING INTERNATIONAL BARRIERS

As a graduate student, I moved from my small home town in Ohio to what I thought was a big city in Texas. It seemed to take all of the bravery I had to start over after driving 24 h from home. I quickly realized that although Texas seemed so far from home it was not at all as the food was similar, there were many Starbucks, and most of all I could speak the language.

Throughout my academic career I have grown to have a strong respect for international trainees. It takes immense bravery to cross oceans, into a new world, in which you are not fluent in the language, to follow your passion for science. For this and many reasons I have worked with an international colleague, Patricia Araujo, PhD, to provide the below guidance.

"Don't be afraid to talk with people. Speak English! Don't be ashamed of your accent. People in the university and around town are quite reasonable and they will have patience understanding you (although sometimes they speak louder, instead of slower, when they notice you are from outside of their country). I always make it clear to native English speaking individuals, that I welcome them to correct my English if I say something wrong. This strategy has helped to improve my English very quickly. Watching American TV and going to the movies also helped me a lot. Avoid only talking to people who speak your language. Try to practice your English as much as possible." Patricia Araujo, PhD, International Postdoctoral Fellow.

Don't be scared to

- Speak the language that you are learning even if you are not comfortable with it
- Admit when you do not know or understand what is being said by a native language speaker

It is thought that individuals who are learning to speak a new language and who are immersed in the country in which that new language is spoken fluently, become reluctant to speak the new language because they are more aware of their mistakes. As children, we make mistakes all of the time as we learn to speak. But we are not aware of the proper grammar or etiquette and quite frankly, as a child we do not care about these things. As an adult however, we are taught the rules of grammar before we are immersed and asked to speak a second language. Therefore, when we make mistakes we know we are making them and even worse, we care that we are making them. This can result in people becoming scared or afraid to speak the new language. This fear can bring the learning process to a halt.

To overcome this fear you need to work to not surround yourself with others who speak your native language. As someone who only speaks one language, I can tell you I am in awe of those who speak 2, 3, 4, or more languages. This skill is one that I value and appreciate. I am not the only one who feels this way and I encourage you to simply communicate the best that you can with native speaking individuals and do just as Dr. Araujo suggested, ask for feedback.

It becomes increasingly frustrating when I recognize that someone is not understanding what I am saying, but when I ask them if they understand they just nod as if they do. This is not a good strategy. (1) This does not help you to grow your skills and (2) this does not help me to learn how to better and more effectively communicate with you. Furthermore, it is my responsibility to pay attention and work to recognize when I am not communicating clearly to my audience. This case is not different.

The key to success is, you guessed it, PRACTICE!

Do not just practice with individuals who speak the language you are trying to learn fluently but practice with another person who speaks your native language and is learning too. This will help you to get over your fear, if you have it, and also to learn from each other. Also, when you are ready, speak with someone who is a native speaker but ask them for feedback. Also, do not forget to watch TV and listen to the radio in the language you are trying to learn. This will further help you to speak in a way that sounds more like a native individual.

Activity: To increase your practice, set aside one day per week to speak only in the language that you are working to learn and perfect, even if you are speaking to friends and colleague who speak your native language.

PERSONAL COMMUNICATION SUCCESS STORY

Now before I send you off to begin to communicate and build your network I need to tell you a story. This one is one of great personal communication success! (Prior to reading further, I need you to watch the video of the 2014 UT Austin Commencement Address,[5] maybe some of you were there. This will provide you with the opportunity to learn a few more tips from one of our nation's best.)

Now you might ask, why that video… well this video was a part of the homework I did before a visit to the UT System offices in Austin as Admiral William H. McRaven, in the video, is now the Chancellor of the UT System. Furthermore, he is my husband's hero… as I was told multiple times before my visit. So, cutting to the chase, the take home message from my visit was always use the restroom when offered and be prepared with an "ask." The visit to Austin was a full day of planned meetings with strong women leaders of the UT System. I was blown away by the support I received and the examples of leadership I was able to learn from. At the closing of the day I had a few moments to myself in the conference room. A conference room, notably named the "Chancellor's Conference Room." When I was delivered there by my escort, I was shown the location of the restroom down the hall in the event that I needed it. I did not but I took the stroll anyway. Imagine a hall lined with four doors on each side. At the end, a door directly in front of you, the restroom. As I made my way down the hall slowly I listened, I listened for the sound of that voice I heard on the video. As I almost reached the end of my hallway journey I heard a door close behind me and as I turned around I was face-to-face with the Chancellor. I extended my hand and we had introductions. This encounter allowed me the opportunity to not only introduce myself, as we discussed above, but also give my "ask." My ask was simply—a picture with my husband's hero. This ask led to a longer conversation, an unforgettable moment in my career and that of my husband's, and was of course followed with a handwritten thank you note So, if you underline or highlight nothing else, remember this: Always use the restroom and be prepared with an introduction and an ask. Oh and don't forget your thank you notes!

REFERENCES

1. Cuddy A. *Your body language shapes who you are, TED talk.* June 2010. http://www.ted.com/talks/amy_cuddy_your_body_language_shapes_who_you_are?language=en.
2. Scientific Communication, Nature Education, J-luc Doumont, http://www.nature.com/scitable/topic/scientific-communication-14121566.
3. Morgan N. To build influence, master how you enter a room. *Harv Bus Rev* September 23, 2014. https://hbr.org/2014/09/to-build-influence-master-how-you-enter-a-room/.
4. Zellner A, InsideHigherEd, editors. *7 Tipps for writing better emails.* September 20, 2013. https://www.insidehighered.com/blogs/gradhacker/7-tips-writing-better-emails.
5. McRaven AWH. *University of Texas at Austin 2014 Commencement address.* YouTube; May 19, 2014. https://www.youtube.com/watch?v=pxBQLFLei70.

PLACES TO GO FOR HELP

http://www.nature.com/scitable/ebooks/english-communication-for-scientists-14053993/contents.
http://www.centerforcommunicatingscience.org/improvisation-for-scientists/.
http://www.hhmi.org/sites/default/files/Educational%20Materials/Lab%20Management/entering_mentoring.pdf.

Section 5

Finding a Job

Chapter 15

The Career Search

Teresa M. Evans, Natalie Lundsteen

Chapter Outline

Things to Consider Before You Begin 183
How to Be What Employers Are Looking For 184
Assessing Your Fit 184
Making a Plan 186
Sample Job Search Plan 187
    Step 1 Assess Your Circumstances 187
Step 2 Begin Your Search 187
Step 3 Network 189
Step 4 Submission and Preparation 189
Step 5 Be Realistic 189
Working With Recruiters 190
Wrapping-Up Your Career Search 193
References 194
Further Reading 194

Chapter Takeaways:

- Your career search must be both quantitative (analyzing your career options) and qualitative (determining careers where you will best fit).
- Assess all aspects of potential career paths before preparing to apply.
- Understand the importance of putting together both self-knowledge **and** career path knowledge.

The career search is a critical piece of the ongoing career planning process. As the title of our book implies, a career search will not occur just once in your life, but will probably occur multiple times. You will *ReSearch* for the right career and then perhaps search again as your priorities and interests change, reinventing your career over time. Up to this point, this book has provided you with help in identifying not only your interests and strengths but also how to identify career fields to align with these interests and strengths. This chapter will outline the important things to consider while conducting a career search, as well as review the methods discussed in other chapters that are key to career search success. A successful career search puts together elements of knowing yourself and knowing your possible options.

It is important to remember that this process really begins with the assessment of both self and personal factors, which is the focus of Chapter 8. It is only after you have identified your strengths and interests that you can start to narrow down the industries, occupations, and workforce needs that best align with your self-assessment measures (see Chapter 3 on the realities of the job market). Your career search process requires research and thought, just like planning a dissertation or a grant proposal. Do not leap into a job before you look thoroughly at your options and do your *ReSearch*!

Have you found yourself asking any of the following questions?

- How do I get a job in _____?
- How do I write a resume?
- What jobs call for my skills?
- Who's hiring?

These are actually not the right first questions to ask because they are too focused on the occupation without any consideration of the best fit for you, the person. There are better ways to initiate and conduct strong career ReSearch. One way to start is with rethinking the questions you ask.

Ask these questions, instead:

- What do I enjoy doing?
- What things am I really good at doing?
- What are various careers **really** like?
- What careers and jobs are a good match to my skills and interests?

Your goal should be not just to find a career, but to find a career that will result in maximum success. Success can be measured by work–life balance, overall well-being, and longevity and growth in a position. It is easy to forget to put our views of the workplace and job search into context. As scientists and STEM professionals we have been in a unique environment for the majority of our training. This environment most often does not lend itself to exposing individuals to the multitude of career paths available to them.

> *Comment from Teresa: As a scientist myself, I remember vividly the feeling that I had when I realized that the laboratory was not going to be my long term career home. I was scared. I was afraid that I might find myself in a career where my PhD would not be "used". Further, I knew that I would not be traversing an established career path but rather I would be creating my own. This last point is key. Once you embrace the fact that gaining your degree gives you the option to create your own career path you can either be horrified or empowered. I encourage you to be empowered. So you need to find what it is that empowers you, what lights the fire in your being, and pursue it with a vengeance.*

Finding all of that empowerment is easier said than done, we know. So if you don't even know where to start answering these questions, look at the self-assessments discussed in Chapter 8, and the information on transferable skills in Chapter 10. These will give you the scaffold that you need to guide your career search.

Activity: Get a notebook and use it to document your responses to the questions below. Pick and choose the questions that fit your search and be sure to think them through and research them thoroughly. Take this notebook or electronic document file with you to meetings with your career mentor.

THINGS TO CONSIDER BEFORE YOU BEGIN

Use the following questions to help begin to assess what is next for your career. You may not have the answers to all of these, but it is important to have them in the back of your mind from the start:

- Do you need a job NOW or do you have time to look (If you answered NOW, See Chapter 18)
- Are you focused on academic, nonacademic career options, or both?
- Is a different profession even an option for you?
- If you are a non-US Citizen, how will your visa status impact your career search? (See Chapter 17)
- Does anyone else have a stake in your career decision-making, such as family?

When considering what careers align with your goals:

- Do your technical skills and areas of interest match the demands of the positions that you are pursuing?
- Do you need to strengthen specific skills? If so, where might you find the training that you need?
- What are your expectations of the companies that you are pursuing? Do these align with reality? (This can be determined with informational interviews, for example.)
- What compensation would align with your expectations?
- Are there opportunities for advancement and promotion? Is this a priority to you?

Defining your target market:

- What industry do you prefer?
- What geographical area(s) are you interested in?
- What size organization is a right fit for you?
- Are there sufficient jobs in the target market?

Finding your workplace cultural fit:

- What type of company structure do you find comfortable? One that is clearly defined or more relaxed?
- What atmosphere allows you to work best and where are you most productive?
- Do you like working with clearly laid out expectations or prefer setting your own?
- Are your interests and values compatible with the type of work environment you are pursuing?
- Do your philosophies and life values align with occupational or company core values and principles?
- What are the business strategies of your target companies? (i.e., product dominance, market share, or R&D focus)

- Is it a financially sound company? What is the compensation like?
- What management style supports your work style? (i.e., lead vs. manage)
- How do companies communicate with their employees and provide feedback?
- Will you have a voice in your growth plan? Will your opinions be heard?

HOW TO BE WHAT EMPLOYERS ARE LOOKING FOR

After you have taken time to identify potential career paths, it is good to also think about what employers in those fields are looking for in exceptional candidates. According to the National Association of Colleges and Employers (NACE) Job Outlook 2016 survey,[1] which included a total of 201 NACE employer members, employers want leaders and team players.

Leadership and teamwork were the top traits desired in new employees, as over 80% of employers who responded to the NACE survey stated that leadership skills must be clear on the candidate's resume, and almost as many employers stated that they also look for indications of a candidate's ability to work in a team.

This same survey, as well as many other employer resources, indicates that communication skills are key! Specifically mentioned in the NACE survey were written communication skills, problem-solving skills, verbal communication skills, and a strong work ethic. You will see in the below table that the attributes employers seek are not all what might be expected (Table 15.1). Specifically, attributes such as creativity are often overlooked by applicants, and as scientists we should remember that creativity is what got many of us into this field in the first place. The pursuit of something unknown requires a keen sense of creativity. Initiative is another skill sought by employers that most scientists possess in some measure. Working independently, running experiments, and finding solutions to problems all demonstrate self-motivation.

For scientists, showing that you have these skills on your CV and resume can be accomplished in multiple ways (see Chapter 16). For example, communication skills are evident not just from your manuscripts but also can be shown via your ability to communicate science to the lay public at science outreach events and through blogs, or finding creative funding sources, as just two examples. As a trained scientist, you are a trained problem solver. After all, science is solving problems. So to make this clear in your resume, you can write things such as: "worked in a team to solve problems associated with experimental design and data analytics."

ASSESSING YOUR FIT

You can find a job, or you can find a career. "Career fit" describes how compatible your skills and personality are to the work you do. To determine your fit for a particular career path and how to package yourself when applying, you must first clearly understand your skills, interests, personal characteristics, and values. This was discussed in great detail in Chapter 8. But when applying

TABLE 15.1 Attributes Employers Seek on a Candidate's Resume

Attribute	Percentage of Respondents (%)
Leadership	80.1
Ability to work in a team	78.9
Communication skills (written)	70.2
Problem-solving skills	70.2
Communication skills (verbal)	68.9
Strong work ethic	68.9
Initiative	65.8
Analytical/quantitative skills	62.7
Flexibility/adaptability	60.9
Technical skills	59.6
Interpersonal skills (relates well to others)	58.4
Computer skills	55.3
Detail-oriented	52.8
Organizational ability	48.4
Friendly/outgoing personality	35.4
Strategic planning skills	26.7
Creativity	23.6
Tactfulness	20.5
Entrepreneurial skills/risk-taker	18.6

Job Outlook 2016. National Association of Colleges and Employers. http://www.naceweb.org/s11182015/employers-look-for-in-new-hires.aspx#sthash.c9HLuCbM.dpuf.

that information you have learned about yourself to your job search, you need to be mindful that the skills you might have do not necessarily mean that you have experience—or enough experience for the role to which you are applying. When you state that you have a skill, this describes how able you are to complete a task rather than describing experience, which is attached to a specific job. For example, the skill of "managing" along with experience of **using** that managing skill is indicated via titles such as Director or Supervisor.

Further, you can think of skills as portable from one career to another, but experience as a director at a cancer institute might not be portable to a career as a start-up CEO. Diving into your skills further, as is outlined in Chapter 8, will help you to more completely assess where your strengths and weaknesses lie.

Your goal is to identify the skills that align with the career that you are seeking, and to determine if these skills are strengths or weaknesses for you. It is important to think about the experience you can show with all of these skills as well.

Once it is clear what skills you have, you must also think about what interests you. If you have strong writing skills, but hate to write (or even just find it difficult and time-consuming to produce good writing) then a career in science journalism might not be your best choice. So, ponder instead on what subject areas fascinate you. Or consider what you would do if you won the lottery. What would you do if you knew you would not fail?

These are all questions and ideas that can help you to dive deeper into finding the career paths that truly interest you. Pull out that pen and notebook again and take some time to think these through. Further, you should have already determined the personal characteristics or traits that make you unique and enhance your ability to perform tasks successfully in Chapter 8, but as a reminder, think about how you might describe yourself and how others would describe you to help you get started.

Finally, the best way to ensure you are on the right track in your career search is to clearly know your values. Knowing your values will help you to stay on track in your career journey throughout your lifetime. Values will change, so be mindful to revisit them regularly. As described in Chapter 8, personal values underlie all that you do in your life—but they can often be the sources of conflict in and out of work. So be aware of your values and work to ensure alignment with your career choice.

Even though Chapter 8 focuses on identifying your skills and strengths, we are emphasizing self-awareness because it is so important and fundamental to the Career Search Strategy we are about to propose: what are your top three skills, interests, personal traits, and values? Once you know these things about yourself, the way that you look at the professional world will be very different. So as you begin to narrow your career search, focus on how that search aligns with your self-assessment.

MAKING A PLAN

Begin making your career plan by establishing professional objectives for yourself. One way to do this is with SMART goals described in detail in Chapter 13. Ensuring that your career search includes goals that are Specific, Measureable, Achievable, Realistic, and Timely will be key to your success. Here is an example:

S: I need a job within six months, preferably as a project manager
M: I will attend a conference and call/email three of my contacts
A: I will tailor my resume and CV and send out at least one job application per week
R: This also stands for ReSearch! Where do my skills fit within the marketplace?
T: By the end of the year I will have...

SAMPLE JOB SEARCH PLAN

Step 1 Assess Your Circumstances

Understand the reason(s) you are looking for a job or exploring careers.

- What is happening in your life? What is the catalyst for action?
- What are you feeling? Is this search motivated by stress or excitement?
- If you are considering a career change, develop the mental strength to make the move you want. It's important to do this **before** you get started.
- Do you have the bandwidth for a comprehensive career search? How much time can you devote to the process, and what is your time frame for searching and applications?

Step 2 Begin Your Search

Begin your search both quantitatively and qualitatively, meaning you will analyze the options that are available, but also determine where you fit best. You can make spreadsheets and grids to analyze types of positions available in different industries, but it can be just as important to get a feeling about how you will thrive (or not) in a certain kind of job. There are also important considerations around who is hiring and how often positions open up in your career path of choice. As we described at length above and in Chapter 8, you must determine how your skills and competencies fit within the marketplace, and, as Chapter 3 advises, you must understand the marketplace before you arrive there.

Here are some steps to get you started with the search:

- Whether you are a superorganized person or not, find some way to capture all the job search information you are going to gather. This might be electronic, in the form of a Word document or Excel spreadsheet, or it might be hard copy information, kept in a special binder or notebook or folder. Whatever works for you, create a system of some kind to keep track of everything you are going to learn and do.
- Create a contact list (information gathering) about who you know and where they are working.
    - Start with your lab and lab alumni. Then consider your program, your department, your wider academic field, peers at other institutions, friends who are not in science, friends of friends, family, friends' families…you get the idea.
- Join interest groups, professional associations, and sign up for listservs.
- Research jobs of interest and fit. Remember to always tailor your materials to link your skills to their needs (more on this in Chapter 16).
- Peruse postings: start looking at advertised jobs well before you are ready to start applying. This way, you will get a sense of the tasks and duties required in a job role, but more importantly, you will see what skills and experience are expected.

- Find your filters: what this means is to figure out the things that are most important to you in a job. It might be salary, or geographic location, or title. It might be the work environment, the opportunity of working in a team or independently, or any number of other factors. Career choices are going to be different for everyone, so the sooner you can recognize what filters are most important to you, the faster you will be able to figure out what job postings are perfect for you.
- Decode descriptions: once you start looking at job postings regularly, you will begin to notice similarities and differences, and how a job with the same title might have a widely varying salary between two organizations. You will also be able to figure out the "code" of job ads: many will list "required" or "essential" experience and skills, along with "desired" or "preferred." Many employers use job descriptions as a kind of "wish list," but the employer may not be expecting every single candidate to have 100% of the desired qualifications.

  - Notice numbers—what percentage of time is described for various job duties/responsibilities? For example, if you are applying for a medical writing job, is the first job duty listed in the posting related to writing, or does it mention research?
  - Scope out similarities—what things are the same (or different) between jobs in the same industry or even the same company? A title such as "Senior Scientist 1" is fairly meaningless when just listed by itself, but looking at job descriptions can help you understand better just what a Senior Scientist 1 does all day!
  - Question qualifications—As mentioned above, most job ads list firm requirements for the position. But don't feel you must meet 100% of those requirements to apply. Take a few chances, especially if you are very excited about the job description. Use your judgment, and don't apply for something that requires 15 years of experience if you only have 2.

- Create job alerts that match your targets (for example, using HigherEd Jobs or other aggregating websites). You can create multiple alerts that focus on job categories, or geographic regions, to give just two examples. You will receive daily or weekly emails alerting you to openings—let the technology do the work for you.

It is very helpful to use general resources to begin exploring types of science jobs. Many of the resources listed below have "career path" or "career resource" sections that give overviews and information to get your career search started:

- Biocareers
- Versatile PhD
- AAAS—Science Careers
- Professional associations (such as the American Society of Cell Biology or Society for Neuroscience)
- LinkedIn or institutional alumni databases

When using any database or website with alumni profiles, investigate in what jobs/companies/industries people with your education are currently working, as well as review their past positions and career history. Searching institutional alumni on LinkedIn is a powerful research tool. Looking at what interest groups alumni or people of interest belong to on LinkedIn may also lead to further clues about career paths.

Don't forget Google—sometimes just using a search engine and typing in, for example, "careers for PhDs epidemiology" might yield some useful results.

My IDP—this tool, discussed in Chapter 8, can give you ideas about career paths to further explore that match your science skills and interests.

Step 3 Network

As Chapter 12 says, 70%–90% of jobs are found informally; therefore the art of building a network can open you up to the hidden job market. This is especially true for PhDs! Many of the case studies that you have read throughout this book point to the value of networks for finding out about careers (and finding jobs!) and we are sure that as you do your own informational interviews, you too will find this to be true. So go forth and set up your own informational chats. Each contact that you cultivate will lead to more contacts. So the more people you talk to, the more complete your picture of a career will be. Chapter 12 has plenty of advice on how to set up and undertake informational interviews.

Step 4 Submission and Preparation

As you begin to submit your application materials for potential career opportunities, the advice in Chapter 16 will be of use. When you are actually submitting applications (or are about to do so), be sure to touch base with previous contacts and/or review previous resources that this book and others have provided. Do not neglect to maintain a good tracking system for your job search activities. You will be sending different documents to each career option as well as speaking with different contacts at each. This can become confusing fast, and the worst thing that could happen is that you send the wrong documents or be mistaken about what you sent. Avoid careless mistakes and stay organized!

Once your documents are out of your inbox and into the marketplace, you need to begin practicing your interviewing skills. Do not wait to do this until it is too late! There are some great tips in the next chapter to get you started.

Step 5 Be Realistic

The unfortunate reality is that you might not find a job quickly and the job you find might not be what you had expected. Therefore, you must consider your alternatives if you can't find the perfect fit as quickly as you thought you would. You might want to investigate options such as contract work or temporary positions. As a scientist, many contract positions exist and we encourage you to investigate them. Remember, the career search is like a "chess game." You might have to make quite a few moves to get where you want to go! And it might feel sometimes like you are going backwards or not moving forward quickly enough, but have patience.

Far more often than not, individuals underestimate how long the job search will take. Being intentional with your plan and actively working on the goals you set will shorten the duration. So stay positive, be patient, and rely on your mentors and network for support!

WORKING WITH RECRUITERS

It's great to imagine a recruiter (or "headhunter") working diligently to find that perfect job for you while you focus on other things—such as research, writing, fieldwork, and teaching. However, the reality is that a lot of effort is required on the part of a job seeker to connect with recruiters, and most recruiters are very specialized in the types of candidates they seek and the level of position they are filling as well as lack the understanding of the specialized fields they seek candidates for. Graduate students and postdocs are not typical candidates for recruiters, but that doesn't mean recruiters should be ruled out entirely. Third-party recruiters (also known as headhunters, search firms, executive search, or just plain recruiters) can be an additional career-searching resource for those elusive PhD-relevant jobs. Think of recruiters as an added bonus to complement all the "traditional" ways you are looking for opportunities, not "magic bullets" for the job search. Knowing the different types of recruiters, how they operate, and why they might be interested in you as a candidate will make it easier to leverage the power of recruiters and recruitment firms.

Recruitment firms and the recruiters who work there come in three varieties: retained, contingency, or contract. Recruiters working on a retained basis charge retainers (up-front fees) to their clients and then conduct searches on behalf of that client. They tend to be very involved and knowledgeable about the positions they are recruiting for (and these also will usually be high-level positions), perhaps with an exclusive relationship with the client organization. Contingency recruiters don't get paid until they present a client with a top candidate who is hired. There is intense competition among contingency recruiters—they are competing with other recruiters and also with internal HR staff or other in-house personnel who are trying to fill the role too—sometimes even working with the same candidates. Contract recruiters are outside firms or individuals who are hired by a client to source, screen, and communicate with candidates. As a novice job seeker applying to an organization, you may not even be aware that the individual conducting your initial phone screen or scheduling your interviews isn't a full employee of the company. Contract recruiters may know an industry well, but may not have full and complete knowledge of individual companies or organizations.

So make sure you understand the differences among types of recruiters. Ask any recruiter you interact with to explain what type of search they are doing and what kind of recruiter they are, especially in regard to how the recruiter is making his or her money on your candidacy. Recruiters usually make 20%–30% (or more) of the salary of the candidates they place, which comes into play when recruiters choose whether or not to spend time with less-experienced candidates such as recent PhDs and postdocs. And no matter the type of recruiter, please do not ever forget their primary motivation is to place candidates, they are usually working on multiple searches, and you should not take their lack of communication with you personally.

Do any of these types of recruiters even want to work with you? Maybe. First of all, recruiters are almost always specialized—whether it is within an industry or for a certain type of candidate (i.e., MD/PhDs) or geographic area. Secondly, while recruiters make their best money placing senior staff and experienced hires, they do occasionally have positions that are suitable for individuals with limited work experience (who might possess subject matter expertise). Unsolicited interest from recruiters is more likely for STEM PhDs than those in Humanities or Social Science, but not impossible.

Recruiters can easily locate PhDs through cultivated relationships with faculty members, as well as alumni networks, professional societies, and online interest groups (LinkedIn and Indeed are the most common). They may also ask university career offices for referrals. Like the majority of job opportunities, "who you know" matters. Finally, remember that recruiters spend about 6 s reviewing your CV, and for recruiters time literally is money.

A comprehensive and polished online presence is key to helping recruiters find you. If your LinkedIn headline says "Postdoctoral Researcher," it's not going to catch the attention of a recruiter looking for immunologists or cancer biologists, and if your online profile summary section doesn't detail specifics on what you have to offer, that recruiter is not going to take the time to meander through your profile looking to make the connections between you and the open position. The CV or resume you send to a recruiter should be equally specific and detailed. Like all your other job-searching efforts, do your homework and tailor application materials for recruiters.

Hopefully recruiters will find **you** via LinkedIn, professional societies, or through peer/colleague referrals. But don't sit around waiting for this to happen (and when it does happen, don't get overly excited because you definitely are not the only candidate being contacted by that recruiter). You will want to do your own research and reach out to recruiters who focus on the industry area you are interested in. You will also want to find an individual you trust at a firm, so that you can establish communication with one person. Then there's the waiting game. The odds are that even if you find a suitable recruiting firm and a great recruiter who "gets" you, the timing of PhD-relevant job openings is sporadic and unpredictable. Be sure to tell the recruiters what they need to know about you: are you location-specific? (i.e., looking to a certain geographic region), or field-specific? (i.e., focused on a definite industry or use of your research expertise). Recruiters will work in a niche area, so seek as close a match as you can find between what you are looking for and what the recruiter is expert in.

Keep track of the recruiters you contact—and don't send your CV to every single recruiter you can find because your overzealousness may backfire (remember recruiters are in competition with each other!). Do update your materials (CV/resume) with the recruiter or firm, and make it your responsibility to stay in touch with your recruiter via follow-up phone calls or emails. When there is a position for which you are a perfect fit, your recruiter will work night and day to get you into that job. There will also be times when a recruiter simply stops responding to you—this is part of the process, don't take it personally, and just like other types of networking, send a thank-you and move on.

Working with recruiters is fairly straightforward, but it definitely requires effort on the part of the applicant—and an understanding of how it all works. Many science PhDs expect there to be a single database overflowing with names and email addresses of recruiters just waiting for awesome grad students to log in and get speedily placed into high-paying industry jobs. Not so—at least not until you've been in the workforce for about 10 years. But once you find a few promising recruitment firms, you will be on the right track. There actually **are** databases of recruiters—but they are listings of firms and their specializations, so as researchers you will find it easy to determine which firms might have postings in your desired industry, and from there you must do the legwork of reaching out and connecting with relevant firms/recruiters. Recruiters have strong presence on social media, particularly LinkedIn and Twitter, so join interest groups, connect with/follow individuals who work as recruiters, and keep an eye out for posts and Tweets about open positions.

Some resources for finding a PhD-suitable recruiter:

The Riley Guide
Oya's Directory of Recruiters
Recruiter.com
Even the "Google-and-pray method" can work, for example, online searching for "media search firm" or "immunology search firm."

For life sciences–focused candidates:

Kelly Scientific
Lab Support
Yoh Scientific
Lab Pros
BioSpace
TheLabRat

For STEM-focused candidates:

K Force (science, healthcare, accounting, finance)
PhDSearchandSelection (UK-based, IT/finance)

Nathan: "Dream Big, Start Small(er)"—some firsthand career search advice.

When I was in graduate school, I wanted desperately to graduate and get a job out in the "real world." So, near the end of grad school, I applied to dozens of jobs in many different areas ranging from project management to science writing and policy. In applying for these jobs, I naively thought that anyone would jump at the chance to hire a PhD. What I know now is that I made several mistakes as I applied for these jobs including not being realistic about the types and level of positions that I could transition into immediately after graduate school; many of the jobs I applied to were more senior level positions and I thought that my PhD would magically overcome the amount of experience the hiring managers were looking for. I didn't realize that to be most competitive, I needed to start in lower level positions and work my way up. So, I transitioned into a postdoc position and then eventually took a job as a science writer/editor. Interestingly, this job actually paid me less than what I was making as a postdoc! I was fine with that though because I came to the realization that I just had to get my feet out of research and into a new career path that could reset my career trajectory.

WRAPPING-UP YOUR CAREER SEARCH

In summary, the career search process is reiterative and ongoing throughout your career. The first time you explore career options builds a foundation for all future career changes and transitions. Definitely take time to plan for an initial comprehensive search, so you can be sure to head in the right direction and find the right types of jobs that truly fit your expertise **and** your desires.

Remember to reach out to your network and mentors as you progress toward your goal for advice and guidance, and keep in mind that your goals may change along the way. If your career search takes some unexpected twists and turns, Chapters 5 and 6 give advice on staying healthy and positive during your job search, including dealing with setbacks and disappointments. Remember, creating a career search strategy gives you the ability to move your career in the direction that **you** choose!

If you put in the effort to truly understand yourself and where you are going in your career search, you will be ready to start the job application journey, and you will find it much easier than if you did not do all the planning we recommend in this chapter. Next step—taking action on applications. Chapter 16 provides advice on how to create application materials and tailor them to fit any opportunity.

REFERENCES

1. Job Outlook 2016. National Association of Colleges and Employers. http://www.naceweb.org/s11182015/employers-look-for-in-new-hires.aspx#sthash.c9HLuCbM.dpuf.

FURTHER READING

1. Smith J. Here's what recruiters look at in the six seconds they spend on your resume. *Business Insider* 2014. http://www.businessinsider.com/what-recruiters-look-at-on-your-resume-2014-11.
2. Lundsteen N. Third party recruiters and PhD candidates. *Inside HigherEd* 2015. https://www.insidehighered.com/advice/2015/09/14/advice-new-phds-using-third-party-recruiters-find-jobs.

Chapter 16

Creating Application Materials, Applying, and Interviewing for Jobs

Natalie Lundsteen, Sharon Kuss

Chapter Outline

Consider the Importance of Timing in Your Applications	196	
Take a Deep Breath Before You Get Started	196	
Preparing and Tailoring Application Materials	198	
Targeting Materials for Each Job Application	200	
Following Application Directions (Dos and Don'ts)	201	
Interviews	203	
Stages of a Typical Interview Process	204	
Types of Interviews	204	
Preparing for Interviews	204	
How to Answer Interview Questions	205	
Structuring Your Interview Answers	206	
Interview Practice	207	
During the Interview	208	
After Your Interview	209	
Getting an Offer	210	
Considerations for Academic Interviews	211	
Postdoc Interviews	211	
Faculty Interviews	212	
Final Words of Application Wisdom	213	
Further Resources for Job Interview and Preparation	214	
References	214	
Further Reading	214	

Chapter Takeaways:

- Different types of application materials are needed for different kinds of jobs (this includes CVs, resumes, and cover letters)
- It is crucial to take your time and follow directions when putting together application materials
- Tailor your application materials—change things up and make sure to target your application every single time you apply for a position
- Be prepared for timing aspects in your applications: certain industries hire on an annual cycle, while other types of jobs are more immediately available
- It is never too early to start preparing and practicing for interviews

ReSearch. http://dx.doi.org/10.1016/B978-0-12-804297-7.00016-1

We hope you have already used advice from previous chapters to reach the point where you know **exactly** (or close to) what type of job you are looking for, and where. Having some career goals already in mind will allow you to create and update excellent targeted application materials that fit the job role in which you are applying. Even if you are not actively job searching, you should begin organizing your job applications as far in advance as you can. It takes time to create a comprehensive CV, write a strong cover letter, turn a CV into a resume, or tailor a resume with keywords and phrases to truly fit a job description. If you have basic job application documents already crafted, it won't be as onerous a task to target and tailor these for specific job roles when you are ready.

CONSIDER THE IMPORTANCE OF TIMING IN YOUR APPLICATIONS

Before starting any type of job application, take a step back and think about when you might actually send those application documents. It is extremely important to understand the issues of timing that surround a PhD job search. You may already be aware that the academic job market runs on an annual cycle, with occasional off-cycle exceptions to the rule. Hiring of PhD scientists outside of academia happens in multiple industries year-round, but it is a rare organization that hires more than a handful of PhDs at one time, and the timing of openings for these PhD jobs may not match up to your project completion or graduation dates. Some companies and organizations only hire one or two PhD scientists per year. Keep in mind that you will have to do a significant amount of research to even find PhD job openings, as many of the giant job-listing sites aggregate postings from multiple sources—so not all jobs you see posted are actually still viable and may be outdated by the time you view those postings on a big online job board. Likely PhD jobs are elusive, often filled by internal candidates or referrals, and, in industry at least, usually are filled in the blink of an eye (meaning, the organization posts a job and wants the position filled as quickly as possible). So, the more knowledgeable you are about the kinds of employers and types of roles you want to pursue, the easier it will be to manage aspects of timing in your job search to find the right job at the right place and right time. Also, remember to include time for the career search process as part of your 5-year plan, which is discussed further in Chapters 4 and 13.

TAKE A DEEP BREATH BEFORE YOU GET STARTED

Many scientists want to leap immediately into action by applying for jobs—rapidly finding job listings and sending off scores of resumes, without taking the time to craft appropriate materials. But just as we advised you in Chapter 15 to take time to assess your own skills and strengths before launching a job search, it is also important to understand the necessity of creating specific materials for each application. Putting together a perfect application is going to take extra time—but it will be worth it.

PhD scientists are great at juggling multiple responsibilities and commitments, but the added stress of new tasks and unknown variables in putting together job applications can seem overwhelming. The advice on balancing and managing your time in Chapter 13 may assist in providing structure to your search, especially if applying for jobs is added on to an already packed schedule of research, writing, and life responsibilities. You may also wish to go back and reread Chapter 6 on staying positive in the job search during the time you are actually engaged in applying for jobs.

As you approach your job applications, try to think of the experience just like you would when planning any big, long-term project. You may need a literal timeline or project plan with milestones and goals, or you could be more general, but you do need to put some thought into the activity. Knowing what you are getting into before you begin will make life easier, and if you create even a broad plan for your job search and creating your application materials, the experience will be a lot easier than if you just jump in blindly sending resumes all over the place. So take a deep breath, and consider the following aspects of the application process.

First of all, how much time do you think it will take you to find a job? The answer to that question depends on many factors: your personality (are you a long-term planner or more flexible?) and the kind of position you are seeking, as well as the industry or organization type you are targeting. There is an "urban myth" (i.e., an unsubstantiated piece of information) advising job seekers to plan a month of job search for every $10,000 of salary you seek, thus a $90,000–annual-salary position would take 9 months to find. This idea has yet to be empirically proven, but it makes sense when considering the time and effort to find types of jobs appropriate for your education and expertise. The average time an American spends unemployed is 9 months, according to the Bureau of Labor Statistics (this includes all levels of education, including PhDs). If you are focused on a particular industry, company, or geographic location, your opportunities may be even more difficult to identify, and thus your time to find a job might take even longer than expected.

Once you understand that it takes time to find any job, you can add more job-seeking time for a PhD or master's level job because graduate education level jobs are more specialized. Jobs at an appropriate level for you are not going to be as widely advertised as jobs requiring less expertise and education, so it will take more time to identify them; then, once you find them, it is likely the job will not be available exactly where you want and/or when you want. Adjust your expectations and prepare for a marathon instead of a sprint.

For the overall timing of your job search, a timeline of 18 months is ideal (as discussed in Chapter 15), giving you the luxury of time to explore options, understand what titles and job responsibilities are, talk to people in those jobs, see how your own strengths and priorities match up to those roles, and then prepare or refine your application materials. But that is often not PhD reality. Attempting to research careers and submit applications while finishing up experiments, a thesis, or a project with vague completion dates could cause you to feel like ignoring the search process entirely. We encourage job-seeking grad students and postdocs to create "lunchtime lists" of websites to peruse or small tasks to accomplish in 5–15 min, such as updating one section on a resume or CV, which can allay the sense that there is so much to do in the job search process and so little time. You're trained as a researcher—so you know that garnering more knowledge gives you more options, which leads to more potential opportunities.

Also consider the timing of different hiring cultures and practices. Academic hiring cycles tend to launch in late summer (August or September) and take about 9 months before hires occur. Even so, be aware that certain disciplines hire only at annual meetings or will list positions in particular publications or Listservs. Don't ever assume "it's a slow time" or "I'm off cycle" because even the most well-established hiring schedules have an occasional blip. Keep an eye out well before you are actually job seeking to get a sense of the timing in your field of interest, and become aware of any unusual patterns in the timing of postings (see where that ideal 18 months for a job search really comes in handy?). The timing of hiring in nonacademic roles will of course be dependent on the industry or organization, but job posting and hiring for most jobs beyond academia is usually immediate. And some PhD jobs (such as policy fellowships or consulting positions) literally are only available once a year. This is a constant dilemma for the PhD job seeker.

PREPARING AND TAILORING APPLICATION MATERIALS

Once you have considered the timing aspects of your job-searching journey, the next step is to ensure that you have the right materials for your applications. Depending on the type of job and employer, you will need a variety of materials that will represent you. You may already have some of these materials (such as a CV) but need to create or revise other types of application materials. The basic application material documents you need are as follows:

- The **CV** (or curriculum vitae, Latin for "course of life") is a document presenting your qualifications and experience. In the United States, the information on a CV represents academic backgrounds and experience, but in other parts of the world the CV is a document describing any education and experience.
  - CV samples can be found in the appendix.
- The **resume** is a summary of your accomplishments—your work history and educational background. Basics of the resume will be your contact information, your education, and your experience. This document cannot be as detailed as a CV because of length. You must keep the resume to one or two pages. You may hear differing recommendations about whether resumes should be one or two pages. PhD scientists definitely have leeway to create and use a two-page resume because of their extensive education and research experience, but there are certain industries, for example, consulting or patent

law, which absolutely require a single-page resume. Formatting your resume in reverse chronological order, with most recent experiences listed first, is the generally favored format because it is easy for a reader (employer) to see your history at a glance. You may consider using a functional or skills-based format for your resume, but this really only works if you have extensive experience and background in a number of skill areas (and if those areas are relevant to the jobs you are applying for).

- Resume samples can be found in the appendix.
- **"Hybrid" CV/resume**—This document is a unique combination of some (not all) of the information generally found on a CV, but organized in a shorter format with focus on results. There is no formal word for this kind of document—our trainees have sometimes referred to this as a "CV-ume" or "Resu-V"—but a hybrid will be most common when applying to an organization that values your graduate research, such as a biopharma business or Medical Science Liaison (MSL) role. Fine details of all your academic background may not be necessary, but you will want to provide more information than the format of a resume allows, for example, listing publications—which you would not do on a resume—but perhaps limiting the extensive listing of awards, grants, and fellowships that appear on your CV.
- **Other documents and supplementary materials**—These will vary depending on the role being applied to but include teaching and research statements for academic applications, diversity statements, and writing samples.
- **Cover letters**—The primary purpose of a cover letter is to allow you to introduce yourself to the reader. A cover letter gives you the opportunity to highlight how your education and experience are a perfect fit for the role or to explain what cannot be seen on your resume or CV—this could include your motivation for the position. Do not be intimidated by the cover letter! It does not have to be long (three paragraphs are acceptable), and cover letters are really just a formula. However, there is room for creativity and a chance to showcase your communication skills. Here's how simple the cover letter formula is, and how it can literally be just three paragraphs long:

$$\text{Introduction} + \text{Selling} + \text{Closing} = \text{Cover Letter}$$

Introduction: The opening paragraph of the letter tells who you are, what you want, and how you heard about the job.

Selling: The middle paragraph (or two) shows what you have to offer that particular role and organization, and why you are motivated for the job.

Closing: The final paragraph is your conclusion, usually wrapping up by saying how excited you are about this opportunity and look forward to an interview.

The more cover letters you write, the easier it will become over time to craft information within that simple cover letter formula. Just as in your resume or CV, use the job description to identify the things a hiring manager is most likely going to be excited to see that you have to offer, and talk about those things in the middle section of your letter. It helps sometimes to write the letter informally, as you might write an email to a friend, to help yourself see what motivates you about the job and how you are a good fit. Then, go back over the document and "professionalize" your writing to bring it to the appropriate tone for a job application.

If a cover letter is truly difficult for you to write, take an objective step back and think about why that may be. If you can't find a reason to describe why you want the job, or cannot come up with a point or two about your skills and experience that make you perfect for the job, you may not have a chance at the role—so do not waste your time. Find something else to apply to that you **are** excited about.

- Samples of cover letters can be found in the appendix.

Most applications ask candidates to "send a CV and cover letter" or "send a resume and cover letter." The cover letter offers you a chance to explain your motivation, highlight how you are suited for the role being applied for, and create a strong first impression. If the job application instructions reference a cover letter, then you absolutely must send one. If the instructions don't mention a cover letter, send one anyway. Basic rule: always send a cover letter with your resume or CV, unless there are explicit application instructions to **not** include one. ALWAYS FOLLOW THE GUIDELINES! The biggest mistake many applicants make is not doing what the employer asks.

TARGETING MATERIALS FOR EACH JOB APPLICATION

One key point about any type of application material is that you will need to adapt and change your materials, offering different versions of your documents depending on where you are applying. We really cannot stress this enough—the same CV or resume does **not** work for every application. You can create a "master" CV, which contains all the information about yourself you could possibly come up with, but it is a rare hiring manager who wants to sift through that document, lines and lines, page after page, to identify exactly why you are a good fit for the position.

Karen Kelsky, author of *The Professor is In*, sums this up succinctly: "Stressed-out search-committee members are not interested in extracting nuggets of brilliance nestled amidst thickets of verbiage."[1] She is describing an academic search in which a human actually looks at most CVs. Nonacademic applications are often scanned by a computer program. When a human does the scanning of applications, the average time spent looking at one candidate's resume can be less than 10 s. In that short time, a potential hiring manger will look at your name, current title and company, current position start and end dates, previous title and company, previous position start and end dates, and education.[2] So your best bet is to tailor your documents and make it easy for the reader to see why you are perfect for the role. Show hiring managers you are **exactly** the person they are looking for.

You will need various versions of your materials, adapting that master document to specific jobs. For example, a consulting resume, a resume targeting MSL roles, an industry R&D hybrid CV/resume, and a CV featuring your grant-writing and communication—you get the idea. Depending on where your career is headed, you can compile information most relevant to that industry, organization, or job role and use that information to tailor your documents. Job descriptions are the best source of ideas for how to tailor your CV or resume, but you can also find articles online (the Naturejobs website often features interviews with scientists in unique careers), or look at LinkedIn profiles of people currently working in that kind of role, focusing on their listed job responsibilities.

FOLLOWING APPLICATION DIRECTIONS (DOS AND DON'TS)

No matter the industry or occupation, if there is an application process, and if there are instructions for your application, you **must** read all the requirements and directions completely through.[3] Even if you are so excited about the opportunity you can't sit still—read the instructions first, before you do anything. Then read them again. And again. Don't take any action until you have read what is required. Take your time. Be thoughtful. Follow directions.

Following directions may seem like the most obvious advice in the world, but scientists are curious creatures and many do not have much experience in the world of applications beyond the bench. You might think it's an easy task to apply for a position because you know how to fill out forms, you've applied for loads of fellowships, how hard can it be? Or sending a simple CV and cover letter in an email—no problem, you've sent hundreds, so you think "I'll just quickly send my application from my phone!" Or perhaps you might think that you know a **better** way to apply or would like to provide information about yourself beyond the formal requirements. No. No, you do not know better.

One evident reason to take your time, read instructions, and follow directions is to ensure that your application is even seen. Make it easy for anyone who might be reviewing or reading your material to see how perfect you are for the position. Do not let application reviewers get distracted from (or worse, become irritated or annoyed by) the process of glancing through materials as they are quickly sorting candidates into "yes" or "no" categories. Why give people an opportunity to put your CV or resume on the "no" pile? Why be the application that makes a reader grimace and lose his or her train of thought?

Hiring managers and recruiters will freely admit that with huge numbers of applicants, it is not difficult to be ruthless during the initial applicant review. They are looking to discard as many candidates as possible to be able to get to a manageable number of "good" applicants. The reasons for a candidate being put into the "no" pile include the following:

- does not have (or did not list) the required experience
- did not list a salary requirement
- did not attach all requested documents
- did not attach **any** documents
- sent a CV instead of the requested resume
- sent a resume and did not fill out the (tedious resume-replicating) online form
- documents contained grammatical or formatting errors
- DID NOT FOLLOW DIRECTIONS (remember, read the directions)

It will of course depend on the job and the organization and the specific processes required to apply, but your application is in a ruthless competition, and whoever is hiring is looking for a way to whittle down the number of competitors. If you can't follow the (usually basic) instructions listed on a job listing, application website, or even a request in an email from a contact, it is assumed that you don't pay attention to detail, and thus are not worth the time to meet.

Don't second-guess, and don't be arrogant when it comes to sending materials or completing an application. Candidates often think it is a good idea to show enthusiasm and send extra materials (extra references, extra writing samples, writing samples in excess of what is required), but it is not. Sticking to what is directed in terms of "extra" is usually a hard and fast rule, although exceptions to it can depend on the situation and the job or industry. However, do not waste time pondering what else those receiving your application materials might want to see—and please do not assume you are smarter than the HR system (or the hiring manager, or the search-committee chair). If a horrific online system asks you to basically retype your entire CV or resume, DO IT, do not say "see attached resume." Should you also send a cover letter when the job ad says send a resume? Yes, probably—that one cannot hurt.

Do include details as required. If you are asked to provide evidence of a skill, do so. For example, if the job description requires undergraduate teaching experience, make sure the word "undergraduate" is on your CV, **and** the online application form (if there is one), **and** in your cover letter, and beyond that, provide detail of the student population you taught: majors, nonmajors, did you develop the syllabus, create and deliver lectures, serve as a TA, train other TAs, get student evaluations? Follow the directions and provide that evidence. Great examples of how to create a CV or resume can be found on the National Institutes of Health Office of Intramural Training and Education website, in the Professional Development Resources section.[3]

Don't leave a required field blank in an application form (especially for an online application system). Yes, the salary requirement question is scary. If the salary field is not required, you **can** skip it. Or, put down a salary range whenever you have that ability (sometimes a hard and fast number is all that fits in the space provided). If you must list a specific number, not a range, and have no idea what to list, make a phone call or send an email to the HR department or even the hiring manager to ask for advice on listing a range. Keep in mind that with any application process, you can ask for clarification about any of the sections or questions or requirements—seek help from a graduate career professional, from a contact within the organization, or even a direct query to the HR department or hiring manager.

Don't send applications or job emails when you are distracted (say, from your phone, or in a few minutes break from the lab). Give the process a laser-like focus. Remember that euphoria and excitement over the "coolest job ever" may also cause you distraction, so don't dash off an email reply or cover letter without putting some thought into the project. Pay attention to details. Don't spell your own name incorrectly, or any name, for that matter. Forgetting to attach documents, or attaching the **wrong** documents is an "oops" in most cases but can be lethal in the job search.

If you take your time with an application, these scenarios are less likely to happen. If and when they do, you will be more likely to realize what you've done and be able to recover quickly and efficiently if you are centered and focused.

After the application is completed, the next step in the application process is (hopefully) an interview. But you might find yourself waiting a while before knowing if you are moving forward. It is sadly very common for submitted applications to be unacknowledged, and this is true across industries and fields. You may receive an automated response of some kind after submitting an application, which is great for peace of mind and making sure your documents actually made it into the system. It is rare to hear more than that at the beginning stage of the application process.

Do ensure, however, that your materials were indeed received if you do not get a response of any kind after submission. Candidates usually receive a notification of some kind at the end of the hiring process letting them know that the position was filled, but again, that courtesy is not always evident. It can be disheartening to apply for multiple positions and hear a deafening silence, but don't waste time dwelling on this. Keep moving forward with the next application, and always be forward-thinking. (Remember to go back to the advice in Chapter 6 on staying positive in your search!)

INTERVIEWS

If you are a viable candidate for the job you have applied for, generally, you can expect an invitation to some kind of brief screening interview followed by a more in-depth conversation. Some organizations prefer multiple levels and types of interviews; other places might make a decision with only one meeting. Much depends on the kind of organization and type of role to which you are applying. Following is a description of a "traditional" interview progression, and description of the types of interviews you may encounter.

STAGES OF A TYPICAL INTERVIEW PROCESS

- First round—usually phone or Skype interviews
    - After an invitation, get your logistics right. Confirm who is calling whom, at what number, or on what website or application. Confirm whom you will be speaking to, for how long, and understand what is the focus of the conversation
    - Know that phone interviews are the most difficult type because you can't see the response of the person you are answering
- Second round—usually in-person interviews
    - These can last a few hours or cover the course of a few days and might be one-on-one or with more people
    - May be multiple rounds (especially in industry)
    - May involve meals, presentations, or other activities (see information on working interviews, below)

TYPES OF INTERVIEWS

There are a few different types of interviews to which you may be invited. When you are invited to interview, do not hesitate to ask your contact (no matter who it is—it might be someone in HR, it might be your potential new boss) to confirm what kind of interview you will be having, and with whom you will be meeting. The more information you have, the better you will be able to prepare. If you don't ask, you won't know!

- *One-on-one*: just you and one interviewer, the most common type of interview
- *Panel*: multiple people interview you at the same time
- *Group*: a group of candidates is interviewed by a panel
- *Meal*: you are interviewed while eating, usually over lunch
- *Working*: you are put to work and observed while undertaking some responsibilities of the role (i.e., in the United Kingdom, most interviews include an "assessment center" activity in which candidates undertake tasks related to the job and are observed while doing so)
- *Telephone/Skype*: often used as a screening tool before an in-person interview

PREPARING FOR INTERVIEWS

The most important things to consider for interviews, both inside and outside of academia, can be distilled down to four important points:

- Know what is happening in that area of work
- Know the organization's mission and goals

- Know the job requirements
- Practice, practice, practice your answers

An important point to remember, if interviewing outside of academia, is to be prepared to answer why you are making the transition from academic research to a new setting. The answer you give should not be a tirade against academic science, or a rant about the unfairness of grant applications. Instead, focus on the future and give an answer that demonstrates you want to use your scientific expertise and skills in whatever environment or field you are targeting.

HOW TO ANSWER INTERVIEW QUESTIONS

Next, understand the role and position for which you are applying. Use the job description to prepare answers about how you fit all the qualifications for the position and are able to assume the responsibilities of the role. If you do not meet all the criteria for the role, do not worry. You have been invited for an interview, so the organization is interested in learning more about you. When responding to questions, don't focus on the negatives or what you lack. Instead, talk about what a fast learner you are (and have specific examples of things you have mastered quickly). Your interviewers want to see you have done your homework about the position and the organization; figure out what you know about the position, and determine how you will succeed if hired.

Most interviewers want to know the answers to three main questions:

1. Can you do the job?
2. Do you want to do the job?
3. Do we want this person as a colleague?

The types of interview questions that may fall under those three categories include the following:

- Can you do the job/does this candidate have the skills needed to do this job?
  - Tell me about yourself?
  - What are your greatest strengths/weaknesses?
  - What can you do for us that other candidates can't?
  - Why do you think you are right for this job?
  - What do you think the main challenges will be?
- Do you want to do the job/is he or she really motivated to do this work?
  - What do you know about our company?
  - What do you think our company is aiming to achieve?
  - What do you know about our products and services?
  - Why do you want to work for this company?
  - Why do you think this job is right for you?
  - What motivates you?

- Do we want this person as our colleague?
  - How would you describe your work style?
  - How would you describe yourself?
  - How would your colleagues describe you?
  - What makes you fit into our company?
  - What makes you a good team member?
    - If you were an animal, what animal would you be? (Okay, you may not get this last one often, but just like when preparing for a PhD defense; it's good to anticipate "left-field" questions!)

STRUCTURING YOUR INTERVIEW ANSWERS

When structuring your answers to interview questions, first look to the job description for ideas and keywords. Almost everything you need to know should be there in terms of what is required for the position—and what the hiring manager may be looking for. You will be asked questions to determine if you can fit those requirements. If you don't have a job description, think about what you know about the job, the organization, and the industry.

Additionally, consider experiences you have had that demonstrate, without a doubt, your analytic prowess, your ability to work independently, or your communication skills (both written and speaking). These areas are asked about in interviews for almost every role to which someone with a science PhD would apply.

Frame your answers in terms of "stories" to make it easier to tell an interviewer about your skills, strengths, or experiences. A story has a beginning, a middle, and an end, and for nervous interviewees who have a tendency to ramble when anxious, the concept of telling a story may help give much-needed structure. You may be asked to describe a time when you worked on a team, met a challenge, or managed a project. These are behavioral interview questions. The best way to answer these types of questions is to use a job-interviewing technique called the "STAR method," an acronym which stands for "Situation, Task, Action, and Result" and allows you to put your story (or example) into a format that is easy for the interviewer to understand.

Structure your STAR answers this way:

S Situation (10%). Present a challenge or situation you experienced.

T Task (10%). What was your goal or assignment? What did you need to achieve?

A Action (70%). What did you do? Why did you do it that way? What were your alternatives? How did you accomplish the task?

R Result (10%). What was the outcome, and what did you learn from the experience?

Novice candidates using the STAR method will get lost explaining the situation and task, but expert interviewees will be able to discuss HOW they accomplished, solved, or succeeded in a situation (or in some cases, were not able to succeed). Give lots of details about the *action* and the *how* in your answer. (Think about "showing your work" in elementary school math classes!) Interviewers want to know how you think, and they should be able to draw parallels from your answers to how you might perform in the job if you are hired.

Here is a facetious example of how to structure STAR answers in an interview, when asked "Tell me about a time when you faced a challenge." Note that the scene is set very briefly yet concisely in the "Situation" and "Task" portions of the answer, and the longest part of the answer describes the "Action":

Interviewer: *"Tell me about a time when you faced a challenge"*

Candidate/Interviewee:

S "My PI asked me to deliver an important talk on our lab's biggest project to a group of visiting researchers/potential collaborators at our annual department research symposium, but the day before the talk I was diagnosed with a case of poison ivy from a hike I had been on the weekend before. I was too contagious to be in contact with other humans."

T "I knew it was my responsibility to find some way to deliver the talk, because it was a key opportunity to connect with these visitors we wanted to collaborate with and I knew the project the best of anyone in my lab."

A "I knew before I went to my PI in full crisis mode that I needed to come up with some solutions. So first I spoke to two of my lab mates who agreed to help me. We spent about an hour and a half on the phone discussing the presentation together. My two lab mates (a postdoc and another graduate student) agreed to take the lead the next day on the talk, but we worked out that also I could be there via Skype. They would explain the situation, present my slides and talk through them as best they could live, with me supporting and commenting via webcam. I also added some graphics of poison ivy leaves to all my slides for a touch of humor. Only then did I call my PI to say we had a situation, but I had it under control."

R "The talk was a success, we ended up getting the collaboration with the visiting lab, and my PI was really happy that I didn't embarrass her or our lab."

INTERVIEW PRACTICE

Once you have considered the types of questions you will be asked, have prepared examples or stories that illustrate your expertise and behavior, possess confidence around how to structure your answers, and have done your research on the organization and the people you will meet, it is time to practice. Actually, you can start practicing for interviews even before you have an interview arranged. The more practice you have, the less anxious you will be!

There is no replacement for answers spoken out loud. Speaking to mirrors or pets is fine for the beginning stages of interview prep, but there is no substitute for saying full sentences out loud to a quizzical human. You absolutely must verbalize your thoughts—simply writing down what you want to say might organize your thoughts, but you eventually have to practice saying the words! Get lab mates, mentors, and/or friends to listen to even just one interview question and ask for feedback. Schedule an interview prep session with a career office if you have one, or record yourself with your phone. If you are really lucky, you will have a career office that offers recorded mock interviews so you can cringe and watch yourself stumbling through interview answers.

Take opportunities whenever you can to practice speaking publicly or to answer questions that require a structured answer. All of this will put you in a good place for your performance in a formal interview situation.

DURING THE INTERVIEW

When your interview day arrives, wear something that makes you feel confident. Arrive early to the interview location, and if you are traveling to an unfamiliar interview location, give yourself much more time than you think you need. Bring a copy of your resume or CV—ideally in a professional-looking portfolio or folder—along with a few sheets of paper to take notes (it's fine to scribble a few notes during your interview!) However, do NOT open that folder to review your own CV when answering questions!

For Skype or telephone interviews, you also need to be prepared. Set up your interview space early, and make sure it is quiet and well-lit (if using video). Lock the door if you have kids or animals (or even housemates) who might unwittingly interrupt you. Don't spread out excessive notes or paper—use the same folder with a CV and notepad as you might use for an in-person interview. It sometimes helps build confidence to dress for a telephone interview just as you would for an in-person one.

When your interviewer greets you, shake hands (and if on Skype or phone, smile!) For many women, shaking hands can be awkward because we don't regularly shake hands with our peers, but it's part of interview culture! Practice giving a decent handshake before you go to an interview. (By decent, we mean not bone-crushing, not floppy. Just professional.) You may also wish to jot down the names of your interviewers, if there is more than one person.

Once you are engaged in the interview, try to stay as focused as you can on the moment, and the question you are being asked. If you "flub" a question, or give an answer you aren't satisfied with, it is absolutely okay to ask your interviewer if you can start the answer over. Having the confidence and maturity to "own" a mistake in an interview is fantastic. You don't want to spend the next few days wishing you had said something differently—go ahead and say something differently while you are in the interview. Or, at the end of the interview, there may be time for you to ask questions, and that is an opportunity to ask to "refresh" an answer or add something to an answer.

Take note of everything around you during your time interviewing. What kind of workspace will you be in? How do colleagues interact with each other? What sorts of personalities are present in your potential new work team? What is the "vibe" you get from the organization and the people there? Your interview is not a one-way interaction. You need to be learning about the organization, just as they are learning more about you.

At the end of an interview, you should be asked if you have any questions for your interviewer(s). Be mindful of time and don't ask a slew of questions if you only have time for one or two. Show you have done your homework about the organization and ask an intelligent question (that cannot be answered from looking at the organization's website!) Don't ask about salary, vacation, or flex time. You can ask about those things when you have an offer! Or, if it is absolutely necessary to know those things, ask separately from the interview situation, ideally to an HR representative. If your interview is with the kind of organization that puts out media or press releases, look at those on the day of your interview and they might provide ideas for suitable questions. Otherwise, it is always easy to ask the person interviewing you what he or she think of their job, or how much they like the organization. A word of warning: do not be overzealous in asking your interviewer questions that he or she may not know. You may think that "showing off" and asking about some obscure topic you found on the company website will impress your interviewer, but it may make the person feel embarrassed if it's not in their area of expertise.

Difficult or "illegal" questions may occasionally be asked in interviews. These can include questions perhaps asked innocently about your family life, your religion, and what ethnicity your last name is. It is not easy to deflect illegal personal questions, and much will depend on the individual situation—there is no single piece of advice to give regarding illegal or uncomfortable interview questions. Refer to the myriad of resources available online, including an article on illegal interview questions written specifically for PhD job seekers.[4]

Certain industries will ask you "specialized" interview questions, such as case interview questions for consulting, or puzzles, and riddles such as those described in William Poundstone's book *Are You Smart Enough to Work at Google?* Preparation for such types of interviews can be best advised by people already working in the field or through consultation with a graduate career advisor who can advise you on specialized resources.

AFTER YOUR INTERVIEW

The first and most important thing to be done after an interview is to write down as much as you can remember about the questions you were asked and your answers. The second most important task is to send thank you notes to every single person with whom you met. If possible, send a brief email thank you note immediately, followed by a hand-written message the next day, but this is not always possible. As long as you send some kind of thank you greeting, you have done the right thing. Your thank you message should ideally mention something that was discussed during the interview ("I really enjoyed hearing about the new drug discovery initiative"), or something that stood out to you ("I got a sense of the real collaboration that happens at your firm").

Some candidates have thank you notes ready to go when they attend an interview and can write the notes in the interview reception area following an interview and then hand deliver them to the receptionist. Other people write them on the flight home or as soon as getting home and mail them the next day. No matter how quickly or in what manner you craft a thank you, send thanks to those who interviewed you.

GETTING AN OFFER

The final step in the application process is receiving and negotiating an offer. When you receive an offer, which usually comes first via telephone, respond positively—even if you may not necessarily be feeling positive. Do not accept any offer "on the spot" or immediately, no matter how excited you are. Give yourself time to be thoughtful and consider all aspects of the offer. Most organizations will follow a telephone offer with something in writing. The reason for this is that there may be some negotiation of terms of the offer, which once finalized will go into the written job offer. So after you have expressed something positive (even "thank you, I'm so pleased!" will do), ask for a few days to be able to consider the offer. It really is important to negotiate, even if you are extremely happy with your offer. Most organizations expect some negotiation from job offers. Organizations that are not open to negotiation will usually tell you this when making an offer. For example, many consulting firms have a set salary with no flexibility for new hires.

Do not negotiate an offer in writing; do as much of your negotiation as possible in conversation. Set up a phone appointment with the HR representative or hiring manager who has delivered your offer and use that time to ask all your questions. There is a difference in negotiating an offer with an HR rep versus the person who will be your direct manager! It is sometimes preferable and perhaps less awkward to talk to an HR representative because he or she is the "middle man" and can convey your questions to the appropriate decision-makers, but it also means that person cannot usually make decisions to bump up your salary or change your start date. No matter who you are negotiating with, you do not want your queries written down because it looks like a list of "demands" that could be forwarded, taken out of context, and make your new colleagues think of you as a diva.

Be clear about what you are asking for and why. If you are asked to justify why you want something, you must be prepared. There are numerous resources available to help determine appropriate salary ranges (such as GlassDoor.com and Salary.com), but try to include other data points in your research as well. Many universities publish graduate salary data, including for PhDs (usually on the career center or graduate school Web pages). If your university does not do this, it can be helpful to look at other comparable universities' PhD graduate salary information.

For other aspects of your offer negotiation, which may include vacation, flexible working hours, benefits, or stock options, to name just a few, it can be helpful to reach back out to contacts you made during informational interviews and ask for their advice. People with experience in the organization or industry will have "insider" knowledge of things that are nonnegotiable, as well as information on aspects of the offer you may not have considered.

Two helpful resources for those who are new to job offer negotiation are *How to Negotiate Your First Job*, by Paul Levy and Farzana Mohamed,[5] and any YouTube recording of William Ury, coauthor of *Getting to Yes*.[6] Negotiation is like public speaking—it gets easier the more often you practice. This is why it's important to always negotiate because even if you love the offer you have been given, you should take the rare opportunity to undertake the give and take experience of a negotiation.

If you are lucky enough to have more than one offer, you may want to create a grid or chart to list pros and cons, or weighing various factors in your offer. You can create something simple on your own, or use existing ones that are easily found online with a search on the keywords "job offer negotiation grid." Dr. Jake Livengood, Assistant Director of Graduate Student Career Services at Massachusetts Institute of Technology has created a fantastic tool to help PhDs consider options with multiple offers in an Excel file that is shared online,[7] see: https://www.insidehighered.com/advice/2016/04/18/tools-help-job-seekers-decide-next-career-steps-essay.

If you have received an offer and are still waiting for an interview (or offer) from another organization, it can be very stressful and tricky to determine how and when to "nudge" an organization. Mentors and PhD career advisors will be helpful to talk with in these cases. The best advice in this situation is to be honest with both the organization that has already given you an offer and the one you are hoping to move forward with quickly.

CONSIDERATIONS FOR ACADEMIC INTERVIEWS

Preparing for the academic interview process is an entire book in itself, and in fact we highly recommend two books: "The Academic Job Search Handbook" by Julia Vick, Jennifer Furlong, and Rosanne Lurie and "The Professor Is In," by Karen Kelsky. Both books are fantastic resources for delving into the specifics of academic interviews and the entire academic job-seeking process. Here are just a few brief tips on postdoc or faculty interviews that may also be of use to you in nonacademic settings.

POSTDOC INTERVIEWS

A potential postdoc mentor may request a video or phone interview prior to inviting you for a visit. Familiarize yourself with his/her research and ensure that you have your research pitch (~2–3 min) perfected. Once you are invited for the visit, which the hosting faculty member typically pays for, you will likely give a semi-nar (see link below for job talks) and meet with everyone in the lab. Remember:

- The postdoc interview usually takes 1 day.
- Practice your talk with your graduate mentor, postdocs, and students.
- Prepare by reading papers from the lab of interest, and think of a potential project you could work on stemming from their research.
- You are not the only one being interviewed. *You should interview them as well.* Ask the lab staff some of the following to get a good feel for how the lab, department, and university function:
  - What do you like and dislike about working here? (university, department, and lab level)
  - What is a typical day like in the lab? How flexible are the hours?
  - Do you have regular lab meetings and meetings with your mentor?
  - What are former postdocs from the lab doing now?
  - Is your mentor open to letting postdocs take their research with them?
  - How well do you like this city? How is your quality of life? What are some things you like and dislike about living here?

Choose a lab that fits you well and has a built-in support system. Even if it is a large lab and you know you will not get lots of face time with your PI, make sure the other lab members are good colleagues that will help you. Also, choose a mentor who is supportive of your future goals and will work with you toward those goals. Take in consideration what former postdocs from that lab are doing now. You can even reach out to them and ask about their experience in that lab. Always write thank you notes to each person you met and the people who organized your visit.

FACULTY INTERVIEWS

Prior to visiting, find out the interview strategy and specifics for each univer-sity. Each institution is different, and the departments and programs within that institution will also vary, but the general theme of the faculty position interview is usually as follows:

- A video or phone interview with the chair of the particular department in which you applied or the chair of the hiring committee.
- Expect each interview visit to be 1.5–2 days. You will be sent a schedule, but often not until the day before your visit.
- A job talk similar to a departmental seminar is standard for an initial visit. Adding some detail (a few slides) about your future directions will give them a good idea of how you intend to shape your research program. You may be required to give a chalk talk on the first or second interview. A chalk talk is how the department is informed of the details of your research program and how you will achieve your research goals.

- You may be invited for a second interview, which will be about 1–1.5 days and either consists of a chalk talk and more meetings with faculty members, core facilities director, and deans. This visit may be the "recruitment interview" in which they attempt to sell you on why this university and city are best for you. Sometimes the university will even arrange for you to meet with a real estate agent. The "recruitment interview" could also happen on a third visit.
- Can you confidently answer questions about why you want to work at that particular institution, and where you see your career going?

Chalk talks are intimidating, so practice mock chalk talks with faculty and postdocs at least 1 month in advance. Instruct those attending to be rigorous and give you as much feedback as possible. Many universities may expect you to outline the research you will propose in your first R01. Know every detail of your research program that you are proposing, and be prepared to answer questions about it, along with your teaching philosophy.

Remember that you are interviewing the university/program/department as well. These are your potential future colleagues, so ask lots of questions to find out about the department chair, graduate student training and expectations, tenure expectations, and guidance/mentoring for junior faculty. Always write thank you notes to each person you met during the interview process, and don't forget to thank the people who organized your visit.

FINAL WORDS OF APPLICATION WISDOM

- Tailor everything in your application—use keywords, make sure your cover letter and CV or resume contain phrases from the job description, and that your experiences illustrate you possess the qualities, skills, and background required to do the job well
- Follow all directions for applying (i.e., if the job posting asks for a resume, do not send a CV!)
- Everything you send in an application should be error-free
- Let your referees know you have listed them well in advance of when they might be contacted by a prospective employer
- If you have any contacts at an organization (perhaps from previous informational interviews), let those people know you are applying/have submitted an application because they might be able to get your resume to the top of the pile or can make sure you are at least considered for an interview!)
- A last reminder about making applications via online job systems: it is unlikely that you will get an interview and probably will not even get a response or acknowledgment that your materials were received. This is a hard and ugly truth in modern job applications. Remember about 80% of jobs are found through networking.[8]

Putting together applications can take up precious time and may seem daunting, but if you start preparing materials and thinking about interviews as early as possible, you can make the job application process less stressful. Remember that any job you get is not a "forever" job, and with every set of applications you prepare you will keep improving your materials!

FURTHER RESOURCES FOR JOB INTERVIEW AND PREPARATION

1. *Oddball Interview Questions: posted annually on.* GlassDoor.com.
2. Poundstone W. *Are you smart enough to work at Google?.* 2012.
3. Green A. *10 reasons your resume isn't getting you interviews.* US News; 2012. http://money.usnews.com/money/blogs/outside-voices-careers/2012/08/13/10-reasons-your-resume-isnt-getting-you-interviews.
4. Vick J, Furlong J, Lurie R. *The academic job search handbook.* 2016.
5. Kelsky K. *The professor is in.* 2015.

REFERENCES

1. Kelsky K. *Stick to two pages.* Chronicle of Higher Education; 2016. https://chroniclevitae.com/news/1464-stick-to-two-pages.
2. Smith J. Here's what recruiters look at in the six seconds they look at your resume. *Business Insider* 2014. http://www.businessinsider.com/what-recruiters-look-at-on-your-resume-2014-11.
3. Lundsteen N. Stay inside the lines: following directions in a PhD job search. *Inside Higher Ed* 2016. https://www.insidehighered.com/advice/2016/03/14/importance-following-directions-when-you-apply-jobs-essay.
4. Lundsteen N. They aren't supposed to ask that. *Inside Higher Ed.* https://www.insidehighered.com/advice/2015/05/18/essay-how-handle-illegal-questions-during-academic-job-interviews.
5. Levy P, Mohamed F. *How to negotiate your first job.* 2014.
6. Ury W. *The walk from no to yes.* TED Talk. TED.com.
7. Livengood J. *How to decide what to do next. Inside Higher Ed*; 2016. https://www.insidehighered.com/advice/2016/04/18/tools-help-job-seekers-decide-next-career-steps-essay.
8. McIntosh B. *80% of today's jobs are landed through networking.* Recruiting Blogs; 2012. http://www.recruitingblogs.com/profiles/blogs/80-of-today-s-jobs-are-landed-through-networking.

FURTHER READING

1. NIH office of intramural training and education guide to cover letters. https://www.training.nih.gov/assets/OITE_Guide_to_Cover_Letters.pdf.

Top 15 Tips for Communicating Your Career on Paper

By Teresa Evans

1. **Your name should stand out**—Use bold to emphasize only the most important features of your resume.

2. **Have professional contact information**—Be sure you have a professional-sounding voice message and a professional email address. You would be surprised how many people do not follow this advice.

3. **Make sure the section headers are clear and easy to read**—Common resume sections include personal info, objective summary education, work experience, special skills, memberships/honors/awards, volunteer experience.

4. **List certifications as education not under awards**—Certifications show ongoing commitment to learning. Be sure not to just take online classes.

5. **Have an objective**—Be sure to have an objective such as "seeking position as an elementary school teacher." This allows a recruiter to quickly scan your resume and also match you to other relevant positions.

6. **Tailor each resume to the job you are seeking**—Resumes should be tailored to the job outlined in the job description. Pay attention to the soft skills. If the job description mentions "commitment to integrity" and "collaborative work experience" be able to point it out in your resume. This could be shown by attending Research Integrity workshops or by having examples of projects that you did as a team. The hard skills get you in the door, but the soft skills get you the job.

7. **Include explanations for gaps in work experience**—It's okay to say "family leave" with the dates specified.

8. **Include volunteer experience**—If you are new in your career and lack work experience, be sure to include membership in community and campus organizations along with volunteer experience. Often this can be the first question an interviewer will ask because it shows what you are interested in.

9. **Keep a master list**—Keep a master list of every activity you have ever done because you never know if something is relevant. This also allows you to go through what's relevant for different jobs quickly.

10. **Only send resumes in pdf**—You do not want people to edit your resume. It is much easier for a recruiter to save a pdf than open a Microsoft Word file.

11. **Proofread**—Send your resume to someone else for proofreading. You rarely find your own typos.

12. **Put what is relevant**—If they ask for a CV, give them a CV. If they ask for publications, be sure to have it in there. If not, do not put extra sections. Also do not list basic skills, which everyone might have such as pipetting or western blots, and be sure to list specific skills that show that you would excel at the job. Also, do not include references unless asked. It is preferred to leave them off so that you can prepare your referees in advance.

13. **Check online**—Google yourself and find what comes up. Also be sure to search PubMed for yourself because research that you participated in while an undergraduate and graduate student may have become a published article.

14. **Abstracts are okay but publications are better**—It is okay to include an abstract, but if you have presented your abstract at three places, pick one. If you have published it then use that instead.

15. **You do not have to include everything in a resume**—While it is important to keep a master list, you do not want to turn in your master list to an employer. Part of job hunting is picking what is relevant and taking off what is not relevant; this makes it easy for the recruiter to see that you have the skills and experience needed for this job. For a CV you keep almost everything but can remove some redundancy.

Case Study

My Experience With Cover Letters
   By Hashem A. Dbouk, PhD

Hashem Dbouk is a medical writer at BIONYC (a division of BGB Group), currently based in New York, New York. He has a PhD from Albert Einstein College of Medicine and a Master's from the American University of Beirut. He was a founding member of the American Society for Cell Biology's (ASCB's) Committee for Postdocs and Students (COMPASS).

The switch from an academic, research-oriented career to the "real world" beyond the bench comes with many obstacles. The one that most don't think about, and yet tends to be the first they stumble on, is the actual job application itself, with the trickiest aspect being the cover letter.

I was no different, after more than 13 years of lab experience, I had really spent my whole adult existence in the safety net/cocoon of the research environment. When it finally came time to apply for a nonacademic job and write a cover letter, I found myself quite perplexed: I could write a lot about my research, detailing the science, techniques, and biomedical implications, but I found myself incapable of describing the crucial points of a cover letter: my strengths and weaknesses, what I bring to the company, or what makes me better suited for the job compared to any other candidates.

It's easy to forget the way jobs actually operate when one is in the academic ivory tower, where the natural progression from graduate student to postdoc (to second postdoc) to faculty seems the expected norm, the way forward is through manuscripts and grants, and what you bring to the table is measured in techniques mastered and marathon hours spent at lab. Suffice it to say, my first attempts at writing a cover letter were, to put it nicely, atrocious, little more than an abstract of my work and my skills. My life in science did come in handy though, as I have learned never to shy away from asking for help to improve.

I started by asking other people to read my cover letter, and these included some coworkers, but also my wife (who is not in science) and my school's career advisor. Feedback from several contacts was essential, particularly from people outside of the lab, with the advice aiming to translate my skills at the bench and in academia to positives for the workplace. For example, my collaborative projects became examples of my ability to work in a team, my diverse research papers were a sign of my ability to work on different projects and produce a high quality end-product, and even my experimental design (and proper controls!) were a clear sign of a meticulous nature and attention to detail! The transformation of my lab skills into attributes that highlight my fit into the company was one great way that reaching out to others helped me fix my cover letter.

In addition to the cosmetic touches that can be applied by others to the cover letter, I personally needed to play a major part in building my cover letter, by making the choice to build my experience in the direction I wanted. My interests lie in science/medical writing, and while writing manuscripts is a bonus, science writing includes a very different set of skills, and I knew I had to learn them the hard way. I found my first opportunity through scientific associations, joining ASCB's COMPASS and becoming a member of its communications committee before

Case Study—cont'd

going on to chair the committee. That allowed me to add leadership experience to my "real-world skills," as well as gave me my first experience doing science writing and editing, writing about science, education and policy to the general public, although the ASCB website was more focused toward people in the sciences rather than the lay public.

To gain even more research experience, I reached out to contacts I had made within ASCB, bona fide science writers, who were happy to give me advice as well as provide me with the opportunities to do some freelance science writing! The insights from that are twofold: the first is that contacts are essential if you are to move away from the bench, and second that professional science writing is very, very different from manuscript writing and you need as much help and practice as you can get. So, with the help of my contacts who served as editors for my science writing trials, I got a lot of pointers regarding the "do's and don'ts" of science writing. These writing experiences were invaluable in shaping and cementing my interest in science writing as well as teaching me the basics of the field, and they would not have happened were it not for a strong network of contacts as well as the willingness to seek out opportunities and take on the extracurricular work beyond the bench.

To sum up, I took two paths to modify my cover letter and apply for my dream job: Asking for help and self-help. Both are essential and complimentary and will feed into transforming your cover letter into one that will make you the perfect candidate for that dream job and land you the interview.

Case Study

Skills that Hiring Managers for Industry REALLY Wish You Had (and you do have them…)

By Vicki Stronge, PhD

Vicki Stronge is Associate Director of Diagnostic Platforms and Systems at Thermo Fisher Scientific in San Francisco. Vicki completed a PhD in Biochemistry at the University of Oxford. She has worked in the life sciences industry since 2007 in various roles from Business Development to Product Management Leadership. She has been on both sides of the interview table many times and has been responsible for hiring science graduates at all levels.

One of the most challenging aspects of completing my PhD wasn't the years of (mostly unsuccessful) experiments, the endless hours (and days and weeks) of paper and thesis writing, or even the lengthy and anxiety-inducing defense. The hardest thing I faced was the daunting prospect of transitioning to a career outside of academia. How could I present myself for a position where I hardly understood the job title, let alone understanding the skills needed for the role and also anticipating what the hiring manager is looking for?

You have probably heard that you need to emphasize skills beyond your academic accomplishments and esoteric technical skills (expertly removing salivary

Continued

Case Study—cont'd

glands from malaria-infected mosquitos isn't the most sought after skill in the board room). Presentation skills, time-management, and ability to prioritize large amounts of work are essential to highlight to potential recruiters, but what is going to set you apart from the rest of the exacademics, as well as potential candidates with ACTUAL BUSINESS EXPERIENCE? Fortunately, if you have a keen interest in business, you do have those skills, and bringing them out in interviews and illustrating them on your CV will be a game-changer in your career search.

As a product management leader who has been in industry for nearly 10 years, I've interviewed hundreds of PhD graduates and postdocs who are keen to make the leap from the bench to the office. And very often I meet a great candidate who I really want to hire: smart, passionate, likable, focused. What I'm really thinking is, "*Can she do the job?*" I need her to convince me she can think outside the lab, and deliver results. I need to know she can think business. Previous experience in product management will tell me that, but without it, she can still convince me. You can provide relevant business experience (not skills) to a potential employer— if you are even slightly interested in business you will have it—you just have to tell me. And how will you tell me? Show it on your CV.

The CV Skills that I want to see from new graduates fall into three categories: "Gimmes," "Next Level," and "Game-Changers."

1. Gimmes

If you don't have these, you probably didn't finish grad school. These are the standard skills that come out of accomplishing a PhD or postdoc. I know you have them, but you must make sure you include them, as they are directly relevant to the work I need you to do. Examples of Gimmes include the following:
- Detail-oriented
- Strong work ethic
- Written communication skills
- Oral communication skills

2. Next Level Skills

These are the skills that set you apart from that academic who just doesn't understand business. These are often called transferable skills, or soft skills. They seem trivial, compared to highly technical skills, but I am looking for them. Emphasize the Next Level skills! Make sure you can provide examples of why you have those skills, and be sure to use examples from both inside and outside your academic career.
- Prioritization
- Problem solver
- Team working skills
- Project management and finally…

3. Game-Changers

Here are the skills that will set you apart, not just from other new graduates or postdocs, but even from other candidates with job-specific experience. The business experience you already have. You might wonder how you can get these skills, and that's where you have to dig deep.

Continued

Case Study—cont'd

- Sales Experience

Sales experience is highly desired by hiring managers. Understanding the activities (and personalities) that go into a sale means you will be able to relate to your sales team, and to the buyers (customers). Look to "bigger" sales experiences to provide deeper understanding of sales cycles. Did you sell a car or house? Tell me about it.

- Business Acumen

Business acumen is something that is highly desired because it can be often difficult to find in new employees. Business acumen can be learned and honed through experience and training, but having a great deal of common sense and an ability to see the bigger picture is usually a natural ability that can set you apart from the rest of the job applicants. Impress interviewers with examples of business acumen in your academic and nonacademic life. Build on your knowledge of business by reading business books, following business and news organizations on social media (*Harvard Business Review* is good), or listening to business or entrepreneur-related podcasts.

- Budgeting/Finance

Use examples of how you have balanced budgets, whether in your personal finances or through a club or small business.

There are many more examples of business skills and experience that can be found in your nonprofessional life if you know what to look for, and these examples should give you an idea. When you next look at a job description and see a requirement that you think you don't possess, try to come at it from another angle and search for another way you might have acquired that skill. Good luck!

Case Study

A Perspective From The Hiring Manager
By Josh Henkin, PhD

Josh is a Program Manager at The Tauri Group and a dedicated entrepreneur. At the Tauri Group, Josh leads teams that provide a full range of technical and programmatic consulting services to the US Department of Defense. In 2014 Josh founded STEM Career Services, a career coaching company aimed at helping science, technology, engineering, and math (STEM) graduates launch and sustain careers outside of academia. Josh and his team of instructors conduct workshops and provide career counseling to STEM graduates at all levels of their careers. These efforts have earned Josh a position on the National Postdoctoral Association Board of Directors where he sits on the Executive committee and serves as the nonprofit's Treasurer. He holds a BS degree in Business Administration, an MS degree in Nutritional Sciences, and a PhD in Cell and Molecular Biology, all from the University of Vermont.

Continued

Case Study—cont'd

I review **a lot** of resumes from STEM-educated graduate students, postdocs, and early, mid-, and late career professionals. The reason why I do this is twofold. First, I currently work as a program manager for a consulting company where I hire candidates and build teams that support my various science and technology clients. Second, I own a prolific career counseling company targeted specifically toward STEM-educated graduates and professionals. In this role, I combine my current knowledge as a hiring manager along with my past experience as a PhD and postdoc to help job seekers create powerful resumes that clearly inform hiring managers about the amazing skills they will bring to an organization and undeniably fill the vacancies for which they seek candidates.

What this means is that I am the person you want your resume to impress. I'm the one who determines whether you get called in for an interview, or if you placed in the "database for future opportunities." In this chapter you have read numerous tips and best practices about how to create a resume, and I can tell you that *all* of them matter. However, as you start your job-searching process, I encourage you to consider taking a look at it from the hiring manager's perspective. Understanding how I think about candidates and resumes might give you a fresh perspective on how to create your resume.

This is a competition; make your resume count.

Typically, I will receive 50 or more resumes for any given position that I advertise. And, I review the resumes as fast as I can because hiring candidates is a task I perform on top of all my other responsibilities. This doesn't mean I don't take it seriously. In fact, it's quite the opposite, because my reputation is on the line every time I bring someone new into the company. You are the one creating a resume, so you can direct my eyes to where I read based on the location, order, and style of how you place content on the resume. Remember this, because you can make my job easier and have your resume stand out by having an attractive resume that is easy to read and clearly points out why you are a good fit for the job.

Finding good talent is not easy.

Just like in dating, it takes time to find the right mate. This is true for finding the right employee. I look to hire employees who demonstrate success in their technical skills, but also who have the ability to communicate and build relationships with multiple stakeholders, fit the corporate culture, are capable of taking ownership of projects, can lead a team as well as participate on a team, and more. The challenge for you is to find ways to convey your abilities in all of these areas on one or two sheets of paper.

The hiring process takes time away from a manager's other daily responsibilities.

Hiring is just one of my many responsibilities. And since replacing an employee who has moved on or been promoted within the company is usually not a regular task, the effort involved in this process requires me to squeeze in extra time for this additional responsibility in addition to everything else I do. A great resume that clearly tells me you are the right candidate for the job will make this process easier.

Continued

Case Study—cont'd

Receiving resumes through an internal referral/networking helps a manager.

An internal referral means that someone I know has already vouched for this candidate. I equate this scenario to the example of would you rather bring your car to a mechanic whom you randomly found on the Internet, or would you rather have a colleague or family members tell you they have been taking their car to a mechanic for years and have had a great experience with them? I'll certainly take the prequalified mechanic and known candidate under consideration. This point highlights the importance of having a solid networking strategy and to utilize that network to apply for as many positions as possible via your network and avoid the dark hole of online job applications.

One final note is that in most cases, managers have to work with the people they hire. Therefore, it helps if you come across as a likable team player that will not only add to the organization's bottom line, but also add value to the workplace culture.

I wish you all the best success in your job search and your professional careers. Feel free to look me up at www.STEMCareerServices.com if you have any questions.

Sample CV

Candidate's Name
Name of Department
UT Southwestern Graduate School of Biomedical Sciences, Department of X
Address, City, State 12345
(214) 123-4567 name@utsouthwestern.edu

Typically, you list an institutional address (i.e. your department and university); you have the option of also including a home address. Include your mobile phone number if that is the easiest way for a search committee to reach you. You may also want to add a second email address (such as a personal Gmail account)

EDUCATION
UT Southwestern Graduate School of Biomedical Sciences, Dallas, TX
PhD in Name of Program, expected May 20xx
Dissertation title, brief summary, mentor's name, and/or committee members may optionally follow here. Could also appear in additional section below entitled "Dissertation," or could be included elsewhere, depending on your preference, the conventions of the field, and the job for which you are applying. There are times when you may also wish to list a particular fellowship or honor here as well.

Previous University, City, State or Country
MS, MA, etc. in Name of Program, June xxxx
Optional: Thesis title, advisor's name

Previous University, City, State or Country
BS, BA, etc. in Name of Program, June xxxx
Optional: Senior thesis title, advisor's name

NEXT HEADING HERE
Choose your first heading with great care, considering the primary focus of the position. If the focus will be research, consider a heading such as "Research Experience." If the focus is teaching, consider "Teaching Experience." The level of detail with which you address either topic should reflect the level of interest that the hiring committee is expected to have in that area. For the purpose of this sample, examples of each follow.
In some cases, the first heading after Education will actually be "Honors and Awards"; in other cases, this category will follow later in the CV.

RESEARCH EXPERIENCE
Organization, Lab, or Project, City, State
Research Assistant, September xxxx to present
Concise but descriptive highlights of your work on this project follow. As you edit and revise these descriptions, keep your hiring committee in mind. Describe your work in a way that is engaging and interesting. Don't just list lab techniques you can perform, but the context in which you undertake them, what research questions are being addressed, and why.

Organization, Lab, or Project, City, State
Research Assistant, September xxxx to present
When describing research experience, the emphasis should be on your contributions and accomplishments, not solely on the project itself. Make a special effort to be mindful of verbs: Coordinated, analyzed, investigated, presented, and so on.

TEACHING EXPERIENCE
Name of College or University, City, State
Lecturer, September xxxx to June xxxx
There is no single, set-in-stone format for describing your teaching on a CV. Depending on your situation and how much teaching experience you have had, you may consider listing it by college or university, as in this example; or you may wish to list it by course, or by some other classification. Sometimes it is sufficient to simply list courses taught; other times it can be tremendously helpful to include a description of your role in the course, including accomplishments that may have been unique to you (i.e., Built an interactive website for course and moderated online discussion, or facilitated small-group problem-solving in 150-person lecture). If you haven't done any university teaching, include mentoring and advising experiences in this heading.

RELATED PROFESSIONAL EXPERIENCE
If you have industry experience that will enhance your candidacy, such as consulting in your field, internships, or other work that will contribute to the committee's understanding of how and why you would be a good fit for a position, consider including it as well. Again, the placement of a category like this is potentially quite flexible. Think carefully about which experience you would like to be part of a search committee's initial impression of you, which experience can be deferred until later in the CV, and which experience may not need to appear in the CV at all.

UNIVERSITY SERVICE
This category might also be titled 'Leadership'. This section is useful if you have served on committees, organized speakers or events for your department, or taken leadership roles in activities on campus. This mirrors the kind of activities a junior faculty member might be expected to undertake. Perhaps you have served as a reviewer for journals in your field; you could re-name this section or add a new one to include that experience.

PUBLICATIONS
Especially for research-oriented positions, this section may be read very carefully. When you list your publications, you may wish to bold your name. You may also wish to include and indicate publications that have been submitted and/or are in press. Typically you would follow the citation conventions of your field, which might include a separate section for 'Peer-Reviewed Publications'.

PRESENTATIONS
As with publications, listing your presentations is helpful as well. In some cases a candidate may choose to combine both sections into one (Publications & Presentations); if you find that you have quite a few of each, it typically works best to keep them in separate categories.

ADDITIONAL EXPERIENCE
Of course, you do not need to include a category with this name. However, you may have experience, volunteer work, or other experiences that do not fit neatly into any of the other categories and have not already been addressed in the CV. Be both proactive and conservative in finding ways to include information that is expected in your field (for someone with a PhD in Drama, this may be a list of performances directed, for example). You may want to have a heading for professional development, media coverage, or other topics. Find ways to include information that will help the search committee better understand who you are as a scholar, a teacher, and a colleague.

HONORS AND AWARDS
When you list awards, consider including a bit of explanatory text if that would help the reader better understand an award's significance (i.e. 'one of four graduate students awarded'). If there is a particular award that might significantly elevate your application, consider finding a way to include it on the first page where it will be noticed immediately. Sometimes specific awards can be included right in the Education section; sometimes this entire category may be moved to the first page.

PROFESSIONAL AFFILIATIONS
Memberships in professional organizations are commonly listed at or toward the end of your CV.

REFERENCES
List your references, along with their titles and contact information, here.

Continued

Glenn E. Simmons Jr., Ph.D.

Postdoctoral Fellow, University of Texas Southwestern Medical Center, Molecular Genetics

5323 Harry Hines Blvd.
Dallas, TX 75390

Phone: 813-766-8707
Email: glenn.simmons@utsouthwestern.edu
www.linkedin.com/in/glennesimmonsjr

EDUCATION

2014- present   **Postdoctoral Fellow, University of Texas Southwestern Medical Center**, Dallas, TX
PI: Jin Ye, Ph.D.

2012- 2014   **Postdoctoral Fellow, Louisiana State University Health Sciences Center,** Shreveport, LA
PI: Kevin Pruitt, Ph.D.

2013   **Ph.D., Biomedical Science**, Meharry Medical College, Nashville, TN
PI: James Hildreth, M.D., Ph.D.

2006   **B.S., Biology,** University of South Florida, Tampa, FL, PI: Scott Antonia, M.D., Ph.D.

RESEARCH GRANT AWARDS

2012-2014   **3-R01-CA155223-02 Research Supplement to Promote Diversity in Health-Related Research,** Louisiana State University Health Sciences Center Shreveport
Role: Postdoctoral Trainee

2009-2011   **F31 AI082950, Ruth L. Kirschstein NIH Predoctoral Research Fellowship,**
Meharry Medical College, **Role: PI**

2007-2009   **T32 AI007281 NIAID Training Grant**, Meharry Medical College, **Role: Trainee**

2002-2006   **NCI 3P30CA076292-15S2 National Cancer Institute/ Project LINK Undergraduate Research Fellowship,** Moffitt Cancer Center, **Role: Trainee**

RESEARCH EXPERIENCE

Current   **University of Texas Southwestern Medical Center**, *Postdoctoral Scholar*
Laboratory of Jin Ye, Ph.D., Department of Molecular Genetics
Project 1: Role of fatty acids in regulation of protein expression.
  • Identified relationship between unsaturated fatty acid and translation.
  • Demonstrated role for fatty acid in protein stability in cancer.
Project 2: Drug screen for novel molecules that block stability of oncogenes.
  • Developed high throughput screen to test effectiveness of small molecule inhibitors in cancer models.

2012- 2014   **Louisiana State University Health Sciences Center Shreveport**, *Postdoctoral Scholar*
Laboratory of Kevin Pruitt, Ph.D., Department of Molecular and Cellular Physiology
Project: Epigenetic regulation of Frizzled 7 receptor in Breast and Prostate Cancer
  • Identified that Sirt1 regulated expression of Frizzled 7 receptor in several cancer models.

2006- 2012   **Meharry Medical College**, *Graduate Fellow*
Laboratory of James E.K. Hildreth, Ph.D., M.D., Center for AIDS Health Disparities Research
  • National Award: Ruth L. Kirschstein National Institutes of Health Fellowship
  • Project: **Mechanism of caveolin-1 mediated suppression of HIV-1 replication**
    o Identified NF-kappa B pathway was required for caveolin-1 to suppress virus replication

Glenn Simmons Jr., Ph.D. Curriculum Vitae

TEACHING EXPERIENCE

2015-present Co-Instructor- University of Minnesota-Duluth School of Medicine,
Pathways to Advanced Degrees in Life Sciences summer program for underrepresented
undergraduates. Designed, taught, and evaluated scientific debate course to
undergraduates relating to gene editing and responsible use of controlled substances.

2013-2014 Co-Instructor- LSU Health Sciences Center Shreveport, Cancer Biology
Taught cancer epigenetics sections to graduate student class, prepared and graded
exam questions.

2010-2013 Co-Instructor- Meharry Medical College Project SAVED, HIV/AIDS Biology
Taught basic HIV-1 biology to community stakeholders and trainers for CDC-sponsored
community-based participatory research projects.

PUBLICATIONS

1. Somnath Pandey, **Glenn E. Simmons Jr.**, Svitlana Malyarchuk, Tara N. Calhoun, Kevin Pruitt. A novel MeCP2 acetylation site regulates binding with ATRX and HDAC1. Genes Cancer. 2015 Sep;6(9-10):408-421). PMID: 26622943

2. Taylor HE, **Simmons GE Jr**, Mathews TP, Khatua AK, Popik W, Lindsley CW, D'Aquila RT, Brown HA. (2015) Phospholipase D1 Couples CD4⁺ T Cell Activation to c-Myc-Dependent Deoxyribonucleotide Pool Expansion and HIV-1 Replication. PLoS Pathog 11(5): e1004864. doi:10.1371/journal.ppat.1004864. PMID: 26020637

3. **Glenn E. Simmons Jr.**, Wendy M. Pruitt, Kevin Pruitt. Diverse Roles of SIRT1 in Cancer Biology and Lipid Metabolism. *Int. J. Mol. Sci.* 2015, 16(1), 950-965; doi:10.3390/ijms16010950. PMCID: PMC4307284

4. Yuyang Tang, Alvin George, Franklin Nouvet, Stephanie Sweet, Nkiruka Emeagwali, Harry E. Taylor, **Glenn Simmons**, James E.K. Hildreth. Infection of Female Primary Lower Genital Tract Epithelial Cells after Natural Pseudotyping of HIV-1: Possible Implications for Sexual Transmission of HIV-1. *PLoS One.* 2014 Jul 10;9 (7):e101367. PMCID: PMC4092063

5. **Glenn E. Simmons Jr.**, Somnath Pandey Ana Nedeljkovic-Kurepa, Madhurima Saxena, Allison Wang, Kevin Pruitt. Frizzled 7 Expression is Positively regulated by SIRT1 and β-Catenin in Breast Cancer Cells. *PLoS One.* 2014 Jun 4;9(6):e9886. PMCID: PMC4045932

6. **Glenn E. Simmons Jr.**, Harry E. Taylor, James E. K. Hildreth (2012). Caveolin-1 suppresses Human Immunodeficiency Virus-1 replication by inhibiting acetylation of NF-κB. *Virology.* 2012 Oct 10;432(1):110-9. PMCID: PMC3767293

SCHOLARLY PRESENTATIONS

Invited Seminars

2016 Inflammation and Tumorigenesis: The Chicken or The Egg- North Carolina A&T State University, Greensboro, NC

2015 Blocking HIV-1 replication: Caveolin-1 and inhibition of virus replication- University of Minnesota-Duluth Academic Health Center, Duluth, MN

2014 "As above, so below…" Cancer Epigenetics- Northwestern State University, Natchitoches, LA

2009 HIV/ STD risk prevention panel discussion- Vanderbilt University, Nashville, TN.

2008 State of HIV/AIDS in South Africa: Update on epidemic and where science is headed- Meharry Medical College, Nashville, TN.

Edited on 5/5/2016

SCHOLARLY PRESENTATIONS

Posters
2015   American Society for Cell Biology Annual Meeting, San Diego, CA
2011   98th Annual Meeting American Association of Immunologists, San Francisco, CA
2011   Keystone Symposium on HIV-1 Pathogenesis, Whistler, BC
2009   Federation of American Societies for Experimental Biology Annual meeting, New Orleans, LA

UNIVERSITY SERVICE

2015-present   Chairperson - UT Southwestern Postdoctoral Association, Career Development
              Committee

2010-2012   Member- Meharry Medical College School of Graduate Studies Admissions Committee

2008-2012   Member- Meharry Center for AIDS Health Disparities Research Advisory Board

COMMUNITY OUTREACH

2016   Visiting Scientist- Children's Chorus of Greater Dallas "Earth, Wind, and Sky"
       performance- Science Policy, Education, and Communications Club (SPEaC) of UT
       Southwestern. Provide live demonstrations of molecular biology and biochemistry to
       children and families at the Schermerhorn Symphony Center.

2015-Present   Guest Speaker- STARS (Science Teacher Access to Resources at Southwestern)
              program. Provide career seminar to high school science classes. Engage in mentoring
              high school students on research opportunities.

2015   Barack Obama Male Leadership Academy STEM Expo. Judge science projects
       presented by students. Provide direct feedback in preparation for regional science fair
       competition for top students.

2009-2012   Poet-Mentor, Southern Word Inc., Nashville, TN.
           Educate youth in urban and academic settings in creative writing and oral
           expression. Coach/Mentor Tennessee national youth poetry slam team.

PROFESSIONAL AFFILIATIONS

2015-present   American Society for Cell Biology
2014-present   UT Southwestern Postdoctoral Association
2011-present   Sigma Xi Scientific Research Society
2010   American Association for Immunologists

PROFESSIONAL AWARDS

2015   American Society for Cell Biology MAC Travel Award to Annual Meeting
       American Society for Cell Biology Mentorship in Active Learning and Teaching Award
2011   Keystone Symposia on HIV Evolution, Genomics and Pathogenesis Scholarship
2009   American Society for Biochemistry and Molecular Biology Travel Award
2009   Federal Association of Societies of Experimental Biology MARC Travel Award
2008   Meharry Medical College Charles W. Johnson Grand Prize for Student Research
2007   Alpha Phi Alpha Michael Singleton Memorial Scholarship Award
2001   Florida Medallion Scholar Award

Glenn Simmons Jr., Ph.D. Curriculum Vitae

TRAINED STUDENTS/SCIENTISTS

2010   Dr. Brittany Burns- Meharry Medical College
- Trained student in basic molecular biology techniques to assist with analysis of caveolin-1 expression.

2008   Dr. Melanie Cruz- Tennessee State University/ Life University
- Trained student in cell culture and molecular biology techniques to investigate the role of caveolin-1 in cholesterol efflux.

Sample Resume

Rajeev M. Harish
5555 Main St., Austin, TX-75555

E-mail: rajeevmharish@email.com
Tel: +1-(555)-555-5555

WORK AND RESEARCH EXPERIENCE

ADVANCED IMAGING RESEARCH CENTER, SOUTH TEXAS MEDICAL CENTER, AUSTIN, USA

Post-Doctoral Researcher (2015-present) and Graduate Research Assistant (2009-2014)   2009 – Present
- Developed novel human brain imaging methods, which brought in +1 million dollars in grant funding to the lab
- Developed new analysis and processing pipelines for multi-dimensional MR spectroscopic data
- Managed multiple clinical research projects data acquisition, analysis and publication
- Co-authored fourteen scientific articles in peer-reviewed journals, including *Nature Medicine*
- Performed 1000+ *in vivo* human scans which lead to simplified imaging methods and increased patient throughput
- Mentored three graduate students and their projects resulting in several publications and international awards
- Created audio-visual learning tools to teach research analysis procedures, which halved the learning time for students
- Built and managed computational and storage resources needed to manage the clinical data

SENSIBLE TECHNOLOGY SOLUTIONS LTD., CHENNAI, INDIA   2008 – 2009
Program Trainee Analyst
- Created customer friendly JAVA-based UI (User Interface) applications for financial services

TECHMED SYSTEMS PVT. LTD., CHENNAI, INDIA   2007 – 2008
Technology Development Engineer
- Developed low-cost dental imaging systems for developing nations, resulting in manufacturing cost reduction by 50%
- Performed comprehensive market analysis identifying potential new sales opportunities and competitive strategies
- Developed strategic research partnerships with universities to discover and develop new products

EDUCATION AND AWARDS

GRADUATE SCHOOL OF BIOMEDICAL SCIENCES, SOUTH TEXAS MEDICAL CENTER, AUSTIN, USA
Doctor of Philosophy (Ph.D.), *Radiological Sciences*   2009 – 2014
- *Summa cum laude* merit award at International Society for Magnetic Resonance in Medicine (ISMRM, 2013) and international travel stipend awardee for three consecutive years

UNIVERSITY COLLEGE OF ENGINEERING, CHENNAI UNIVERSITY, CHENNAI, INDIA
Bachelor of Engineering (B.E.), *Biomedical Engineering* (with honors)   2003 – 2007
- First prize in technology contest -2006 at IIT-Mumbai, India
- First prize in biomedical device design contest -2006 at Chennai University, Chennai, India
- Stood in Top 4 percentile in Indian-national aptitude test (2004)

LEADERSHIP & ACTIVITIES

SOUTH TEXAS MEDICAL CENTER, AUSTIN, USA
Biomedical Innovation (Clinical Innovation Program for Medical Students)   2014 – Present
- Designed new program for medical students with focus on innovation and entrepreneurship
- Taught design innovation course to medical students, and to identify unmet clinical needs
- Mentored teams of medical and graduate students on medical device design projects and developed novel solutions
- Served as a liaison between medical school and UT Northern Engineering school to develop design prototypes

Safe-T Inc. (Innovating and Improving the safety of deliveries)   2012 – Present
- Co-founder and Director of Product Development
- Designed a low-cost surgical assist device for safer cesarean section births
- Lead biomedical engineering efforts for design, development, prototyping and testing of products
- Obtained a seed non-diluting grant of $25k for initial prototyping and business model development
- Created value propositions and designed documents to secure the IP rights for the device

UNIVERSITY COLLEGE OF ENGINEERING, CHENNAI UNIVERSITY, INDIA
Chief Student Representative for Career Development office   2007 – 2008
- Student community representative and liaison between university and industry
- Developed and organized sustainable recruitment training for 600+ strong student body, resulting in 100% placements

Co-Convener of MEDITECH-2007
- Led a team of 30+ students to raise $5K to organize technical symposium on biomedical innovations and advancements

Autism Awareness Program
- Participated in autism awareness program for rural population on national television

SCIENTIFIC RESEARCH IMPACT

Published 14 scientific papers in the last six years with 300+ citations and cumulative h index of 7
- Harish RM, Miller P, Choy Q *et al. Magn Reson Med* 2015 (cited 1)
- Harish RM, Andrews M, Boyett S *et al. NMR Biomed* 2014; 27(10):1232-1276 (cited 2)
- Choy Q, Harish RM, *et al. NMR Biomed* 2013; 26(10):1272-1296 (cited 6)
- Harish RM, Boyett S, Patel T *et al. NMR Biomed* 2012; 25(4):573-632 (cited 18)
- Choy Q, Harish RM, DeVore R *et al. Nat Med* 2012; 18:824-9 (cited 202)

HOBBIES: Travelling, collecting old music (vinyl), book clubs, writing short stories
LANGUAGES: Proficient in English, conversant in Hindi and Telugu

Sample Hybrid (CV/Resume)

Charlie Jackson PhD

Big Texas Medical Center
Department of Cellular Biology
1000 Lone Star Way
Metropolitan, TX 77777

Charlie.Jackson@bigtexas.edu
Phone: 777-777-7777
Fax: 888-888-8888

Summary Statement/Qualifications

I am an ambitious and enthusiastic cancer biologist with a desire to transition to a role as a Medical Science Liaison. During my time at BTMC I have collaborated on several projects developing an extensive professional network across the United States. I have demonstrated innovation, motivation, and entrepreneurial spirit through the creation of the BTMC Consulting Club. I have also tapped into the Angel Investor and Venture Capital network, creating the first biotech consulting organization in Metropolitan. My skills, professional network, and a decade of oncology research will allow me to add immediate value to your company.

2013   Ph.D. Cancer Biology, Big Texas Medical Center, Texas
2006   B.S. Biochemistry, Scientifica University, California

Education

Big Texas Medical Center, Metropolitan, TX
Doctor of Philosophy, Cancer Biology   Aug 2008- Sept 2013
Mentors: Dr. Joe T. Garcia, Director of Therapeutic Oncology Research; Dr. Rick Callahan, Professor at Medical Center Institute;
Project: Highly classified scientific work

Scientifica University, West Coast, CA
Bachelor of Science, Biochemistry   Jan 2005- May 2006
Honors: Dean's List Fall 2005 & Spring 2006, Cum Laude graduate

Research Experience

Big Texas Medical Center, Metropolitan, TX   Oct 2013- Present
Postdoctoral Fellow II
Mentor: Dr. Samuel White, Distinguished Chair for Research in Oncology.
- High content, genome wide scientific findings
- Implementing scientific things
- Lead investigator managing a $200K annual budget aimed at molecular stuff
- Regularly interact with clinical residents on collaborative projects.

Big Texas Medical Center, Metropolitan, TX   Aug 2008- Sept 2013
Graduate Student
Mentors: Dr. Joe T. Garcia, Director of Therapeutic Oncology Research; Dr. Rick Callahan, Professor at Medical Center Institute
- Identified things with cells
- Presented cell findings

Scientifica University— Molecular Biology Department, West Coast, CA   Sept 2006- Aug 2008
Research Specialist
Mentor: Dr. Emma Brown, Important Fellow
- Gathered, processed, and interpreted data as part of a multi-institutional research collaboration on the functional characterization of science stuff in a lab

Charlie Jackson PhD

UT Southwestern Medical Center
Department of Cellular Biology
1000 Lone Star Way
Metropolitan, TX 7777

Charlie.Jackson@bigtexas.edu
Phone: 777-777-7777
Fax: 888-888-8888

Professional Experience

President and Founder– Big Bang Theory Consulting Metropolitan, TX   March 2015- Present
- Created the first biotech focused consulting organization in Metropolitan, Texas. Our clients include a family office, private equity group, and biotech start-ups
- Delivered market reports, technology assessment and valuation to executives and investors.

Market Analyst- Science Advice Inc, Enzyme, NY   Oct 2014- April 2015
- Provide services to angel investors, private equity groups, and venture capitalists on the life science market.
- Interacted with both key opinion leaders and C-level executives, acting as a conduit and distilling information into actionable business solutions or strategic moves.

Intern Market Analyst — Big Bob's Biosciences, Metropolitan, TX   Sept 2014- Feb 2015
- Develop market research reports on key healthcare areas of interest for Big Bob.
- Presented competitive market analysis, estimated market growth rates, product valuation, and exit strategies.

Consulting Club Founder and President— BTMC Metropolitan, TX   Sept 2013- March 2015
- Lead a five member executive board and 35 member general body.
- Coordinated with large firm recruiting departments to organize recruiting events and implemented resume and case workshops held both on and off campus.
- Initiated a partnership with Giant Texas Medical Center consulting club.
- Created in-roads with Metropolitan area angel investors and firms in the providing expert insights and recommendation on potential investments.
- Efforts have yielded two offers at two firms for club members and affiliates.

Scientific Consultant— BTMC Metropolitan, TX   Nov 2013- April 2014
- Advised a biotechnology company on experimental design, clinical and treatment leads on novel based treatment option of cancer
- Project was terminated as a result of our analysis due to lack of specificity and general toxicity.

Awards

Training Fellowship, NIH T32: Cancer Biology, 2014
Travel Award, AACR Special Conference: **Noncoding RNAs and Cancer,** 2012
Outstanding Graduate Student Presentation, Texas Science Society, 2011
Research Fellowship, Scientifica University, 2004

Professional, Academic Activities & Additional leadership roles

Professional activities: Reviewer of several scientific articles, STARs inner Metropolitan high school mentoring program, and tutor at local county colleges.

Academic Affiliations: American Association of Cancer Research, AACR, (2009-current), Texas Science Society (2009- current), BTMC consulting club member, Phi Theta Kappa Honor Society member

Postdoctoral Association Career Development Committee - Grants Panel Chair - formed a panel of successfully funded postdocs, grants managements, and faculty grant reviewers aimed to inform postdocs of the grant application and review process. **Symposiums planning committee** – organized annual postdoctoral association symposiums consisting of two poster sessions and several talks scientific and career development talks.

Charlie Jackson PhD

Big Texas Medical Center
Department of Cellular Biology
1000 Lone Star Way
Metropolitan, TX 77777

Charlie.Jackson@bigtexas.edu
Phone: 777-777-7777
Fax: 888-888-8888

Oral and Posters Presentations (2 of 12 listed)

C. Jackson, L. Green and A. Patel. Laboratory Shenanigans: science and such. Big Texas Medical Center, Metropolitan, TX, February 12, 2011. **Oral**

C. Jackson, L. Green and A. Patel. Laboratory Shenanigans Unveiled. Annual Meeting of the Texas Science Society, Texas Hospital for Children. Metropolitan, TX, March 30th-April 1st 2011. **Oral**

Publications (2 of 6 listed)

Jackson C, Wang C, Lawson J, Miller L, Jones C, Wiley II, Pratt JD, Blanchard A. (2015). molecule pathway and stem cell maintenance in the human body. (Under review)

Reed AA, Hanson Y, Wyatt Y, Sorkin C, Jackson C, et al. (2013) *Science shmience*, a New System for Naming Stuff. Journal113 (1): e153438

Sample Cover Letter

Your Street Address
City, State, Zip

Date

Employer's Name
Title
Company/Organization/Institution Name
Street Address
City, State, Zip

Dear Mr./Ms./Dr. Last Name:

Who are you and what do you want? Your opening paragraph should briefly introduce you and your interest in the organization or position. If you are aware of a specific position or opening, refer to it now and how you learned about it. This paragraph could also mention the name of an individual who recommended that you contact the employer, or cite other research that prompted you to write. It is important to indicate why you are interested in their organization.

Why are you a good candidate? The middle paragraph(s) should consist of a selection of highlights from your background that would be of greatest interest to the organization and consequently create the notion of "fit." Focus on your top 2-3 skills and experience and include supporting evidence for any claim of skills or accomplishments. Again, try to display knowledge of the field and organization. Use action verbs to describe relevant skills and expertise and mention specific knowledge you may have (i.e., lab techniques or computer applications.) that would be needed in the work. You can also touch on a particular topic that seems important in the job description that the employer developed. Catch the employer's attention and entice them to read your resume in detail and schedule an interview.

What will you do next? Your closing paragraph should outline next steps. Express your willingness to provide additional information and desire to further discuss the position in an interview. Include your phone number and email address. If you will be in the area, let them know. Thank the reader(s) for their time and interest.

Sincerely,

(Your handwritten signature; although you may omit extra spaces if sent electronically)

Your Typed Name

Continued

Sample Academic Cover Letter

Name of Your Current Department
Name of Your Current Institution
Address
City, State/Country 12345

Date

Name of Recipient
Recipient's Title
Name of Department
Name of University
Address
City, State/Country 12345

Dear Dr. Recipient (or Dear Hiring/Search Committee, or Dear Professor Recipient):

In the first paragraph, you will want to formally apply for and express interest in the position, and introduce yourself. You may share that you are in the process of completing your PhD/postdoctoral fellowship in your particular discipline at (your institution). You can also introduce your specialty or area of focus. Ideally, you will also use this first paragraph as an opportunity to begin personalizing your letter to this department and institution.

In the next paragraph, you can choose whether you would like to focus on your research or your teaching. This will depend on the job description. In either case, be clear and descriptive. An academic cover letter can be one or two pages, so you are not limited in terms of space. When describing your dissertation and/or your research, provide sufficient context to help the reader understand why your work is interesting, new, and compelling. Your description will likely be two to three times as long as this paragraph (thus, this letter will be about two pages long). If a research statement has also been requested, try to maintain consistency between the two descriptions without sounding repetitive. On other words, don't write in great detail about your research in a cover letter if you are also attaching a research statement. But if you are not including a research statement, discuss your research in this letter. In addition to your past research, your future research is also likely to be of interest to the hiring committee.

This paragraph will focus on your teaching. When you write about your teaching experience, consider whether or not a teaching statement has also been requested. If it has, you will want to reinforce your message without actually repeating it word for word. This paragraph is not only about your teaching experience, but can also address the courses you would like to teach, particularly at the institution to which you are applying. This will require a certain degree of familiarity with their department and curriculum, as well as the student demographics.

You also have the opportunity to address accomplishments, interests, or experiences that are relevant to the position including, but not limited to, service to your university or your field. If the culture of the department or institution is particularly unique or appealing to you, consider addressing that here as well.

In your concluding paragraph, it is appropriate to reiterate your interest in the position and to offer thanks for the committee's consideration. You may also make reference to the other materials you have submitted, and let them know that you look forward to hearing from them. It can be helpful to include your email and phone number in the final paragraph for their convenience.

Sincerely,
(include a handwritten signature here!)

Your Name

Chapter 17

The International Perspective

Natalie Lundsteen

Chapter Outline

Manage Expectations in Your Job
Search   234
Understand Your Visa and Work
Options   235
Build Your Transferable Skills   237

Building and Expanding Your
Network   238
References   240
Resources   240

Chapter Takeaways:

- If you are seeking work outside your home country, manage your employment expectations.
- Understand your visa and work options.
- Identify and develop transferable professional skills to make yourself more marketable.
- Develop your networks, especially if planning to remain in a foreign country.

Science is a global enterprise. Therefore, this book would not be complete without providing some advice and support for international graduate students and postdocs. Taking an international view applies to all of us, since career opportunities in science (and work in general) can take us anywhere in the world. When considering who might be an "international trainee," we don't necessarily assume a US-centric view. I was an international student, having completed my PhD in the United Kingdom (as a US citizen), where I experienced the joys of navigating work and student visa requirements, along with the challenges of starting my post-PhD job search in a country different to the one where I planned to find work. My coauthors and I have also worked with and advised international students and researchers at universities in the United States and abroad. It is a rare scientist who does not work alongside international colleagues!

This chapter aims to give general advice to those who study or work (or both) in a country other than their own, whether you are an international trainee in the United States planning to stay, are in the United States planning to return to your home (or another) country, are a US citizen looking at work in another country, or are someone who is studying/working out of the United States and

ReSearch. http://dx.doi.org/10.1016/B978-0-12-804297-7.00017-3

focusing your job search on the United States. There may be other combinations or descriptions, but basically—if you have any international concerns, this chapter is for you. The general advice in the rest of this book is completely relevant to international scientists, but there are a few areas of additional consideration in your job search, which will be covered in this chapter.

MANAGE EXPECTATIONS IN YOUR JOB SEARCH

Your strategy as an international job seeker means almost all jobs you are interested in will be open to you (with a few exceptions), but you will need to do a little more advance preparation than other candidates. Our advice on understanding the realities of the job market in Chapter 3 discusses the importance of thinking about your career path as early as possible, and being realistic about what is needed to succeed in various careers. You should know your career options and narrow down your career choices. However, you must also always be aware of immigration laws and visa restrictions, along with perceptions and misunderstanding on the part of people who select you for interview or make decisions about hiring you. Therefore, knowing as much as you can about your own situation will allow you to dispel incorrect information and provide positive education to others while you are job seeking. In addition to understanding your right to live and work in various locales, you must also understand where the types of jobs you are interested in are plentiful (and thus, perhaps more available to you).

You have many science career options, but be realistic about the kinds of opportunities you target. For example, non-US citizens are not going to be hired into certain government labs, just as US citizens are not eligible for foreign government work. But beyond that type of limitation, most career avenues are open to you. You will just have to navigate hurdles that might not be present for others if you are seeking work in a country other than your home. There is one potential area of restriction: Some of you may be studying in the United States on scholarships that require you to return to your home country to work. If you have such a requirement, honor the agreement and don't try to evade that commitment—it's just really unprofessional and at some point in your career you may well have to return home, so don't burn bridges.

When considering an international job search, think broadly about labor markets. Your international science job opportunities can be affected by geography, economic policy, national politics, trends in specific industry, or all of the above. Be aware of where opportunities might be plentiful and where it will be more difficult to find work. There are countries that are "immigrant-friendly" and others that are not. Certain countries (or even regions) can be economically robust and thus perhaps in need of developing their workforce. Others may be struggling or in a time of change, and thus not a good bet for job growth.

Constantly changing political landscapes, as well as economic variables, will affect both immigration and visa regulations. Large countries might have dramatic variances from state to state (or region to region) in labor markets and economic strength, which then might dictate immigration and work visas and/or availability of jobs. Alongside that, different industries may be affected by these economic and political variables in different ways. In the US pharmaceutical industry right now, for example, many of the global firms with multiple locations across the country are reducing workforce and consolidating research and development functions. This means fewer jobs, in fewer locations, and more competition. As a job seeker, it is necessary for you to understand the bigger picture of the country (and industry) you are targeting, to get a realistic view of potential for employment.

Remember, too, that work and study visa regulations change every year, often multiple times in a year. Know where to go to find information, and *remember that the responsibility to learn and stay up-to-date about this information is all yours.*

UNDERSTAND YOUR VISA AND WORK OPTIONS

Be constantly proactive in managing your visa status and paperwork. Do not depend on the international affairs office of your institution to do this for you. You must ASK questions and stay informed. Read every piece of email or mail that comes to you regarding your visa, and don't ignore requests to update information. Do not listen to friends, family, or someone who "knows someone who knows something" about visas. As a career advisor, I am often asked questions about work visas, and my response is that "I only know enough about visas to be dangerous," meaning: I am not an expert and might give you misinformation. Bottom line: The only advice you should take on immigration and visa matters is advice from the international affairs office staff or your immigration attorney.

There is no doubt that visa issues cause science job seekers extra anxiety. However, a job seeker under stress doesn't make the best choices in his or her job search. Confidence can come from being as educated as possible about your work options. Know the big-picture legal aspects, and know your own personal options. This includes being knowledgeable about your Optional Practical Training (OPT) if you are in the United States, or any right to work, or right to remain after study if you are a trainee elsewhere. Be sure you know what is currently legislated and also the exact amount of time you might personally possess to work. When you are applying for jobs, if you are in the process of applying for a US green card, or permanent residency in another country, there may be restrictions on your ability to change employers while in that process. Know everything there is to know about your situation, so there are no surprises.

Attend any workshops on your campus that have to do with immigration or visas. Events taking place on campus will usually involve legitimate speakers or information. There is a lot of misinformation available online, so if you must read blogs or websites about work visas, please do so as a trained critical researcher, and remember: only trust advice from an immigration attorney or international affairs office professional. Also, if it sounds too good to be true (i.e., a website advertising a scheme that guarantees green cards), it definitely is not true.

The worst way to go about a science job search is to start with companies that grant a lot of H-1B visas. Yes, you can find information online about US companies sponsoring the highest number of work visas to foreign nationals—but I don't see a lot of companies on those lists that are focused on scientific expertise. One of the most common situations I come across with the international graduate students and postdocs I advise is the idea that any job that grants right to remain in a country is sufficient for them. They don't seem to care about finding the right fit for their education and expertise; they just want the job because of the visa. These scientists submit applications and waste time applying to companies because they have heard from friends that work visas are granted, or perhaps they know of a handful of companies who have hired science PhDs in the past, so that's where all their application efforts are directed. But a job that isn't a good fit for you is not a job you are going to get. There's way too much competition out there.

Instead, take the time to go through the career search process (as is provided in this book). If you know what your strengths are, the career areas you are interested in, and how you will provide value to a company or organization, you are much more likely to be a "fit" for that place and be considered for the job. An organization that must sponsor you for a working visa will have to undertake the cost and time of applying on your behalf, and they are only going to do that if they are sure you are going to add value as an employee.

Dan Beaudry, author of *Power Ties: The International Student's Guide to Finding a Job in the United States*,[1] suggests the best strategy for finding a job with H-1B sponsorship is to offer the company a compelling reason to hire you. Company hiring managers may ask why they should grant an "outsider" (i.e., foreign national) this position when there might be a domestic worker who can fill the post. Both in the European Union and the United States, a visa can only be granted for a post if there is proof that the applicant is more qualified for the role than a resident/ citizen. So, if you apply for jobs that are a "stretch" (meaning you possess very few of the qualifications and required experience) or if the positions are unrelated to your scientific training, and you have the additional hurdle of needing visa sponsorship, there is little chance an organization is even going to interview you.

I generally advise international students and postdocs to include "right to work" information on a CV or resume, if they have it, but otherwise not to draw attention to the fact that visa sponsorship is needed. Your scientific expertise should create interest from an employer, but if your credentials are being reviewed by a nonscientist, or someone without an understanding of the value you could add to the organization, drawing attention to your nonresident status or your need for a visa might cause you to be passed over in favor of another candidate who won't need a visa and isn't as "complicated." (You may be asking: "how do I get my CV or resume to someone who will value my scientific expertise and credentials?" The answer to that is networking, discussed later in this chapter.)

Once you are invited to interview, be prepared to alleviate any concerns the employer may have about your visa sponsorship. If you have OPT (or similar), explain exactly what time you have remaining to work under that program, and how the employer can use that training time. Hopefully, the employer will have previously sponsored work visas, but you may find yourself in the position of describing the employer-sponsoring process. If you don't know how to explain these things about yourself and your right to work, set up a meeting with your institution's international affairs office and get educated.

Keep in mind that while large companies may have extensive experience sponsoring work visas or hiring foreign nationals, they also may take a very long time to make that happen, and they are probably inundated with requests from international students and scholars wanting to work there, so your competition will be fierce. Small or medium-sized companies may not know everything about visa sponsorship, but it is much more likely that you will get a chance to prove your worth to the organization to a hiring manager, who then will be willing to listen to your explanation of how straightforward the process is for the company to sponsor your work visa. Again, I must suggest Dan Beaudry's book for international students as a fantastic resource for understanding more about how to work with US employers and get past work visa hurdles.

Stay positive, because there are thousands of scientists around the world being hired and sponsored to work in foreign countries. Start your job search early, target the right kinds of companies, and be patient with the time it takes for these processes to happen (in the United States, the employer-sponsored visa can take many months to finalize).

BUILD YOUR TRANSFERABLE SKILLS

Finding a job that comes with a work visa is much more likely if you determine where your best-fit industry and type of role in that industry will be. Identifying and developing your transferable skills is a constant challenge for job-seeking scientists, but it is an extremely crucial part of positioning yourself as a "best-fit" candidate with the expertise needed to assist an organization or company with their work, product, or mission. Your scientific expertise is usually the primary reason an organization will be interested in you, but be aware of what else you have to offer that is of value. Employers want to know what skills you have that can meet their needs, whether those skills are in problem solving, data analysis, organization, or communication (as just a few common examples). The transferable skill identification and development discussed in Chapters 8 and 10 will help you get started thinking about your transferable skills and how to present them appropriately to an employer.

But since you have the added challenge of the work visa hurdle in your job search, you will need to identify any of your skill areas that need work and polish them. Teamwork, communication, and adaptability are the most important transferable skills for international trainees to possess and develop. Chapter 14 provides advice on improving your communication skills, but you may need to put extra effort into your language facility. Employers really do value your foreign language skills, but if you can't communicate confidently in the business language of a company during an interview, you will not be offered the job. This is going to mean pushing yourself outside of your comfort zone to speak publicly in a language that you may not feel confident about, but practice makes perfect.

Teamwork is also a challenge for scientists accustomed to working independently on the bench, but remember that you are almost always part of a lab group team, which you can discuss in an interview. You can also easily improve your teamwork skills by joining an organization or two, whether at your institution or in your community, and hopefully eventually taking on some responsibility or leadership in that group.

Adaptability is the easiest of these three key skills for international applicants to demonstrate, because your experiences studying or working outside your home country show your ability to adjust to new situations and environments. Business organizations in particular value a candidate's ability to learn new things and manage change.

In addition to your basic communication skills (speaking and writing), be aware of the value of your intercultural competence: your ability to communicate appropriately and effectively with those from other cultures. This is a great thing to highlight during interviews and even in your cover letter if applying to a large multinational firm. It's a good idea to also take advantage of any opportunities you have to learn more about the culture where you are job seeking. If you are in the United States and want to remain there for work, attend any available career development workshops on resumes, interviewing, and other career search topics, to gain as much knowledge as possible about the mindset of your competition and what employers expect from applicants.

BUILDING AND EXPANDING YOUR NETWORK

In any career search, establishing networks early is advised because when you are actually job seeking and need contacts, you are already connected to people who might be able to help you. For international applicants, having a contact inside a company to refer you to the hiring manager may be the only way your resume gets past HR screeners who don't want to deal with the perceived complication of visa sponsorship. But you can't ask someone you don't know to endorse or refer you. You actually can't really expect an existing contact to go out of their way for you either! That is why you must build relationships early and often, and make sure you are a known, trusted, and a credible candidate for that position. In the United States, there is much reference to the "hidden job market," the available job roles that are rarely advertised and are found through networks. This is true in many countries around the world—**what** you know is not as important as **who** you know.

The best way to build your network is to start where you are. For example, if you know you want to stay in the United States, expand your network in simple ways—make friends with American colleagues, ask them for advice on your job search, and join organizations that will not only build your teamwork skills but will also connect you to others in the group. Professional or career-focused groups are the best types of organizations in which to get involved, since you will build teamwork skills, meet other people, and also be working on career topics that increase your career knowledge. Make efforts to integrate more fully into the culture/society where you are based, rather than associating only with people from home. That is not to say you won't need the comfort of speaking your own language and hanging out with people who understand the way you think, but if your goal is to work in a new culture, you need to integrate into that culture whenever possible.

If you know you want to return to work in your home country, it's important to maintain, and expand, your network there. This can be difficult when you are away for years at a time. I found it a challenge returning home to find work in the United States after 8 years in the United Kingdom, primarily because my network was so much stronger in Europe than at home, and even though I had tried to keep connections, I wasn't as known to people in my field in the United States. It is also a challenge to build networks if your home country isn't big on networking, but adjust your activities as needed. Some simple ideas to keep your home network robust are as follows:

- Maintain occasional correspondence with former professors or colleagues. Let them know what you are working on, or update when you reach milestones such as promotions or publications.
- Offer to give a talk in your old department when you go home for visits, or even reach out to new universities and offer your expertise.
- Set up informational interviews or coffee meetings with people working in companies or industries of interest when you are on home visits.

The networking and informational interviewing advice in Chapter 12 will be useful to you for these kinds of activities.

If you are trying to make contacts in a country different to both your home country and the one in which you are currently living or working, learn as much as you can about the place before you embark on your search. The great thing about being a scientist is you probably already know people from your country of interest, (and if not, someone in your lab probably knows someone) so start with contacts close to home and begin building your country-specific knowledge.

Scientific professional societies may also provide an opportunity to find international contacts.

When seeking individuals to connect and meet with in your target country, alumni of your various educational institutions are another great resource. The reason for this is you have at least one thing in common (studying or working at the same place). There may be international alumni groups you can join, or you can ask to be added to an email list so you are aware of activities of the group or within a certain country. You can usually find this information on the alumni or development office Web pages of your institutions. Do this type of activity well in advance of the time you will be relocating to or returning to that country.

LinkedIn is a very powerful research tool for connecting with people in the country, company, or job role of focus, as you can search institutional alumni by cities around the world. Beyond your alumni connections, you can use LinkedIn to search for people more generally in a certain country, but the connections will be less strong and people will be less likely to respond to a total stranger. Joining interest groups on LinkedIn is a great way to show some connection or similarity. You may wish to include information on your LinkedIn profile that indicates your desire to work in a certain country, and be sure to include your language skills in your profile.

Remember, your reasons for making connections and networking must be genuine, but if you have made real connections, your network will be a powerful asset when you are actually applying for jobs. No matter the country or culture, people are your most valuable resource for information and making things happen in your job search.

REFERENCES

1. Beaudry D. *Power ties: the international student's guide to finding a job in the United States.* 2014.

RESOURCES

1. Goinglobal. Country-specific career and employment information. http://www.goinglobal.com.
2. International Postdoc Survival Guide. National Postdoctoral Association. http://www.national-postdoc.org/?page=SurvivalGuide.

Case Study

Global CV and Resume Styles
By Abby Evans, PhD

Abby Evans is a Careers Adviser at The University of Oxford. She specializes in advising science students, researchers, and graduates on UK and international careers in academia, industry, and beyond. She has a PhD in Geophysics from the University of Cambridge.

In a global jobs market, it can be a challenge to understand the expectations of international employers and determine what is culturally appropriate for CVs and resumes. Cultural norms of CV/resume style and content vary greatly around the world. Here are just a few examples.

While the inclusion of a photo would be a no–no in the United States or the United Kingdom, it is standard procedure in many European countries. In Germany CVs ("*Lebenslauf*") are usually signed and dated. Some countries also require you to submit a "statement of veracity" signed by a third party who can vouch for your information. Even standard paper size varies—US standard (8½ × 11 in.) compared to European A4 (210 × 297 mm).

Beyond the practicalities of content and format, style variations also exist. In Europe, for example, the style of writing is generally more direct, straightforward, and stripped back than the self-marketing and more effusive language of a US resume.

So the upshot is that you shouldn't assume that the resume format you would use in the United States will be the best option everywhere. Getting the cultural nuances wrong is a clear indicator to an employer that you haven't done your homework. Find out what is appropriate for the culture of the organization and the country. Review as many relevant CV/resume samples as possible.

If you can, get someone who is familiar with the country to which you are applying to review your documents before you submit them. Your aim should be to gain an understanding of the organizational and regional culture and convey that understanding to potential employers.

Case Study

Career Experiences Outside of My Home Country
By Sina Safayi, PhD, DVM

Sina Safayi is currently Assistant Director of Career Development at the University of Texas MD Anderson Cancer Center UTHealth Graduate School of Biomedical Sciences in Houston, Texas. He previously oversaw a career professional advisory scheme for postdocs at Okinawa Institute of Science and Technology in Japan, and prior to that was a postdoctoral researcher at Iowa State University and Clemson University. His PhD is from University of Copenhagen in Lactation Physiology, and he also has a DVM from Shiraz University, Iran.

As a Refugee

Refusing to call myself "immigrant," I consider myself a "refugee" from the Middle East in self-exile for the past 12 years. I escaped the existing dictatorship, social injustice, and inequality for a better future to achieve my dreams in the "ideal" land of so-called "liberty, democracy, justice, and equality." I was among a few of my lucky fellows who had the opportunity to use continuing education as a means to emigrate, rather than fleeing illegally. I respect both groups from the bottom of my heart, since I endured the hardships of dictatorship myself. The cause for which you fled will always haunt you, unless luck finds you along the way. In other words, there can be a great deal of anxiety over the expiration date of a temporary work visa, especially since your greatest fear is being faced with having to return to your homeland. Inevitably, you usually end up taking an option, which is usually better than the latter, but certainly is not the best. Therefore, because time is of the essence, visa holders cannot hold out for better opportunities to come along.

Another universal factor would be the biased nature of humans. Living 12 years outside my homeland and exploring various countries across Asia, Europe, and America, I assure you that this "ideal" land of so-called "liberty, democracy, justice, and equality" does not exist. However, countries like Denmark or the United States are decades or maybe centuries closer to that dream than where I come from, the Middle East. No matter where in the world you go, you face "racism" or a "glass ceiling." To avoid some of these barriers, here are a few suggested solutions based on my experience:

- Choose a multicultural country with immigrant-friendly policies, considering barriers such as economy and job market, as well as culture and language.
- Stay there as long as you are not considered an "alien" on your job applications. This corresponds with the fact that you will not need visa sponsorship for work after your education, which could be a huge obstacle during the job-hunting process for internationals.[1]
- Pick colleges in or close to the large cities where you can find more networking, and therefore, job opportunities. Also, large cities tend to be more multicultural (alien-friendly!) than small cities.
- Try to fit into your host society rather than isolating yourself in small alien societies such as those from your own country. This integration helps you to be seen and be considered to work your way up the ladder more quickly.

Continued

Case Study—cont'd

As a Scientist

With a DVM from Shiraz University in Iran, I left what I used to call home to continue my education at the University of Copenhagen in Denmark. During my stay there, I passed graduate courses in Germany and Sweden and as part of my PhD education, did sabbaticals at Aarhus University in Denmark and the University of Arizona in the United States. Six years later, I came to the United States and did 2 years of postdoc work at Clemson University and 3.5 years of postdoc work at Iowa State University. Having two doctorates, 5+ years of postdoc experience, 70+ publications and presentations including 20+ peer-reviewed publications, 16 years of teaching and mentoring experience, and being co-I or co-PI on a few grants, I decided to choose the route of Science Policy in a new country, Japan.

I have always held a keen desire to challenge myself in leadership roles. This became particularly apparent at the beginning of my undergraduate education and has sustained itself through a number of opportunities over the past couple of decades. These 18+ years of exposure to a range of professional and leadership activities in international higher education across three continents, along with my unique pathway of graduate and postdoctoral training, helped provide a strong backdrop for me to build on in the way of taking an administrative role in Japan's higher education. Last year, I joined the Okinawa Institute of Science and Technology, a newly founded international university in Japan, as their Postdoctoral Career Development Program Lead, the first program of its kind in Asia. Looking back over the entirety of my experience, I suggest to other scientists following an international career journey to:

- Pick your PI and institute wisely. The best assurance for your success would be to consider the record of your potential PI; how much support she/he provides for her/his mentees and finally, where her/his alumni landed careers in the job market.
- Notice the "The Iceberg Illusion." Individuals erroneously believe they belong to a top echelon of candidates who will succeed in securing a faculty position, dismissing the significant effort and dedication required of those who have achieved that goal.
- Be aware of the reality of job markets. Roughly 80% of PhD grads desire a faculty position, yet ~3% in the United Kingdom and ~15% in United States end actually achieving that goal.[2] Also based on a US study, the majority (70%–85%) of career-track positions are filled by alumni from 25% of elite institutions.[3]
- Understand the difference between "real self" and the illusion of "ideal self." This can be the most important in a chosen career path; the illusion of believing that a faculty position is the best career choice without a thorough self-assessment of your "skills" (what they are good at; e.g., grant writing, managing people, or teaching), "interests" (what makes them excited; e.g., helping others or the advancement of science), and "values" (what they value most; what is most rewarding?).
- Stay connected. Since most job opportunities happen through networking, it would be wise to stay in one country/region and take short sabbaticals, rather than moving to another country starting your social and professional network

Case Study—cont'd

from scratch. Also, feeling more secure by having a circle of social and professional support around you, you will find yourself taking more risks and hence, will have more chances to succeed.

The End of the Tunnel

Bottom line, it is never too late to define a strategy for an effective goal-oriented doctoral or postdoctoral experience. Try not to limit yourself to a few options; look at the big picture and think out of box. Assess yourself, explore your options, set an informed career goal, and go for it full-engine ahead, knowing that "a goal without a plan is just a wish."… "May the Force be with you."

---

[1] What you will be called as foreigner/international resident on official papers in the United States.
[2] Powell K. The future of the postdoc. *Nature* 2015;**520**(7546):144–47.
[3] Clauset A, Arbesman S, Larremore DB. Systematic inequality and hierarchy in faculty hiring networks. *Science Advances* 2015;**1**(1):e1400005.

Case Study

Knowing Who Can Help You

By Tracey Wells

Tracey Wells is Director of the Careers Service at the University of Bath (UK). She has worked in University Careers Services for 15 years, and has particular interests in international careers and working with international students. She has presented at conferences in China and Europe, as well as in the United Kingdom. She has a degree in Chemistry from the University of Durham, and previously worked as an Information Officer for the Royal Society of Chemistry.

If you are seeking work outside your home country, don't try to go it alone! As well as the invaluable advice and insights you can gain from talking to fellow students, academics, and colleagues, think creatively about where and from whom you can seek additional support.

So, who can help? As well as your Careers Service, your institution may provide you with access to international networks through alumni databases and LinkedIn groups. Are there additional organizations that can support your global careers search? Find out about recruitment intermediary organizations promoting opportunities in particular countries—some of these organize "Career Summits" and "Career Forums" bringing together companies and job seekers across the World. Professional bodies and trade associations may have access to international networking groups, publish lists of member companies, or provide labor market information and advice for job seekers within a particular sector.

The websites of embassies of particular countries vary in the amount of information they provide, but in addition to publishing details on any relevant visa options (if required), they often provide a gateway to labor market information and possibly resources for job seekers.

And finally, if you are making applications in a language that isn't your first language, getting a second opinion from a speaker of that language can help you to avoid errors in grammar and language in your written documents—helping to make your applications stand out for the right reasons!

Case Study

Are You a Scientist Thinking of Living and Working Overseas? (I Did, and Here's What I Would Tell Myself If I Could Do It Over Again)
By Cath Latham, PhD

Cath Latham is Senior Research Officer at the Burnet Institute for Medical Research and Public Health (Melbourne, Australia), where she works on developing drugs for viruses affecting global health including HIV. She has a PhD in Biochemistry from the University of Queensland (Brisbane, Australia) and completed a postdoctoral research fellowship at Columbia University (New York, NY, USA) before returning to Australia.

The great thing about science is how truly global it is. You will always find people around you in your lab or workplace who have already made an international move who can give great advice. Although, it's not without its challenges! Having made a huge leap from Australia to the United States for my postdoc, I would tell myself three things if I were to do it over again:

1. Listen closely to advice from others and let people help you. Before you go, and when you arrive in your new international home, you will need to reach out to others for all sorts of reasons, even just getting a bank account open or buying furniture, or knowing how to get paid in your new workplace. There's no need to make it harder for yourself even if you're determined to "do it on your own." So don't be afraid to accept that help when its offered!

2. While everyone's story is unique, you will find that all expats have common experiences, and you can help each other get used to your new surroundings. Everyone's experience will be different, depending on where they've come from and where they are headed but in a lot of ways, you will have a lot in common with others who have moved internationally and are away from their home country. This happens regardless of your personality and any challenges you've faced in the past. Reach out to others and you might be surprised how much you can help each other out!

3. If you choose to move back to your home country again after your international experience, don't underestimate how much things might have changed while you were gone. It's tempting to think that your home is in stasis while you are having the time of your life but the changes can be quite shocking, but exciting too! Also, it is really important to keep the networks you make once you leave. Not just your work contacts, but also the friends you have made while you've been there. My New York friends, wherever they are now, are still a constant source of support and advice, and we catch up whenever we can!

There are really two main reasons why I went overseas to live and work after my PhD. First, I wanted to challenge myself and succeeding in a safe, familiar environment of my home city and country, which seemed so removed from the rest of the world, didn't satisfy me for the long term. I am Australian, born in the country town of Bundaberg in Queensland. I moved to the city of Brisbane for university, then went on to do a PhD there. If you haven't heard of Brisbane, it's a lovely city, but at the time I was living there it was more like an oversized country town and not somewhere perceived to be a buzzing urban hub of style and culture like Sydney or Melbourne, or other famous cities around the world! Regardless of where you are in Australia, it is far away from the rest of the world. REALLY far away. Basically it's like living on the moon!

Case Study—cont'd

I'd always wanted to live and work overseas, and as my science career developed, it encouraged and facilitated the idea of an international living/working experience. As a scientist, I had so many questions about what the rest of the global scientific community was doing. I would read leading papers in my field from United States and European collaborators and competitors, and I thought "How do they think? How to do they design experiments? Is it different from the way that I and my mentors and colleagues think about our scientific problems? If we are different, then what do we/I do well and what could I learn from my scientific colleagues overseas? How do my scientific methods and training translate to another culture?" But the second reason for going overseas, beyond the international aspects of science, is that I just had an incurable wanderlust. New York City, baby! YOLO.

It's important to remember whatever international move you make; you're going to get some form of culture shock. In moving to the United States, I had more of a culture shock than I expected. I thought Australia and the United States wouldn't be too different—both young countries, both settled by Europeans, and in the present day we are multicultural, diverse, and vibrant. And most obviously, there isn't really a language barrier because we're both speaking English (in one form or another). If you move to Europe or elsewhere, you will probably speak English at work, but all the other life stuff is a hell of a lot tougher if you don't speak the language. All I can say is, do NOT let this deter you from the amazing experience of moving to a new, exciting, foreign country. Surely, that's half the fun! And if you return to your home country, you might also find that you get some "reverse culture shock" as you try to remember how life works at home!

But for all the fun and adventure, it was hard to get out of my comfort zone and there were challenges. I took a pay cut by taking a postdoc in the United States, the international move was at my own expense, and I moved away from my friends and family. That first 6–12 months in a new place is really hard. Whether you move as a couple or as a single, you still need to set up a new network at work and in your home life, as well as getting to know new projects and colleagues in your workplace and that takes a while. Seemingly mundane tasks in your home country, such as opening a bank account or sorting out where to buy your groceries or doing your taxes, can be tricky to sort out in a new country. And that's just the practical stuff. Before I moved to New York, people who had been through a move like this had told me about how it takes ages to make friends, but I didn't quite believe them till I went through it myself. And was it worth it? Oh hell yes! Learning about how other people and cultures do things—in life as well as in science is enriching and confronting at the same time. It smashes through preconceptions, and gives you a perspective and compassion that it is only possible to develop by immersing yourself in a new way of life. You will make friends and colleagues who will stay in your network for years after you have all moved on to the next stages of your life. One thing I found invaluable was that once I finally got the hang of living in NYC, it was an incredible boost to my self-confidence. Occasionally, I'd be out with my friends, look around at the Manhattan skyline and think "Hey! I really did it!"

Continued

Case Study—cont'd

My last piece of advice to scientists thinking about moving beyond their home country is: wherever you move to or from in the world, we are all speaking the language of our scientific field. Now I'm back working on the moon (Melbourne, Australia) and my international experience has stayed with me and helped me see my own country in a different way. Living and working overseas after your PhD can make you realize how lucky we are that our jobs bring us together with like-minded people all over the globe. Pretty cool.

Section 6

Quick Tips, Summary and Conclusion

Chapter 18

Career Planning Quick Guide

Teresa M. Evans, Lily Raines

Chapter Outline

Quick Guide	**250**	Step 6: Acquire Additional	
Step 1: Seek Help	250	Marketable Skills Quickly	253
Step 2: Assess the Time You		Step 7: Network: Assess Current	
Have Available	251	and Identify Future Allies	253
Step 3: Determine Your Short-		Step 8: Prepare Your	
Term Versus Long-Term		Documents	254
Career Goals	251	Step 9: Know Where/How	
Step 4: Make a Plan	251	to Apply Efficiently	254
Step 5: Determine Your		Step 10: Stay Positive	254
Current Marketable		**References**	**254**
Skills	252	**Further Reading**	**254**

Chapter Takeaways:

- This chapter serves as a summary and quick guide to career planning.
- The more time you have to plan you career the better, so START EARLY.
- The less time you have to plan your career, the more focused you need to be.
- Refer to this chapter often and ask others for help.

This chapter is a summary of material covered in depth elsewhere in this book and will serve as a quick guide to the steps necessary to quickly change your career path.

Has your lab lost funding? Is your mentor moving to another state? Was your significant other offered a promotion that requires you to move in a matter of months? Did you finish your degree faster than you anticipated (yes, this happens!)? Although it's never too late to start developing the skills you will need for your desired career, whether it is academic or otherwise, it is critical to begin as early as you can. The earlier you begin, the earlier you can self-assess to narrow your career path (Chapter 8) and thus optimize your limited free time. Chapter 13 has advice for how best to make

ReSearch. http://dx.doi.org/10.1016/B978-0-12-804297-7.00018-5

time for your critical career development work while also making time to take care of your health (Chapter 5).

Refer to the following flow chart below as a guide to determine where you are in the career planning process and the next steps you should consider.

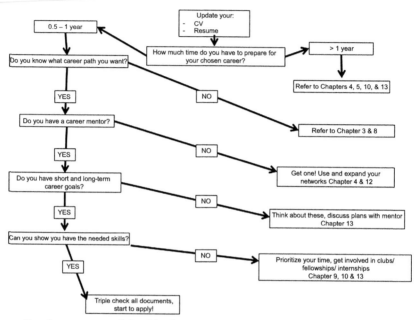

For the purposes of the this chapter, we will assume that you are in need of a career path change in less than 6 months and that you are starting from scratch.

QUICK GUIDE

Step 1: Seek Help

Although it is theoretically possible to make a major career transition on your own, it is incredibly difficult and completely unreasonable if you only have a few months. Help in a difficult transition can come from many places. This book is one of the many resources you should use, no matter how much time you have to determine your career path. However, you must find additional guidance anywhere you can. Often you can find help through interactions with various mentors, even if they are not laboratory mentors. Counselors, coaches, and professors help graduate students make these transitions, and many universities have professional development offices to make finding them easy.

Step 2: Assess the Time You Have Available

First, think about how much time you have to prepare for your career move. You need to maximize this time, and as of this moment on your priority must be transitioning into a new career and expanding your network. Your goal is to move toward your career goals without sacrificing the funding you need to support yourself. The best way to do well going forward is to do well in your current position, and you must continue to perform your laboratory and graduate duties (such as writing your dissertation). While you are in lab, make the most efficient use of your time. You will have to choose your career-building activities judiciously. Please refer to Chapter 13 for advice on balancing all of your activities and responsibilities. If, after honest and thorough reflection, you cannot find additional time for career activities, you must focus most on assessing the skills you already have. These are the transferable skills described in Chapter 10. If you have more than 6 months and can efficiently manage your responsibilities, you should aim to acquire experiences to add to your resume or curriculum vitae (CV).

Step 3: Determine Your Short- Term Versus Long-Term Career Goals

Now that you know how much time you have to focus on your career, you need to determine your short- and long-term career goals. For example, a short-term goal might be finding another laboratory to work in, while a long-term goal might be to pursue a career in science policy.

You must realize that, regardless of how much time you have available, it is possible you will not achieve your long-term career goals immediately after graduate school. However, preparing for and achieving short-term goals are important steps in realizing your ultimate career goals. It is not "giving up" to take an intermediate position while you leave a toxic work environment, or take a lower paying position to gain the experience you need for your next step. Keep your long-term goals in mind as you make all of your career decisions.

Step 4: Make a Plan

This book has many activities and suggestions on how to plan your career, but these suggestions are generally focused on taking the long view of career planning and having the luxury of time. While long-term planning is also necessary, quickly adjusting your career path requires special actions. Use the below checklist to stay on track. Tear it out and keep it in your pocket. Make a copy and stick it on your wall. Do whatever it takes to use this list to keep you focused.

◯ Find a Career Mentor

◯ Establish a Timeline

◯ Know short term and long term goals

◯ Determine skills required for career

◯ List your marketable skills

◯ Engage in activities to gain additional skills

◯ Update Resume

◯ Update C.V.

◯ Write Cover Letter

◯ Research job postings

◯ Reach out to recruiters in the field you are interested in

◯ Call on your network

◯ Informational interviews

If you are still unsure of exactly what career path you will follow or how to prepare for it, a great place to start is getting involved in activities outside of the lab that you enjoy. Volunteer for programs that you think are important, or start your own program if none exists. For example, if you feel strongly that the public can benefit from increased science literacy, volunteer with a program dedicated to this mission. If you want to inspire children to enjoy science and relate to diverse mentors, sign-up for an after-school or summer school program. If you feel passionate about improving patient care, volunteer with your local hospital. If you enjoy teaching, offer to be a tutor. Volunteer work provides proof to prospective employers about what you value and what your skills may be.

Once you find an activity you like, pursue a leadership role. Leadership and project management are desired skills across all careers, and being involved with something you enjoy is a good way to be "productive" regarding your career even while you're still undecided. Don't overcommit—refer to Chapters 9 and 13—but really look at how you spend your time and where your interests lead you.

Step 5: Determine Your Current Marketable Skills

Employers look to your resume to find proof of the skills you claim to have, so use all of what you have already done to your advantage. The only way to do this is to make a list of these skills both in a resume and in a less formal "skill list" of your own. Refer to Chapter 10 to learn more about the transferable skills acquired in lab and how to market them to employers.

Graduate school trains you to be a research machine. Breaking this down, you are acquiring the skills to think critically, defend arguments, research unfamiliar areas to distill your own opinions, communicate your ideas in writing and oral presentations, and write research papers and/or grants. If you have been able to secure your own funding or publish papers, you have shown persuasive writing and communication skills. If you have ordered supplies and managed the budget for your lab, this is experience with budget management. Managing and maintaining communal equipment is both a technical chore and a position of responsibility. Each of these is a transferable skill valuable in any career path, and you can focus on the skills most relevant to the career path you have chosen to pursue.

Step 6: Acquire Additional Marketable Skills Quickly

Once you determine what career path you will pursue and have a thorough list of the transferable skills you already possess, there are several ways to identify and gain the additional skills you might need. To explore this in more detail refer to Chapter 9.

Some universities have clubs or organizations dedicated to the career path you are interested in. For example, many graduate schools have consulting and biotech clubs that are involved in local or national competitions. If time allows, you can look for an internship or fellowship in your desired field. For example, the Mirzayan Fellowship[1] and AAAS Mass Media Fellowships[2] are available to those interested in science writing. Look to NSF, NIH, and AAAS for other opportunities.

You must focus on one or two things you can do very well rather than trying everything. If time is limited, use your network to find opportunities to make maximum impact toward the skills you need. Remember your short-term goals and only engage in activities that are required for you to attain those goals.

Step 7: Network: Assess Current and Identify Future Allies

As addressed in Chapter 12, networking is hugely important for career success. It is even more important when you are looking for a career change in short order. You have a network already and may not realize it. Who wrote your graduate school recommendation letters? Who is on your thesis committee? Does your campus have a professional development office? These are established people who are on your "team" who want to see you succeed. Even if you are pursuing a nontraditional career against your advisor's wishes, you can find people who can and will want to help you. Ask your friends and colleagues if they know someone in the field you're interested in. You never know who can introduce you to someone until you ask.

Even without a personal connection, you can directly contact people you think can help you in your career. As long as you are clear in what you are asking for (i.e., a brief informational interview), are polite in your contact, and make sure to follow-up and thank those you connect with, you may be pleasantly surprised by how helpful former strangers can be. For more on informational interviews, read Chapter 16.

Step 8: Prepare Your Documents

Update your CV and resume immediately. You may need other types of documents depending on the career you are pursuing, so know what you need before you apply. Do whatever it takes to get your documents perfected as fast as possible. You will need these to get your next position, whatever it may be, so do not wait to prepare them. If you are still unsure of your path, prepare updated "skeletons" of the documents that you can then customize for each position as it arises. Your documents must be perfect, so send your drafts to colleagues and professionals for feedback. For more on these refer to Chapter 16.

Step 9: Know Where/How to Apply Efficiently

The process of executing a career search has been outlined in great detail in Chapter 15. You need to remain focused on the goal at hand and be sure to execute the application process in the most efficient way possible. If possible, use your network to get help to directly contact the people who will review your application. The goal is to submit a wide range of applications while consistently preparing the best application you can. Stay organized, and budget the time needed to ensure that every application you submit is the strongest it can be.

Step 10: Stay Positive

Even with ample time, making a career transition can be very stressful. At an accelerated pace, these stresses are amplified. Please refer back to Chapter 5 and stay mindful of your mental health as you proceed in your career plans. You must take care of yourself to ensure that you provide the best interviews that you can. Keep your career mentor updated to ensure that you are staying on track, both professionally and personally.

The authors wish you the best of luck in your career transitions, and encourage you to use this book, your networks, and all resources available to you as you prepare for and research your future career paths.

REFERENCES

1. Christine Mirzayan Science and Technology Policy Graduate Fellowship. The National Academies of Sciences, Engineering, and Medicine. http://sites.nationalacademies.org/pga/policyfellows/; June 19, 2016.
2. Science & Technology Policy Fellowships. The American Association for the Advancement of science. http://www.aaas.org/program/science-technology-policy-fellowships; June 18, 2016.

FURTHER READING

3. Pasteur L. *Dans les champs de l'observation le hasard ne favorise que les esprits préparés.* Lecture, University of Lille; December 7, 1854. June 18, 2016. https://en.wikiquote.org/wiki/Louis_Pasteur.

Index

A

AAAS Science and Technology Policy
    Fellowship Program, 93
Academic interview process, 211
Academic professionals, 64
Acute stress, 33
American Association for the Advancement of
    Science's (AAAS) Mass Media Science
    & Engineering Fellows Program, 92
American Society for Biochemistry and
    Molecular Biology's (ASBMB)
    Science Policy Fellowship Program, 92
Analytical skills, 108
Association for Women in Science (AWIS), 91
Association of Health Care Journalists, 95

B

BALSA Group, 91
Biomedical sciences career landscape, 12
Bioscience community, 20
Branding process, 133

C

Companion support, 36
Career characters
    conclusion changer, 5, 7
    data collection process, 5
    Facebook feed, 6
    midway modifier, 5, 7
    optimized observer, 5–7
    planning, 5
    trainee career planners, 6
Career planning
    and motivation, 26f
        bioscience community, 20
        career mentor, 22–23
        case study, 27b–28b
        event selection, 21–22
        finding opportunities, 21
        graduate training, 20
        information gathering, 22

know yourself, 25
long-term career goal, 23
professional goals, 25
self-knowledge and career tools, 26
social media connection, 22
Stan's plan, 23, 24f
teaching courses, 25
work–life balance, 26
quick guide
    activities and responsibilities, 251
    career development, 249–250
    document preparation, 254
    flow chart, 250, 250f
    future allies identification, 253
    long-term plan, 251, 252f
    marketable skills, 252–253
    positive attitude, 254
    process execution, 254
    seek help, 250
    short-term *vs.* long-term career goals, 251
Career search
    candidate's resume, 184, 185t
    career-fit, 184–186
    employer resources, 184
    goal, 182
    leadership and teamwork, 184
    network and mentors, 193
    planning
        assess your circumstances, 187
        be realistic, 189–190
        decode descriptions, 188
        filters, 188
        job alerts, 188
        network, 189
        peruse postings, 187
        resources, 188
        skills and competencies fit, 187
        SMART goals, 186
        submission and preparation, 189
    questions to begin, 183
    with recruiters
        career-searching resource, 190
        high-paying industry jobs, 192

Career search (*Continued*)
    life sciences-focused candidates, 192
    PhD-suitable recruiter, resources, 192
    retained, contingency/contract, 190
    STEM-focused candidates, 193
    types, 191
  self and personal factors, 181–182
  self-assessments, 182
  target market, 183
  transferable skills, 182
  workplace culture, 183
Chronic stress, 33
  risk for, 34
  symptoms, 34
  unhealthy coping behaviors, 34
Cognitive load management, 108
Communication, 74–75, 111
  international barriers, 176–177, 176b
  and mentoring, 171–172
  nonverbal communication, 171–172
  oral communication. *See* Oral
    communication
  personal communication, 177–178
  self-confidence, 166
  thoughtful, 166
  verbal communication, 165, 172–173
  written communication
    email communication, 165. *See also*
      Email communication
    thank-you notes, 175
Conclusion changer, 5, 7
Cover letters, 124, 126, 199–200

E
Elevator speech, 124, 127–128, 167
Email communication
  "Slow Down" post-it note, 173–174
  strong email/letter, 174–175
Emotional support, 36
Event selection
  anticipated crowd, 22
  event length, 21
  "fun", 21
  meeting new people, 21
  one-on-one discussion/lecture format, 22

F
Facebook profile, 124, 130
Faculty interviews, 212–213
Federal and state government, 14
Freelance business, 16
Functional skills, 75, 75f–76f

G
Gallup StrengthsFinder tool, 80
Guest blog postings, 125

H
Hybrid CV/resume, 199

I
Imposter fears, 48
Individual development plan (IDP), 80
Informational interviewing
  act polite and professional, 146
  admissions requirements, 146–147
  admission tips, 146–147
  application statistics, 146–147
  background verification, 145
  brief phone call/brief in-person
    meeting, 145
  definitions, 144
  friends and family, 145
  gratitude, 147
  HR system, 147
  laboratory and university alumni, 144
  LinkedIn, 144
  list of questions, 146
  professional societies and organizations, 144
  timing, 146
Informational support, 36
Insight Data Science Fellows Program, 92
Institute for the Future (IFTF), 108
International barriers, 176–177, 176b
International Council for Science
  (ICSU), 91
Interpersonal skills, 111
Interviews
  academic interview process, 211
  answers, 205
    structuring, 206–207
  difficult/illegal questions, 209
  faculty interviews, 212–213
  in-person interview, 208
  organization and role type, 203–204
  postdoc interviews, 211–212
  practice, 207–208
  preparation, 204–205
  professional-looking portfolio/folder, 208
  questions, types, 205
  resources, 214
  stages, 204
  thank-you notes, 209–210
  types, 204

J

Job application, 213–214
  academic hiring cycles, 198
  application directions, 201–203
  career communication, paper, 240b
  career goals, 196
  case study, 241b–246b
  documents, 96, 196
  factors, 197
  getting an offer, 210–211
  giant job-listing sites, 196
  interviews. *See* Interviews
  job-seeking time, 197
  lunchtime lists, 197–198
  material documents
    cover letters, 199–200
    CV, 198
    documents and supplementary materials, 199
    hybrid CV/resume, 199
    resume, 198–199
  materials creation, 196
  multiple responsibilities and commitments, 197
  nonacademic roles, 198
  responsibilities, 197–198
  targeting materials, 200–201
Job market, 119–120
  academic landscape changes, 12–13
  Big Bang Theory, The, 15
  career choices, 14–15
  career options, 13–14
  day-to-day tasks, 11–12
  design and construction, 16
  freelance business, 16
  teaching communication concepts, 16
  tenure-track position, 12
  unexpected obstacles, 16–17
Job search
  adaptability and resiliency, 46–48
  career support, resources, 53
  confidence
    academic research culture, 48
    imposter fears, 48
    negative self-talk, 49
    positive self-talk, 49
    voice tone change, 50
  consulting jobs, 54
  graduate career advisors, 53
  growth mind-set, 50–51
  imposter syndrome and self-doubt, 55b–56b
  impractical expectations, 54
  learned helplessness concept, 51
  Learned Optimism, 51
  low-stress situations, 52
  mentor–mentee relationship, 52
  multifaceted project, 45
  opportunities to learn, 55
  stress, imposter syndrome and depression, 56b–57b
  support option, 53–54

K

Knowledge and experience gaps
  academic commitments and career-related pursuits, balance
    academic career long-term stages, 97–98
    be realistic, 98
    organized schedule, 97
    policies, 98
    support network, 98
  academic responsibilities, 89
  career goals, 87
  career-related knowledge
    adult education, 94
    courses, 94
    creative and realistic, 93
    massive open online course (MOOC) platforms, 94–95
    professional organizations, 95
    transferable skills, 94
    workshops/online trainings, 95
  case study, 99b–103b
  day-to-day job responsibilities, 97
  experience, types, 88
  extracurricular opportunities, 88–89
  governmental organizations, 93
  graduate training, 88
  internships/volunteer opportunities, 88
  job application documents, 96
  paid work experience, 88
  practical career experience gain
    fellowship programs, 92
    internships, 89–90
    personal connections/network, 89
    supplementary work, 92
    temporary consulting/ freelance work, 92
    temporary/short-term work, 91
    volunteering, 90
  practical experience, 88
  project management skills, 97
  science communication, 96
  solid internship, 96
  support nonacademic career preparation, 99b
  work experience, 88
Knowledge-based skills, 75, 77

L

Leadership skills, 111
Learned Optimism, 51
Letters of reference, 124, 126–127
Life and career balance
  business plan, 156
  case study, 161b–163b
  eulogy, 156–157
  one thing, planning, 157–158
  opportunities selection, 156
  personal mission statement, 157
  responsibilities, 159
  SMART goal setting, 158
  speed read and write, 160–161
  time management, 155
  workaholic lifestyle, 158,
    159f
Life sciences-focused candidates, 192
LinkedIn profile, 124, 128–130
Long-term career goal, 23

M

Massive open online course (MOOC)
    platforms, 94–95
Me Brand
  branding process, 133
  case study, 134b–137b
  cover letter, 124, 126
  elevator speech, 124, 127–128
  employment rates, 121
  entrepreneurial enterprise, 121
  Facebook profile, 124, 130
  four w's, 121–122
    career choice, 124
    What, 123
    Where, 123
    Who, 122
    Work, 123
  guest blog postings, 125
  in-person and electronic methods, 124
  job market, 119–120
  job-seeking game, 120
  letters of reference, 124, 126–127
  LinkedIn profile, 124, 128–130
  online website, 124, 130–131
  personal blog, 125, 131–133
  resume, 124–126
  science blog, 125, 132–133
  short- and long-term success, 121
  social media platforms, 133–134
  turbulence and uncertainty, 120
  Twitter account, 124, 130

Mentor–mentee relationship, 52
Midway modifier, 5, 7
Myers–Briggs type indicator (MBTI), 80–81,
    112–113
myIDP tool, 80

N

National Institutes of Health's (NIH) Office
    of Intramural Training and Education
    (OITE), 95
Negative self-talk, 49
Nonverbal communication, 171–172

O

One-on-one discussion/lecture format, 22
Online website, 124, 130–131
Optimized observer, 5–7
Optional Practical Training (OPT), 235
Oral communication
  delivery plan, 169–170
  elevator speech, 167
  formal introduction, 167
  guidelines, short introduction, 167
  introducing others, 168
  room/stage command, 170
  show confidence, 170
  slide images and plan, 169
  story telling, 168–169
  TED presenters, 168
Organizational skills, 111

P

Personal blog, 125, 131–133
Personal communication, 177–178
Personal inventory
  career-counseling, 74
  career counselor, conversation, 85
  career options, 73–74
  interests, 81–82
  job roles and environments, 85–86
  personal beliefs and priorities, 83
  personal traits and qualities, 82–83, 82f–83f
  self-assessment, 73
    resources, 85
  self-awareness, 74
  self-reflection exercises, 74
  skills
    career paths and opportunities, 80
    classification, 75
    communication skills, 74–75
    knowledge-based skills, 75, 77

lab evaluation worksheet, 77, 78f–80f
personal traits/attitudes, 75
and strengths assessments, 80–81
transferable/functional skills, 75, 75f–76f
work values, 84f–85f
Personal mission statement, 157
PLoS One, 13
Positive self-talk, 49
Postdoc interviews, 211–212
Practical career experience gain
fellowship programs, 92
internships, 89–90
personal connections/network, 89
supplementary work, 92
temporary consulting/ freelance work, 92
temporary/short-term work, 91
volunteering, 90
Problem-solving skills, 108
Professional behavior, guide
academic professionals, 64
age barriers, 68
be assertive, 65
be proud, 68
casual *vs.* professional business attire,
62–63, 63f
colleagues' needs, 61
communication, 65
dress code, 63
family and work integration, 66
GENUINE smile, 60–61
identities, 66, 67f
professional dress, budget, 63–64
professionalism expectation, 60
reciprocity styles, 61–62
senior men interaction, 65–66
splash size, 68
timing, 64
tit for tat behavior, 61
unprofessional behavior, 64
women leaders, 65
women professionals, 65
Professional network
career exploration, 147–148
career research activity, 140
case study, 149b–153b
conference with mentor, 142
definition, 140
diverse career backgrounds, 141–142
friends/colleagues break, 142
informational interviewing, 140. *See also*
Informational interviewing
information/resources sharing, 140
job searching, 140–141

leadership roles, 142
linear path, 141
practice, 143
seminars, 143
social media, 142
unexpected connection, Twitter, 148–149
Project management skills, 97

Q
Quantitative skills, 108

R
RAND Corporation, 91
Research and development positions, 13
Resume, 124–126, 198–199

S
Science blog, 125, 132–133
Self-assessments, 50, 182
Self-confidence, 166
Self-knowledge and career tools, 26
SkillScan, 81, 113–114
SMART goals, 158, 186
Social intelligence, 108
STEM-focused candidates, 193
Stress management
acute stress, 33
chronic stress, 33
risk for, 34
symptoms, 34
unhealthy coping behaviors, 34
fight-or-flight response, 33
graduate training, 32–33
life-threatening attacks, 33–34
physiological and emotional issues, 31–32
prestress conditioning, 35
companion support, 36
cognitive restructuring, 39–40
communication, 38–39
emotional support, 36
hobbies, 41–42
informational support, 36
mindfulness practice, 40–41
physical activity, 35–36
social skills and thoughtful
strategy, 36
stress levels, 37–38
tangible support, 36
psychobiology of, 33
"self-care" and "balance", 31–32
trust process, 42–43

T

Tangible support, 36
Teaching careers, 13
Teaching communication, 16
Teaching courses, 25
Tenure-track (TTT) professors, 16–17
Time management, 155
Tit for tat behavior, 61
Transdisciplinarity, 108
Transferable skills, 75, 75f–76f, 94, 182,
    237–238
  academic accomplishments, 115b–116b
  analytical/quantitative skills, 108
  case study, 116b–117b
  cognitive load management, 108
  computational thinking, 108
  cross-cultural competency, 108
  design mindset, 108
  extracurricular activities, 108
  graduate and postgraduate studies, 107
  Institute for the Future (IFTF), 108
  new media literacy, 108
  nonacademic job, 106
  novel and adaptive thinking, 108
  problem-solving skills, 108
  recognition
    accomplishment statements, 114–115
    assessment instruments, 112–114
    hidden skills, academic profile, 109–110
    nonacademics, feedback, 111–112
    tools, 109
    work, sports and leadership profile,
      110–111
  sense making, 108
  skills employers, 107–108
  social intelligence, 108
  strong work ethics, 108
  teaching and concentration, 106
  transdisciplinarity, 108
  virtual collaboration, 108
  written communication skills, 108
Twitter account, 124, 130

U

Underrepresented minority (URM), 16–17
Union of Concerned Scientists' Science
    Network, 95
Unprofessional behavior, 64

V

Verbal communication, 165, 172–173
Virtual collaboration, 108

W

Workaholic lifestyle, 158, 159f
Workshops/online trainings, 95
Written communication, 108
  email communication, 165. *See also* Email
    communication
  thank-you notes, 175

Edwards Brothers Inc.
Ann Arbor MI. USA
May 18, 2018